Inside the Banking Crisis

Inside the Banking Crisis

The Untold Story

Hugh Pym

B L O O M S B U R Y

LONDON • NEW DELHI • NEW YORK • SYDNEY

First published in Great Britain 2014

Bloomsbury Publishing Plc
50 Bedford Square
London
WC1B 3DP

www.bloomsbury.com

Bloomsbury is a trademark of Bloomsbury Publishing Plc

Bloomsbury Publishing, London, New Delhi, New York and Sydney

A CIP record for this book is available from the British Library.

ISBN: 9-781-4729-0287-0

10 9 8 7 6 5 4 3 2 1

Design by Fiona Pike, Pike Design, Winchester
Typeset by Hewer Text UK Ltd, Edinburgh
Printed and bound in Great Britain by CPI Group (UK) Ltd, Croydon CR0 4YY

To Susan

Contents

Preface and Acknowledgements

Much has been written about the banking crisis, from the credit crunch and ensuing rescue of Northern Rock in 2007 to the ongoing debate five years later regarding what to do about Royal Bank of Scotland. Thousands of pages have been generated on the economic boom and bust which paralysed leading industrialised nations. There is no shortage of books on how banks went on a lending binge till the music stopped and the the punchbowl of cheap credit ran dry.

The astonishing downfall of Royal Bank of Scotland has been well documented – Iain Martin's *Making it Happen* is an authoritative account. The marriage of Halifax and Bank of Scotland and subsequent unravelling of the combined entity HBOS has been outlined by Ray Perman in his book *Hubris*. The Northern Rock fiasco of 2007 was chronicled the following year by Alex Brummer in *The Crunch*.

So why another book on the banking crisis? This is not an attempt to go through again in great detail the causes of the financial crash. It does not provide a blow-by-blow account of the boardroom upheavals at RBS and HBOS. But it does tell a hitherto untold story – how a small group of officials, advisers and ministers coped with the financial hurricane which battered the UK. Even five years on, the scale of the threat to the British economy in 2008 may still not be fully appreciated by voters and consumers. Britain was on the brink, standing alone, and somebody had to come up with answers. This book will explain who was there to repel the grave threat to UK plc. It was, arguably, the peacetime equivalent of 1940. Decisions made then have shaped the path of the economy since the darkest hour of crisis and affected millions of business and household borrowers.

The fact that a parliamentary Banking Commission was established in 2012, including the bishop who would subsequently become the Archbishop of Canterbury, is proof that interest in the taxpayer bailout of banks is not waning. Based on this author's experience, there is still a strong public demand for information and explanations. This was a defining episode in postwar British politics and economic history.

I have talked to many of the participants in the Government and regulatory arena during the crisis, as well as highly placed sources in the banking industry. Most did not wish to be quoted but gave freely of their time and I can only thank them warmly for that. Their over-riding sentiment was that these once-in-a-lifetime events should be chronicled and analysed before memories faded. I hope they are not disappointed. When people are quoted directly, their comments come from interviews I carried out. Other quotations are sourced, with fuller details in the bibliography.

My sincere thanks are due to Stephen Rutt and Alana Clogan at Bloomsbury who always showed great faith in the project and their colleagues who helped take it through to publication. Thanks, too, are owed to my agent Andrew Lownie. Colleagues at the BBC Business and Economics Unit have been tolerant and patient as I took time off to research and write. Laurence Knight and Malcolm Balen were expert and very helpful critics.

My biggest vote of thanks must go to my family – to my wife Susan especially for her unstinting love and support, and Andrew, Jonathan and Kirsty. My brother William and his family (Claudia, Ambrose, Polly and Isaac) and my mother Caroline deserve thanks as well. They were very tolerant of my tendency to disappear with my laptop for lengthy periods of our holiday together. I hope they all feel it was worth it.

Introduction

It was 4.30 in the morning on a dank October day in 2008. A gangling, dark-haired figure was walking as fast as he could from his flat in Pimlico towards Westminster. It was not something James Leigh-Pemberton was accustomed to do. He was one of the City's most experienced investment bankers and the son of a former Governor of the Bank of England to boot. Eton-and Oxford-educated, hurrying through the centre of London in the early hours did not square easily with his urbane image.

But this was a crisis. Leigh-Pemberton feared that a complicated deal to rescue Britain's leading banks could unravel. And if it did fall apart by 7 o'clock. that morning, when the financial markets opened for business, there could be a catastrophe. No deal would mean a rapid loss of confidence and the probability of queues building up outside bank branches. The cash machines would run out of notes. Leigh-Pemberton was deeply concerned about all those things, not to mention the untold social consequences if Britain's financial infrastructure collapsed.

He reached the Treasury and found his way through the maze of corridors which he now knew well to the rooms full of civil servants who had been up all night. They were completing the paperwork requiring leading banks to take government bailout cash. Lloyds had been trying to question some of the fine print in the documents and was pushing to change parts of the deal. Treasury staff had called Leigh-Pemberton with news of that development as he climbed into bed in his flat. He had been tempted to ignore it and get the sleep he craved. But this required one more push. He convinced the Treasury team to play hardball with Lloyds. Their tough line held and the final documentation was ready for a formal announcement. It was duly conveyed to the London Stock Exchange's regulated news feed service known as RNS. Shortly after 7 a.m., it was flashing on screens in trading floors. The markets took the news in their stride. Nerves held and panic was avoided.

Leigh-Pemberton was one of a handful of people battling against a tide that was threatening to engulf the financial system. He headed a team from the investment bank Credit Suisse, engaged as an adviser by the Treasury. The momentous decisions on the part-nationalisation of Lloyds, which was taking over the stricken HBOS, and Royal Bank of Scotland were taken by the then Prime Minister Gordon Brown and the Chancellor Alistair Darling. The gravest crisis facing the UK in modern times happened on their watch and they rose to the challenge. But the planning and execution of the rescue deals was the work of a small number of individuals, some part of the government machine and others from outside.

A key player was Shriti, now Baroness Vadera, formerly a banker but since 2007 a minister and close adviser to Gordon Brown. Born in Uganda, her family had fled to India after the expulsion of Ugandan Asians. The Oxford-educated Vadera quickly marked herself out as a high-flyer in the City. After her appointment as a Labour minister she became well known in Whitehall for her no-nonsense and often pugnacious approach.

Paul, elevated to Lord, Myners had become a minister only one week previously. He was a Labour-supporting City grandee, formerly head of the fund manager Gartmore and at one stage chairman of Marks & Spencer. Myners was a gregarious character at ease in the worlds of finance, politics and the arts. He found himself in a firefighting exercise only days into the job.

At the Treasury two senior civil servants had had their lives consumed by the financial crisis: Tom Scholar and John Kingman. Both had worked hard to grasp the essentials of the banking industry's problems well before they swirled around the gates of Downing Street. There was also Geoffrey Spence, a soft-spoken Northern Irishman, who had moved from the banking world to head the Treasury's Private Finance Initiative operation. By the time the crisis hit he had become Alistair Darling's special adviser on banking issues. Dan Rosenfield, a young career civil servant running the Chancellor's office, witnessed scenes unprecedented in modern British political history.

From the City there was a small team of investment bankers headed by the experienced troubleshooter David Soanes and his colleague Robin

Budenberg. They had spent much of their careers as highly respected executives at UBS, where Vadera had also spent some of her time as a banker. Their role, with a few UBS colleagues, had been under the radar before October 2008 and not in any official capacity.

Looming over the team at Westminster and the City's financial advisers was the towering intellectual presence of Mervyn King. Dogmatic, sometimes stubborn and aloof towards what he felt was the vulgar world of investment banking, King was at the helm of the Bank of England for a crisis as severe as anything his predecessors had seen in the previous three centuries. His lieutenants on deck, Sir John Gieve, Paul Tucker and Andrew Bailey, had to fight the financial fires raging around the Bank.

These officials and advisers found themselves at the centre of an unprecedented financial disaster. The banking system was close to the edge. There was nothing in the textbooks or civil service manuals to explain how to tackle the emergency. There was no safety net. They had to work things out for themselves and with time always against them. Haunting them was the fear that banks would fail and social disorder might break out on Britain's streets. Shriti Vadera still has nightmares about those days, imagining herself going over the top of a trench and charging towards the enemy before realising she is on her own.

They had learned valuable lessons during the Northern Rock fiasco the year before. Britain had been caught napping by a funding market crisis in August 2007. In little more than a month, a bank had fallen apart. The banking system was pathetically under-prepared and the situation had been compounded by a series of policy mistakes. It had been a humiliation for an economy which prided itself on providing world-class financial services. In some senses it was a Dunkirk moment – a heavy defeat but a chance to regroup and lick wounds ready for the next battle.

At various times in 2007 and during the spring of 2008, Soanes had warned Downing Street about an impending bank funding crisis. Memos were sent to senior officials. Number 10 and the Treasury at that stage had been reassured that British banks were capable of plugging holes in their balance sheets. The Royal Bank of Scotland had launched the largest cash-raising exercise in British corporate history, bringing in £12 billion from shareholders who were later to rue their decision and, in some cases, launch legal action.

At the same time, the US investment bank Bear Stearns had keeled over and been rescued by the American government working with the Wall Street giant JP Morgan. The fact that financial markets were not severely undermined by the Bear Stearns debacle provided a false sense of reassurance to many investors. But, unknown to the markets and media, the mortgage giant HBOS was on the brink. Rumours swept the City of London and the HBOS share price plummeted. That forced an unprecedented denial by the regulator, the Financial Services Authority (FSA), though top-secret preparations for a possible collapse were underway.

As the City of London emptied in August 2008 for the summer holidays, there were few warnings of what was to come. The US state-guaranteed mortgage giants, nicknamed Fannie Mae and Freddie Mac, were struggling but the administration seemed to have the situation under control with a rescue deal on the table. There was no sense in the Westminster village or amongst the media commentariat that any storm was looming. At the end of the month, the Chancellor Alistair Darling suggested that the UK economy was facing its worst economic crisis for 60 years and was ridiculed by anonymous briefers at Number 10 Downing Street.

But Vadera, walking down Whitehall on one of those August days, was suddenly struck by an alarming thought; the major banks would need a lot more extra capital and no private investor would provide it. That left only one obvious but terrifying conclusion – it would have to come from the taxpayer. In a series of emails she and Tom Scholar at the Treasury ran their numbers and assumptions. At the same time, Mervyn King and colleagues at the Bank of England were banging a drum for the extreme option – making all the banks take funding from the government.

The Lehman Brothers crash in the middle of September had been like a lightening bolt across financial markets and in political corridors of power on both sides of the Atlantic. It changed the face of British banking at a stroke. The tottering HBOS fell into the arms of Lloyds, a deal unthinkable only a month before because it so obviously flouted competition rules. Bradford & Bingley closed its doors as usual one Saturday lunchtime and never opened them again as an independent bank. At the Treasury it was a race against time to come up with a comprehensive plan for the whole system. The leading civil servant Scholar pulled together the threads. He sat in a City boardroom with Soanes, Budenberg, Vadera and other banking advisers to flesh out a plan. When the chairman of RBS Sir Tom McKillop phoned Alistair Darling on 7 October warning him that his bank would run out of cash by that evening, the Chancellor decided it was time to act and he had a blueprint to fall back on.

After an all-night session at the Treasury during which takeaway curries were procured to feed the exhausted civil servants and hangers-on, the plan was ready to go. But would it satisfy the markets? The Prime Minister and Chancellor could only wait and hope. Some feared a bank run at RBS with crowds on the streets and social disorder. The scheme helped restore an uneasy calm, with its readiness to inject hundreds of billions pounds into the system. The assumption was that several more days, perhaps weeks, might be needed to finalise the arrangements with the banks and hammer down the legal technicalities.

By the end of the week, though, the financial markets were in turmoil once again. It dawned on the exhausted Treasury ministers and advisers that the final deal had to be hammered out that weekend. Bank chiefs were ordered to report to the Treasury on the Saturday. A momentous weekend followed, during which Myners and Vadera went from room to room at the Treasury addressing the bosses of each bank in turn. They and Leigh-Pemberton knew that they had only until early Monday to thrash out an agreement. Darling and Brown signed off within hours of the markets opening for business. They got there, just.

Armageddon had been avoided but at what price? Gordon Brown's Labour administration was determined to steer clear of full nationalisation. He was convinced that such a move would torpedo their chances at the general election. New Labour had strained every sinew to bury the economic policies of the past, including commitments to state ownership. Northern Rock had been nationalised but at the time, in early 2008, it had been portrayed as a special case with no precedent set for further such action. Taking RBS and HBOS onto the state's books, aside from crippling the public finances, would look like a return to Labour's socialist ways.

But pumping tens of billions into RBS without nationalising it was tricky. If the government was to hold a majority stake in the bank, with the rest held by private investors, the taxpayer would have to pay more for each share than otherwise would have been the case. So sparing the government's blushes and steering clear of full nationalisation came at a cost. With Lloyds/HBOS it was possible to keep the government stake at just under 50 per cent. Management was left to manage and the Treasury would let them get on with it. Alistair Darling's aim was for the banks to be nursed back to profit with a return to the stock market as soon as possible to allow the government to get its money back through share sales. It seemed like the best idea at the time and was not seriously challenged. Indeed, George Osborne continued the policy when he took office in 2010.

But the consequences of these fateful decisions are still being felt across the economy. In effect, the government had paid too much for their stake in RBS. The Americans had gone down the same route but had struck harder bargains with the banks over the bailouts. So whereas the US government stakes in banks across the Atlantic were sold off some time ago, British taxpayers are still saddled with RBS in an arm's-length relationship with Whitehall. Shares in Lloyds are being sold off but an RBS privatisation seems a lot further off. The UK economy needs a vibrant banking sector to generate credit for a long-lasting recovery. The state-controlled banks, still burdened with problem loans dating back to the boom years, have struggled to provide that.

Some senior policymakers at the highest levels of the Bank of England and the Treasury now say it would have been better to have broken up RBS. Taking the political pain at the time and getting direct political influence at the helm of these banks would have allowed for a more radical strategy to be implemented. Stripping out the bad assets and keeping them in government hands while preparing the remaining 'good bank' for an eventual flotation to repay some of the taxpayer's investment might have been the best course. This was what the Swedish authorities did after their banking crisis in the early 1990s. Nationalising

HBOS and letting Lloyds continue on its own were seriously considered at the time.

Leigh-Pemberton, Vadera, Myners, Scholar and Kingman and others helped the government win a decisive battle at the height of the financial crisis. The threat of banks imploding and ATMs closing was averted. But with hindsight they did not secure the peace. The banking crisis of 2008 and 2009 still casts a very long shadow over the British economy. Growth has been impaired and businesses have not secured the loans they need to ensure dynamic expansion and job creation. That's why it matters.

The causes of the banking crisis are many. Suffice to say that in a world of low interest rates and fast growing developing economies accumulating savings, there was a flood of cash swirling around the global economy. Banks were the intermediaries, lending to almost anyone who wanted to borrow. House prices soared. People who could never afford mortgage payments were lent money they were never likely to pay back. Traditional banking was based on taking in deposits and lending to households and companies. But soon after 2000, banks discovered they could borrow money from markets as well as depositors. Easy profits were to be made as they borrowed from each other or international investors and lent to customers at higher rates of interest. And the authorities allowed markets to think that the largest banks were too big to fail and would always be bailed out if there was no other option. It was bound to go pop, and it did.

Understanding the crisis involves grasping only a few basics of banking. The first rule is that not everybody who deposits cash in a bank can get it back at the same time. The bank might have lent £100 to borrowers, such as companies, for terms of three years or more. But that could be funded by £100 of savers' money on instant access accounts. If all depositors choose to exercise the right to pull their money out, the bank cannot call it all back instantly from the borrowers. To cover the likely day-to-day requirements, banks need what is called liquidity, that is, easy access to cash or investments which can be instantly converted into cash. Without liquidity, a bank runs dry.

The banks also need capital, that is, money put in by shareholders or accumulated from profits. The point of capital is to provide a buffer against future losses. In other words, if a bank has lent out £100, it might expect if things get tough for £95 to be returned. If so it needs £5 of capital to cover that potential loss.

Capital needs to be held as secure assets which can be easily sold to raise money or cash on deposit. On one side of a bank balance sheet are bank loans, known as assets – that is, the bank's 'use of funds'. On the other side are liabilities, or 'source of funds' – they come usually from deposits and borrowings from markets. If after covering losses on the asset side, a bank's capital runs out and liabilities are bigger than assets, the bank is insolvent. Banks can raise capital by holding on to profits, going to shareholders and asking for money or simply cutting back their loans so that retained capital rises as a percentage of assets.

Regulators watch banks' capital like hawks. However, they were not watching closely enough before the crisis. Capital is usually expressed as a percentage of assets. To make matters more complicated, it is expressed in most cases as a percentage of 'risk-weighted assets'. What this means is that the banks are permitted to hold less capital against the safer loans but have to set aside more against the riskiest lending. These 'risk-weightings', worked out by the banks, proved controversial. Before the crisis they were allowed to take too optimistic a view of their assets and set the weightings accordingly. Since the crisis regulators have called for banks to hold higher percentages of their assets as capital.

From Northern Rock onwards, capital and liquidity dominated the thoughts of policymakers and bankers. The big question was who would provide them if investors would not? All roads led back to the Bank of England and the government.

Some said it was a solvency crisis, others said it was a liquidity crisis, still others said it was both. The brutal truth was that if a bank is in trouble and investors lose confidence, liquidity is harder to find. And if that happens, markets start questioning whether the bank has enough capital. If they believe there is insufficient capital, they will fear insolvency so will all try to get their money back at once with the inevitable consequences.

As banks discovered, confidence and trust could vanish in an instant. As policymakers discovered, there was no repair kit for a banking system that was on the verge of imploding once confidence had evaporated. They had to make it up as they went along. The stakes were terrifyingly high. They could not afford to get it wrong. This is their story.

Chapter 1

The Rock crumbles

Nothing like it had been seen on Britain's streets since the late nineteenth century. Queues outside bank branches were images that most people associated with grainy footage from Germany or the United States in the 1930s. It just wasn't British. But it was on 14 September 2007. First a handful, then a dozen and then a few more began to congregate in streets. They were queuing to get into branches of the Northern Rock bank. They were behaving in a way which was 'perfectly rational' according to the Governor of the Bank of England. With the official deposit protection scheme covering only a proportion of their savings, why take a risk if they had a tidy sum in a bank which needed emergency loans? Rational it might have been, but the episode proved disastrous for the country's international image and will remain etched in the history books as a shameful chapter. International TV coverage of the Northern Rock queues, according to one horrified MP, made the UK look like Zimbabwe.

There were many causes of the Northern Rock debacle. One of the main reasons was the dramatic reversal in market conditions which took its toll on most banks – Northern Rock was among the first to be knocked over. The seizing up of financial markets in August 2007 has been well documented. Put simply, there had been a credit bubble and it had burst. In the early years of the decade, major central banks had lowered interest rates in an attempt to stimulate growth after the internet and technology boom had turned to bust and the Iraq war dented international confidence. Savings and surpluses built up in fast-growing Asian economies needed to find a home. The result was a flood of funds surging around the world markets. Official interest rates were low so the hunt was on for higher returns from more exotic investments. Banks were falling over themselves to lend. The sub-prime mortgage debacle was the result of this credit binge. Low-income US borrowers were targeted and persuaded to sign up for mortgages which they had little chance of repaying. In a constantly rising housing market defaults are not a problem as the lender can easily sell the property. But the crunch comes, as it did in 2007, when house prices start to fall. Borrowers hand in the keys and banks are left with properties worth a lot less than the original loan.

The US sub-prime disaster had such a huge impact on financial markets because exposure to vulnerable American borrowers was so widely spread around the international banking system. US lenders sliced and diced the mortgages and packaged them up as sophisticated instruments with names like 'collateralised debt obligations' and 'asset-backed securities'. They were created, sold and re-sold and ended up on the balance sheets of US, Asian and European banks. When house prices started to fall and defaults rose, the music in this global financial game stopped. Suddenly everyone wanted out. They scrambled to cut their losses on the sub-prime mortgages. But they were selling into a falling market. Valuations of the assets became impossible. And as every bank began to take stock of its own problems, the next question was how badly other institutions were affected. If a bank was suspicious about the extent of a counterpart's sub-prime losses, it would want to reduce lending to the other institution. A vicious downward spiral developed with banks reducing exposure to other banks and thus the supply of credit around the system was severely impaired.

Warning lights had been flashing in early 2007 as mounting sub-prime losses were unveiled by some lenders. In July, the US investment bank Bear Stearns announced that two of its hedge funds that had invested heavily in sub-prime securities had lost almost all of their value. On 9 August 2007 the markets really took fright. The French bank BNP Paribas froze three of its funds because they could not keep up with investor demands to get their money out. Selling the funds' assets to raise money to repay those investors who wanted to quit was proving impossible. Global stock markets plummeted. The European Central Bank (ECB) pumped nearly €100 billion into the system to boost liquidity. The credit markets seemed, alarmingly, to be seizing up.

It is easy to blame highly paid wheeler-dealers and traders on Wall Street and in the City for blowing up the banking system with excessive risk-taking. But the first high-profile collapse was a former building society based in Newcastle-upon-Tyne. Northern Rock was not involved in sub-prime lending in the United States. It did not even have much sub-prime exposure in the UK market. It most certainly was not a high-rolling casino bank, staffed by pinstripe-suited City bankers with red braces. Its core business was providing supposedly plain 'vanilla' mortgage and savings products. Northern Rock had expanded aggressively since it converted from building society to bank and floated on the Stock Exchange in 1997. Increasing market share in a highly competitive mortgage market was the strategy and to achieve this, making loans easily available was the main task of management. Lending up to 125 per cent of the value of the property was not unusual for Northern Rock.

The main reason for the Rock's downfall was not so much the quality of the lending, although that did not help, but rather the way the bank financed its loan book. Traditionally banks raised money from depositors and then lent it to businesses, mortgage borrowers and other customers. Liberalisation of financial markets and the surge in the availability of cheap credit opened up new funding avenues for banks in the early years of the twenty-first century. Rather than relying on deposits as the sole source funding, banks started tapping wholesale credit markets. They could borrow from one another 'unsecured', in other words without collateral for defined periods from one day to a couple of years. In addition they could parcel up their loans and 'securitise' them; in other words, sell them on to other investors and bring in more cash to then invest in more lending. According to one estimate, by the end of 2006, Northern Rock customer deposits covered just under 23 per cent of its loan book, the rest coming from wholesale markets or securitisations of mortgages. The Treasury Select Committee of MPs, which carried out its own inquiry, 'The Run on the Rock', noted that this was a sharp drop from a figure of nearly 63 per cent when the bank had demutualised and was low compared to other building societies which had converted to banks.

Put simply, Northern Rock needed financial markets to fund more than three quarters of its lending activities. And this borrowing from markets was much shorter term than the average loans made, typically 25-year mortgages. A householder will usually pay back a bank or building society at regular intervals over those 25 years. But the lending institution may well borrow to fund that mortgage over a much shorter period and keep repeating the borrowing every time repayment is due. In good times, that is straightforward. A bank can borrow short term at low interest rates and lend at higher rates to mortgage customers for longer time horizons. That way healthy profits are made and credit to keep rolling over the short-term loans is always available. But when those credit markets dry up, the short-term wholesale funding is suddenly no longer available. The lenders can no longer keep rolling over their own borrowing. That mortgage loan will not be fully repaid for another couple of decades. But the money the banks and building societies borrowed to provide the mortgage has to be paid back immediately. Northern Rock, like many others, was caught in this squeeze and found itself desperately short of funding.

The bank was also generating a high volume of short-term fixed-rate mortgages. These loans and others would be 'warehoused' every three months and placed into a Jersey subsidiary called Granite. They would be then be parcelled up and sold on via securitisations to outside investors. The money raised would subsequently be lent out for new mortgages, which were in turn bundled and the process repeated. The advantage for Northern Rock was that the securitised mortgages were 'off balance sheet', in other words, were not included in the loan book because they had been sold to outside investors. The strategy was to keep on generating new mortgages and to achieve that, the business had to grow. There was a constant need for momentum and expansion. If the production line stopped, the whole structure would become unstable. One senior policymaker said later that the model was unsustainable and would eventually fall over 'like a car which runs out of road – a monster which was out of control'. Looking under the bonnet of Northern Rock, then, revealed a bank that might have been impossible to save even with a takeover or bailout.

Northern Rock was not the only bank to be teetering on the brink of disaster because of the near-closure of credit markets. Four German banks at various stages in August and early September 2007 were revealed to be struggling because of exposures linked to the sub-prime market. The largest US sub-prime lender, New Century, had filed for bankruptcy protection back in April. But Northern Rock was to be the UK's first casualty and one that would have a much higher profile than the plight of institutions in other economies. As noted above, it was the televised images of the queues which brought the Rock's problems onto the global stage and dented the UK's reputation for financial competence. Since then a debate has raged over whether Northern Rock should have been better handled by the regulators and whether, even if it had been placed in some form of 'special measures', the queues and ensuing bank run could have been avoided.

Northern Rock's vulnerability was certainly known about by British regulators before the wholesale markets started to implode in August 2007. The problem was that nobody seemed quite sure who should be responsible for dealing with it. The Labour government had reformed banking regulation soon after taking office in May 1997. The Bank of England, after a series of embarrassing failures such as BCCI and Barings, was stripped of its traditional sole responsibility for overseeing banks. This was handed to a new body, the Financial Services Authority. The Bank was tasked with the job of maintaining and monitoring financial stability without direct powers to tell financial institutions how to behave. In the years of steady economic growth and easy credit before 2007, the FSA was principally focussed on consumer protection. A light-touch approach to regulating banks, backed by all the main political parties at Westminster, was seen as the most appropriate stance. After all, the City of London was a world-renowned financial centre and an important source of jobs and wealth for UK plc. Heavy-handedness by the regulators, it was widely agreed, would make it more likely that international banks would scale back their UK operations in favour of investment in more liberal centres elsewhere.

The Bank of England, for centuries the guardian of financial rectitude in the famous Square Mile of the City of London, had other fish to fry in the years leading up to 2007. Stripped of the responsibility to monitor the health of the banks and prescribe remedial action by individual institutions, the Bank focussed on its core mission – control of inflation. While the decision by the new Chancellor Gordon Brown in 1997 to transfer bank regulation to the FSA rankled at the highest levels of the Bank of England, there was great satisfaction at being handed full independent control of monetary policy. And no one was more satisfied than Mervyn King, then Deputy Governor of the Bank and before that its chief economist. Control of interest rates and a mandate to keep inflation at a target rate of 2.5 per cent (later amended to 2 per cent on a different inflation measure) was the ultimate train set for a monetary economist to play with. And King was the country's pre-eminent mone-tary economist at that time.

There was no doubting Mervyn King's academic credentials. His family background was modest – his father was a railway clerk who retrained as a teacher. After Wolverhampton Grammar School he progressed to King's College, Cambridge, taking a first in economics, before a master's and then a stint as a Kennedy Scholar at Harvard. His teaching career including a spell at Massachusetts Institute of Technology where he shared an office with Ben Bernanke, who later became chairman of the US Federal Reserve. After seven years as a professor at the London School of Economics, he joined the Bank of England as chief economist in 1991. King was one of the architects of the inflation-targeting regime adopted soon after Britain crashed out of the European Exchange Rate Mechanism in 1992. It was formalised with Bank independence in 1997 and has remained in place ever since. King ascended to the post of Governor, succeeding Eddie George, in 2003.

King was certainly a brilliant and widely respected economist. But to say that he did not suffer fools gladly was an understatement. He was, with good reason, supremely self-confident about his own judgement on economic affairs. Differing with him on such matters was likely to be met with a stern riposte and intellectual counterblast. One senior banker, preparing for his first meeting with King, asked for guidance from a Bank of England contact and was told not to disagree with the Governor. The banker laughed and suggested that might be difficult at times. The response from the Bank executive was 'No, you don't under-stand, do not disagree with him – he really doesn't like it'. Another lead-ing player in the City who sat on the Bank of England's governing body, the Court, recalled the atmosphere inside the Bank during King's gover-norship: 'It was like boarding a plane – anyone with a double first in economics turn left and everyone else head off down to the right.'

The Governor had a frosty relationship with some close colleagues at the Bank. Paul Tucker was a Bank of England 'lifer' who had worked in almost every part of the institution. He was head of the Bank's market operations, had an easy-going affinity with City bankers and was well-respected by leaders of the financial community. But he and King had not seen eye to eye for some time. At the height of the crisis they just about rubbed along together, doing the minimum required to maintain the right degree of professionalism. They may have worked together for many years but Tucker continued to address his superior at the Bank under the traditional title, 'Mr Governor', as did others who were part of the Bank hierarchy. Tucker was later to become Deputy Governor covering Financial Stability.

The Governor looked every inch the economics don rather than smooth City slicker. Owlish in appearance, he wore round-frame glasses which had thick lenses, giving him a beady-eyed aspect that could be quite unsettling in discussions about policy or high-level economics. King was a music lover, an enthusiasm he shared with his wife Barbara, a Finn. They were students at Cambridge and then lost touch. Thirty years later she called him from Finland, having recently divorced her first husband. King later told the BBC: 'We met at Frankfurt airport and I felt exactly the same about her as I had in 1970 – the moral of this story is never change your telephone number.'

King's enthusiasm for sport was well known to journalists who sat through his press conferences and others who listened to his speeches. Sporting metaphors and allusions would frequently be woven into complex arguments about economic policy, sometimes leaving lesser fans scratching their heads. As a lifelong Aston Villa supporter, football was one of his passions. In one speech King managed to compare a brilliant World Cup goal by Maradona against England to the conduct of monetary policy – the Argentinian star had run in a straight line while the England players moved left and right anticipating what he might do rather than what he actually did.

Cricket was another passion of the Governor. He took great pride in selecting former Test stars, including Graeme Hick and Andrew Strauss, to join his team for the annual match against the Bank of England's regular side. He would tell colleagues, only half-jokingly, that such a prerogative was highly likely to ensure victory for his Governor's Eleven. It was tacitly accepted by the Bank's team that getting the Governor out cheaply or smashing his slow left arm bowling around the ground was not done thing. Watching his county (Worcestershire) play or keeping tabs on England's progress in Test Matches were always King priorities. He devoted time and energy to a cricket charity which aimed to

promote the game in state schools. The Governor was sometimes criticised for popping up in the Royal Box at Wimbledon while some financial crisis was raging. This always seemed a trifle unfair as King was on
the committee of Wimbledon's All England Club and would make only
brief visits to the tournament.

The Governor had little time outside work, sport and music for socialis-
ing in the City. He recoiled from the idea of glad-handing bankers.
Senior hands in the City remembered with exasperation being invited
to a dinner with him in Threadneedle Street. They were bewildered
when King stood up after the starter and said he had to leave to deal
with important business, leaving his guests to continue with the rest of
the meal. When the crisis descended on the Bank in August 2007, the
banking industry was frustrated that the Governor seemed aloof and
unsympathetic to their plight. They felt that Eddie George and his
predecessor, Robin Leigh-Pemberton, had been more willing to hear
them out, often over a whisky in the Governor's parlour. They believed
the Bank of England's job was, at least in part, to stand up for the interests of the City of London and that the Governor was failing in his
duties. King – and he probably had considerable sympathy beyond the
City – never felt it was his responsibility to look after the trade union of
bankers or follow their agenda.

In the midsummer of 2007, all seemed well with the world. The economy was growing steadily, with six successive quarters above the long-
run average rate of expansion, and inflation was gliding down towards
its 2 per cent target. Mervyn King could reflect with some satisfaction
that the Bank was getting its job done, quietly and efficiently below the
radar of most political and financial comment. And that job, as far as
King was concerned, was keeping the lid on inflation. Monitoring
conditions in the banking markets with a view to maintaining financial
stability was not something the Governor gave much thought to.

Gordon Brown's long campaign to take the mantle of Prime Minister
from Tony Blair had finally borne fruit in June 2007. He moved from
the Treasury to 10 Downing Street and appointed Alistair Darling, a
long-standing ally from Scottish politics, to the post of Chancellor. A
shake-up of junior ministerial posts saw Kitty Ussher join the Treasury.
A professional economist and former adviser at the Department of

Trade and Industry (as it was then named), she had been elected as Labour MP for Burnley in 2005. Ussher's ministerial brief was to cover the City and financial markets and soon after her appointment she was invited to the Bank of England for a 'get to know you' breakfast with the Governor. King was pleasant and welcoming but suggested there was not much to talk about in areas covered by Ussher's post. Financial stability, he suggested, was a low priority and there were no obvious problems looming. The Governor noted that the team at the Bank covering stability in markets had been cut back as there was a reduced need for their services. Ussher was surprised, but acknowledged later that 'we weren't on the case either'.

By late July, though, a stronger breeze was ruffling the calm waters around the Bank and the City of London. The sub-prime mortgage woes of the United States were beginning to be seen as a threat to markets on both sides of the Atlantic. The scale of losses at the stricken Bear Sterns hedge funds was becoming clear. The Federal Reserve chairman, Ben Bernanke, warned that losses linked to sub-prime could mount to $100 billion. World stock markets wobbled and shares plunged in the final week of the month. That same week saw Northern Rock announcing an upbeat set of half-yearly results, mortgage sales up by 47 per cent over the year and an outlook described as 'very positive'. But some senior policymakers were having doubts about the Newcastle-based bank.

Northern Rock's funding model and vulnerability was well known amongst regulators. A share price fall of 10 per cent on one trading day in June, following a management warning that funding costs were rising, showed that there was nervousness in the market too. The Deputy Governor of the Bank of England with responsibility for financial stability, Sir John Gieve, was among those in the high level group known as the triparite (the Treasury, Bank of England and Financial Services Authority) who had been aware of the issue since the previous year. Gieve was an affable former civil service mandarin. At the Treasury he had worked for Chancellors Lawson, Major and Lamont, and then had taken the top job at the Home Office. His tenure, at a department where damage limitation was often the main focus of efforts, had been undermined by rows over foreign prisoners not being deported after serving jail sentences and management of departmental funding. Gieve knew his way around government and had long experience of financial policymaking but had a difficult relationship with the Governor, probably reflecting King's disdain for financial stability issues.

Staff at the Bank had drawn up a paper in the autumn of 2006 highlighting the vulnerability of some British banks to the possibility of the wholesale funding market drying up. Officials ranked the banking institutions in order of exposure to this credit market. Alliance & Leicester was at the top of the list because of its reliance on short-term borrowing from other banks and financial institutions. Northern Rock was a bit lower down because it depended more on securitisation – the bundling-up and sale of mortgages to raise money to lend to new customers. Securitisation at that stage was seen as a more stable source of funding than inter-bank borrowing. When the credit crisis struck the markets the following year, however, Northern Rock was forced to resort to short-term wholesale borrowing. This paper, signed off by Sir John Gieve, was sent to the FSA. It was duly noted but no action was taken. The Bank of England's Financial Stability report published in April 2007 had talked in more general terms about the risks of banks' reliance on funding other than customer deposits: 'Securitisation still leaves the UK banks exposed to a deterioration in market conditions. If they were unable to securitise existing assets, new lending would need to be financed through other wholesale sources, which may be difficult or costly to access during times of stress.'

Gieve was ultimately responsible for the Financial Stability reports, published bi-annually. He had asked Bank staff working on the analysis to produce a slimmer, more readable document than hitherto and one which was more accessible to the markets and the media. He later reflected that the Bank did not realise at the time how telling the analysis was: 'We did spot elements of the vulnerability quite well but we didn't see how big or how imminent the threats were.' With hindsight, he admits they should have done more to highlight their opinions with counterparts at the FSA and in the Treasury rather than writing reports and then not following them up. The problem at the time, though, was that there was an assumption at the highest levels of the Bank that their responsibility was to flag up concerns rather than to take action.

The FSA later owned up to failings over the policing of Northern Rock before the crisis. In March 2008, it published details of an internal performance audit. The chief executive, Hector Sants, said at the time: 'Our supervision of Northern Rock in the period leading up to the market instability of last summer was not carried out to a standard that is acceptable.' A litany of errors was set out, including neglecting to hold enough meetings with Northern Rock and to follow up concerns about the funding model. A high turnover of regulatory staff, some lured to higher paid roles in financial services, was also cited as a factor in the failure to hold the bank to account. Sants, however, argued that it was impossible to say whether the FSA's failings affected the outcome at Northern Rock. Defenders of the FSA have consistently argued that it was not the only global regulator caught short when the credit markets froze. They also stress that political leaders of all parties wanted light-touch 'principles-based' regulation rather than the heavy-handed enforcement of rulebooks.

The complacency of regulators infected Northern Rock itself. The bank had ploughed on through the summer of 2007 with few reasons to be concerned about the future. The chairman was Matt Ridley, an intellectual scion of an aristocratic Northumberland family. He was the nephew of the late Conservative Cabinet minister Nicholas Ridley and would later inherit the title Viscount Ridley on the death of his father, who in his time had also served as chairman of Northern Rock. Matt Ridley, who was tall, bespectacled and looked suitably boffin-like, had worked as a journalist and written extensively on zoology and political philosophy. By his own admission he saw himself as a non-executive chairman without banking expertise and relying on seasoned operators in the financial world serving as non-executive directors.

Ridley and his non-executives had discussed Northern Rock's funding model from time to time. They were aware that the bank was heavily reliant on wholesale markets functioning normally. But on each occasion someone in the group had pointed out that regulators seemed unconcerned and if they were not voicing any worries there could hardly be any reason for the bank to change policy. A friend of Ridley's from a business background had warned him that the bank was dangerously exposed. But that was the only Cassandra-like voice. The Northern Rock chairman had a good relationship with Mervyn King as the

Governor had read some of Ridley's books and warmed to a fellow intellectual. A dinner with King in early 2007 attended by some of the Northern Rock directors had got round to the subject of liquidity in the system. The Governor had not demurred from a consensus that there was no obvious threat to the smooth operation of that part of the financial machinery.

When the financial volcano erupted on Thursday 9 August and the European Central Bank pumped emergency liquidity into the markets, British policymakers did not make much noise. As a deliberately planned strategy it might have had some merit because of the need to maintain calm and refrain from excitable media interventions. But the truth was more prosaic – the Chancellor was on holiday in Majorca and did not know what had happened till he caught sight of a *Financial Times* the next day. Kitty Ussher was on duty at the Treasury but she was on other business on the day in question. Like Darling she realised there was a problem in the markets only when she picked up a newspaper the following morning while waiting to do a radio interview at the BBC's Westminster studios. Treasury officials had not thought it necessary to disturb the Chancellor on holiday or provide a briefing note to the junior Treasury minister.

At the Bank, King was in his office and monitoring developments. The previous day he had told journalists at the quarterly Inflation Report media conference that 'our banking system is much more resilient than in the past', though he did not deny that he and other Bank policymakers had discussed developments in the markets at some length. Gieve was away. The Deputy Governor's mother had died and he had been organising the funeral. After that he took a long, planned holiday. Gieve phoned in each day and offered to come back from his leave but was encouraged by the Governor not to break his trip as there was no evidence at that stage of a systemic crisis. The Bank had been taken aback by the speed and scale of the European Central Bank's response on 9 August. Some senior sources in the tripartite believed the ECB had panicked by turning on the funding taps that day and claimed later that the US Federal Reserve had been furious. The ECB, it was argued, had generated a sense of crisis with its unexpected and large-scale intervention.

The following day, Friday 10 August, saw a stock market rout and the beginnings of a severe contraction in the availability of short-term bank funding. Federal Reserve policymakers had taken a similar stance to the Bank of England at their regular meeting three days previously. They had held interest rates and played down the idea that the sub-prime drama might hold back what was otherwise a growing economy. By that Friday, though, it was all change at the Fed and emergency funding was being hosed into the US market with one of the central bank's lending rates reduced. The Bank of England did not follow suit. There was no special extra liquidity operation. It was not long before Mervyn King would face a rising tide of criticism for refusing to turn on the Bank of England's taps to flood a credit market that was drying up.

Crisis or no crisis, it did not take long for Northern Rock to realise that the game had changed dramatically. The bank was preparing to launch a new securitisation exercise that would see another tranche of mortgages sold in the markets to raise funding to cover impending liabilities and new lending. But that was several weeks away. In the meantime, plans to raise short-term funding had suddenly turned sour. Persuading lenders to roll over loans rather than demand repayment had become considerably more difficult. The inter-bank funding market had seen benchmark lending rates, known as LIBOR, escalate over two days. Northern Rock was going to have to use those markets to keep plodding along but they had become dramatically more expensive.

The Northern Rock board decided quickly that a takeover by a bigger bank was their only escape route. The bank's brokers were instructed to put up a 'For Sale' sign and find buyers. Barclays, RBS and Santander were all approached as obvious candidates for a deal with Northern Rock. But the timing was unfortunate. All three potential suitors were embroiled in another corporate battle, as bidders for ABN Amro. The message back to Northern Rock from all three of the banks was positive but with a suggestion that the issue be postponed until October, by which time the ABN Amro situation would be resolved. But October would be too late for Northern Rock. It was another piece of bad luck for the Newcastle bank.

In the week beginning 13 August, the Rocks' bosses were contacting the FSA to alert them to their problems. The bank regulators, however complacent they might have been in the months before, were now on high alert. Northern Rock was code-named 'Elvis' and the Newcastle headquarters 'Memphis' as FSA executives began to draw up contingency plans. Matt Ridley, given his personal rapport with Mervyn King, put in a call directly to the Governor to notify him of the bank's troubles. The Northern Rock chairman was anxious not to spook the Governor while not downplaying the board's concerns – he also wanted politely to enquire whether the Bank of England might do more to boost the supply of liquidity.

King's response was surprising. He quoted the Nobel prize-winning economist George Akerlof's 'The Market for Lemons', a treatise based on the second-hand car market. The theory was that a seller should never under-price a poor second-hand car (known in the US as a 'lemon') as buyers would assume it was dodgy. If the price is too low, nobody will make an offer. King's advice to Ridley was not to appear too desperate in the wholesale money markets by being prepared to pay more than others to secure funding. In the same vein as the 'lemons', nobody would be prepared to lend to Northern Rock if the interest rate looked too high.

Though few in the City beyond Threadneedle Street were thinking of lemons at the time, most bankers were aware that offering too high an interest rate in a stressed money market would raise eyebrows. Paying too much would smack of desperation. There was a clear incentive for a bank to talk down the rates it paid in the LIBOR market. These rates were reported each day to the compilers of the LIBOR data. It was an issue which exploded into scandal when it was alleged that Barclays was under-stating the rates it paid to borrow. An FSA investigation concluded five years later revealed that managers at Barclays had instructed staff who submitted data on borrowing costs to reduce the figures to avoid negative publicity in the markets. The findings resulted in total fines, including US regulators, of nearly £300 million. Other leading banks, including RBS and UBS, were also fined over LIBOR by authorities on both sides of the Atlantic.

From the middle of August, Northern Rock's bosses were concerned about their predicament. But it would be another four weeks before its problems became public knowledge and its battle for survival as a private sector bank was over. Right up until the end of the month, the Rock's directors hoped that the funding markets would warm up again and a mortgage securitisation might be possible. They felt they had enough cash to keep going at least until the middle of the following month. Within the tripartite group there was scepticism about that but there was still hope that a takeover by another bank might be engineered. The traditional way of doing things in the City was for the Bank of England Governor to call in members of the bank bosses club over a weekend, bang their heads together and leave them to come up with a lifeboat solution for whichever institution was in trouble. Older City hands remembered when the distressed bank Barings was rescued by ING of the Netherlands, with the then Governor Eddie George getting both sets of directors round the table at the Bank and a symbolic £1 being passed from purchaser to seller.

At the Treasury there was mounting frustration at what was perceived as Bank of England inaction. The Governor, it was felt, had the powers to intervene and boost the supply of funding to help Northern Rock under a blanket liquidity window opened to the whole market but was refusing to do so. As one source put it: 'People would stomp up and down corridors saying "Bloody hell, the Bank must do this – we have got the risk and they have got the levers"'. Kitty Ussher was not the only one at the Treasury who was perplexed that the Bank of England was not making use of the extensive powers at the disposal of a central bank. On one occasion while in the car driving back to Westminster after a meeting with Mervyn King, she had discussed with a senior Treasury official the Bank's apparent reluctance to get more involved. 'What will it take to make the Governor change his attitudes?', she asked. 'Probably a run on a bank', Ussher answered her own question flippantly.

A Bank of England-engineered solution involving a bidder being sounded out for Northern Rock looked tricky given the febrile state of financial markets. But feelers were put out to two would-be suitors, RBS and Lloyds. Interest at RBS quickly waned but Lloyds, at that stage cautiously run and well-capitalised, was certainly ready to do business with Northern Rock. For a little while, talks between the two over a rescue takeover proceeded smoothly. The difficulty was that the Lloyds board had identified a funding gap of £60 billion. Lloyds was prepared to cover half that liability but believed it needed a guarantee from the Bank of England to provide up to £30 billion of funding until the wholesale markets reopened and Northern Rock could finance itself again. This opened a hornet's nest as far as the Governor and Chancellor were concerned. There was reluctance to extend credit lines to one bank in a commercial deal with another. This, it was feared, would penalise other banks who had not had the same opportunity to borrow on the same terms. And for King, the theory of moral hazard was a guiding principle – bailing out banks on less than punitive terms would only encourage the others to take more risk in future in the knowledge there was always a Bank of England safety net.

On 30 August, Ridley came to London for a meeting at the Bank of England. The FSA got to hear about it and demanded that he spend time with its senior regulators. The FSA was still hopeful that the Lloyds deal could be successfully negotiated and offered support to the Northern Rock chairman in his attempts to pursue it. But when Ridley sat down at Threadneedle Street with the Governor, he got a very different impression. King informed Ridley that the Lloyds offer was too low and Northern Rock deserved to continued as an independent business. The Governor had earlier voiced his confidence that Northern Rock would be successful with its securitisation exercise in September. Ridley left confused at the mixed messages he was getting from different parts of the tripartite authority and concerned that his bank would be allowed to fall between the different stools.

Up in Newcastle, there was still optimism that the Lloyds deal could be made to work and would get the nod from the authorities. Lloyds had a 100-strong team combing through the Northern Rock books in a specially constituted data room. The 'Black Horse' bank was known to be cautious. It had shied away from takeovers in the past and did not have the same aggressive approach as RBS. Late on Friday 7 September, Lloyds did begin to draw back. But, encouraged by the FSA, the talks were revived over the weekend with a Bank of England guarantee still on the table. Nervously, Ridley, the Northern Rock chief executive Adam Applegarth and other directors waited by the phone in the North-East. On the Monday came the call which they had dreaded – the tripartite authority could not approve the Lloyds deal.

Fingers were pointed at Mervyn King for refusing to agree to the request for a £30 billion loan. He later made clear that the Bank of England could not agree to such a drain on its balance sheet without the approval of the Chancellor. The ball, as far as the Governor as concerned, was in Alistair Darling's court. If the Chancellor wished to give a guarantee to the Bank of England to backstop the credit line then of course it was possible to provide it. Darling's recollection was that none of the other banks was interested in Northern Rock and that Lloyds never made a serious offer: 'There is always someone sniffing around something – never at any stage did they come and say they were interested in even half an offer – if they had come and said they are serious about buying this that would have been helpful.'

An added brace of problems which contributed to the failure of the Lloyds plan was what should be revealed to financial markets and what might constitute state aid under European Union rules. As Northern Rock had told markets before 9 August it was confident of its sources of commercial funding, the fact that it now needed help from the authorities represented a material change in its circumstances. The secret talks with Lloyds would have to be declared to investors at some stage to avoid a false market for Northern Rock shares developing. EU rules might well bar such a large guarantee being given by a central bank to a single institution. In the end trying to make a takeover of Northern Rock work part-funded by the Bank of England proved beyond the wit of the regulators and lawyers. With hindsight, though, many have said the Governor, backed by the Chancellor, should have gone ahead and brokered a deal rather than bowing to the views of lawyers. The extent that the possible Lloyds bid was ever a runner fell at a fence some way from the finishing line.

The FSA's chief executive Hector Sants was convinced a marriage could have been arranged, so avoiding the ensuing debacle, and he told the BBC five years later: 'I think things would have been very different if the government and the Bank had taken my recommendation that they should provide liquidity support to Lloyds to purchase Northern Rock'. But some senior players at the Bank of England and the Treasury were never fully convinced. They have since argued that because the Northern Rock business model was so fundamentally flawed, a deal with Lloyds and support from the Bank of England would only postpone the day of reckoning. One senior regulator described it as 'a bridge to nowhere'.

The Northern Rock train was now hurtling out of control of the regulators. The board threw in the towel and asked the Bank of England to act in its traditional role of lender of last resort. King and his colleagues agreed. On Wednesday 12 September, the Bank published a letter the Governor had written to the Treasury Select Committee chairman John McFall. King, in what seemed like a high-brow treatise, argued his case for not risking moral hazard by lending banks money just because they had made bad decisions about strategy. But one sentence tucked away in the letter appeared to make an exception:

> "Central banks, in their traditional lender of last resort (LOLR) role, can lend 'against good collateral at a penalty rate' to an individual bank facing temporary liquidity problems, but that is otherwise regarded as solvent."

The Governor appeared to be clearing the intellectual road to a bailout of Northern Rock. While rejecting the blanket demands for more liquidity that had been made by the banking industry, King was explaining how the Bank could make an exception for a single institution which was the victim of temporary and unforeseen factors rather than the legacy of rash lending. It was an elegantly written document, typical of King's intellectual approach to banking and markets. But it would not save Northern Rock.

Chapter 2

The Rock rescue

In the early evening of Thursday 13 September, a meeting of members of each branch of the tripartite authority took place at the Treasury. Chaired by Alistair Darling, it had been convened to finalise the details of the Rock bailout. The intention was for the announcement to be made the following Monday when the markets opened for business at 7 a.m. It was hoped that a low-key technocratic-style statement would be published setting out details of the loan from the Bank of England to Northern Rock. The theory was that the authorities would be seen to be in control and moving in a business-like way to assist a bank experiencing temporary turbulence. As one source put it: 'The idea was to keep it on the business pages rather than the main news.' But the plan began to unravel when, from a corner of the room, a Treasury press officer interrupted the proceedings. 'Robert Peston has been on again and this time he's asking the right questions', was the unexpected message. Darling abruptly ended the meeting and moved off swiftly with his advisers.

Robert Peston, then the BBC's business editor, had started to ask questions on the state of Northern Rock a few weeks earlier. He had been sceptical about the Rock's financial model for some time and the market crisis of August 9th had rekindled his suspicions. Initially, it had been possible for the Treasury and the Bank to stonewall his enquiries. But Mervyn King's letter had provided the final piece of the jigsaw. By Thursday evening, Peston was asking directly whether the Bank of England would be providing a loan to Northern Rock and it was impossible to deny. As Darling had feared, the cat was out of the bag. Peston went on the BBC News Channel just after 8p.m. to break the story. Kitty Ussher, who had been at the tripartite meeting, had taken a train to Stockport en route to her Burnley constituency. She got into her car, parked at the station, turned on the radio and was flabbergasted to hear the BBC broadcasting details of a plan which had been discussed only a couple of hours earlier. Ussher had planned as usual a week in the constituency to deal with local issues ahead of the party conference season. It would not be long before the Chancellor summoned her back to London warning that 'soon none of us may have constituencies to go back to'.

Peston had broadcast his scoop on BBC outlets stressing that while Northern Rock was being provided with emergency liquidity this did not mean there was anything for savers to worry about. In his BBC News blog he said: 'None of us – not even Northern Rock's depositors – probably need to panic that the Bank has had to step in'. He pointed out that if the authorities had thought Northern Rock was not a viable bank, they would not have agreed to rescue it. But the news report lit a touchpaper. Within a few hours Northern Rock's website had crashed. Many of the bank's savers watching the news on TV that night only had to pick up a laptop, go to the website and move their money out of the Rock. The fact that the website was down created a sense of crisis around the bank from which it never recovered. The IT staff had been caught on the hop – they did not get the website running again until it was too late. More preparation might have kept the site going longer at the outset and avoided the early panic.

Caught on the hop too was the rest of the banking industry. Angela Knight, chief executive of the British Bankers' Association, was hosting a reception on a passenger boat on the River Thames with many City financiers and others from the markets. She had to move away from the crowd of well-refreshed guests to take a call on her mobile phone. The news about Northern Rock came as a bolt from the blue to Knight and others with her. Stuck on the boat, the event continued but the bankers' revels were subdued. All the talk was of how the Rock could have got itself in the position of needing a Bank of England lifeline. And there was inevitably speculation about who would be next.

The following morning, Friday 14 September, saw a torrent of media calls directed at Northern Rock, the Treasury and the Bank of England. There were incessant demands for interviews. But the Chancellor and Bank Governor had flown to Portugal for a meeting of European finance ministers – Alistair Darling felt that not showing up would add to the sense of crisis. Adam Applegarth made a few media appearances, arguing that his bank must be sound if the Bank of England was prepared to lend to it. But the stalwart of most media outlets that morning was Angela Knight, doing her best to extol the virtues of the British banking system and reassure audiences their money was safe. She clocked up 19 back-to-back interviews on TV and radio. Her son, travelling in the Far East and for a while out of contact, called later that day to tell his mother he had seen the story on local TV. It was the only cheerful moment in Knight's day.

Whatever was being said by broadcasters and their guests, Northern Rock customers began to make their way to branches. Small clutches of people gathered outside a few outlets, waiting patiently to get inside to speak to staff and withdraw their money. For BBC News and other TV channels there was a dilemma – show the pictures and risk the accusation of inciting people to queue or keep the pictures off the air and face the charge of suppressing information. But by lunchtime it was clear there were queues at every branch. Northern Rock's second major misfortune, after the shutdown of its website, was that it did not have a large number of branches – just 70 around the UK, few of which were in the populous South East of England. As a result, there were fewer locations than at other high street banks at which customers could go and withdraw cash, hence the larger number of them appearing at each one.

Northern Rock staff had not been briefed on how to handle the flow of customers building up outside branches – there had not been time because of the unexpected revelation of the emergency loan. There was no grasp of how to organise the queues and to get as many people as possible in and out of the branches with their money. At the same time, at Northern Rock headquarters in Newcastle there seemed to be a lack of recognition of the scale of the impending disaster as hundreds of millions of pounds were withdrawn by depositors. The website had slowed to a crawl because of the volume of traffic attempting to get money out, yet the bank's IT experts appeared unable to resort to contingency measures, if indeed there were any back-up plans in place. The press office was overwhelmed with calls yet offers of help from the British Bankers' Association and other sources were rejected. It was hard, however, to blame the beleaguered Rock management and staff, as there was no template on how to deal with a bank run.

If there was no template for the Rock's executives, there was no certainly
no emergency plan stored away in the Treasury for the Chancellor to
dust down and enact. Alistair Darling flew back from the meeting in
Portugal, in his own words, jammed in the back seats of a small chartered plane with Mervyn King. There was time to get to know each other
a bit better on the flight, whiling away the time with talk of football as
well discussing how to deal with the Rock. They had seen TV footage of
the queues on rolling news channels, highly and embarrassingly visible
on screens around the conference hall. But there was nothing in the
Treasury or Bank of England playbook that could be deployed. No
Chancellor or Governor had been confronted with a run on a bank
since the nineteenth century.

Back at the Bank of England that day, senior officials were coming to
the conclusion that the only way to reassure customers and stop the
queues was to offer a blanket guarantee of all deposits. That had to
come from the government because while Threadneedle Street could
manage a £20 billion loan to the struggling bank, it could not afford to
underwrite £80 billion of Northern Rock deposits on its balance sheet.
It was the logical, though unpalatable, next step once the taxpayer,
through the Bank of England, had offered to pump in enough cash to
save the bank. The emergency loan had been announced but the fact
that savers were not reassured and were demanding their money neces-
sitated further action, so the Bank's thinking went. It was inconceivable
that Northern Rock would be allowed to fail once the decision to save it
had been made. Sir John Gieve's view was that 'it was double or quits –
we had already decided not to quit, we had already decided to save this
bank so we had to get on and save it – this seemed an absolute
no-brainer'. The Bank's view that a blanket guarantee of deposits was
required was conveyed to the Treasury late on the Friday. But from then
right through the weekend until the Monday, the government did not
take the advice. Gieve later concluded that the failure to offer the guarantee while the queues built up for another three days was
'cack-handed'.

On Friday and over the weekend, either in physical withdrawals from
branches or via the bank website, it is thought that about £2 billion was
taken out by customers. The queues continued at some branches
through Monday and late that afternoon Alistair Darling announced

that the government would guarantee all Northern Rock deposits, including those by local authorities and commercial lenders. Over the weekend, the Chancellor had revisited the Lloyds takeover idea, supported by a Bank of England loan guarantee. But it had not gone anywhere. Lloyds' bosses were contacted again and insisted on the same official backstop if any deal was to go ahead. There were concerns in the Treasury about using the government's balance sheet to underpin a struggling bank. Guaranteeing one bank's deposits might prompt questions about others. Ministers and officials wondered whether the rot might not be stopped and whether customers of Alliance & Leicester and other banks seen to be vulnerable might start pulling out their money. Darling was not convinced that underwriting all deposits on the Friday or Saturday would have made much difference. The government guarantee was finally announced by the Chancellor in the bizarre setting of a press conference with US Treasury Secretary Hank Paulson, who was visiting London at the time. That did the trick as far as the queues were concerned. It looked more like business as usual at Northern Rock branches by the following morning.

The damage had been done. The government had the daunting task of working out a way forward for Northern Rock and juggling the need to find a private sector buyer while ensuring that the taxpayer's interest was protected. But hanging over the tripartite group and, ultimately, Downing Street, was the whiff of incompetence. The run on the Rock was a humiliation for a government and banking industry which sought to ensure the UK was globally respected as a financial centre. The recriminations were swift. Mervyn King and Sir John Gieve were summoned to account for themselves before the Treasury Select Committee of MPs. In a bruising session, Gieve took many of the punches. The committee chairman John McFall accused him of being 'asleep in the back shop while there was a mugging out the front'. King was asked at one point which of the members of the tripartite had been in charge during the weeks before the run on Northern Rock. The Governor, to the surprise of MPs, answered 'it depends what you mean by in charge'.

One of the areas probed by the Treasury Select Committee was the state of readiness of the government and other regulators before the market crisis flared up in August 2007. Their investigation and subsequent revelations revealed major shortcomings in what might charitably be termed the UK's defences in the event of a financial hurricane. No regulator or government in any leading economy had anticipated anything like the severity of the credit market freeze which developed. To suggest that the Treasury, Bank of England or Financial Services Authority should have had comprehensive contingency plans in place would have been unfair. But it transpired that the UK was, in some key respects, the least well protected of any of the major industrialised nations. And one of the most exposed areas was deposit protection.

To expect customers of high street banks to assess the financial health of institutions as they decide where to deposit their money is unrealistic. A deposit protection scheme exists to ensure that in the event of a bank failure, most ordinary customers are left with the bulk of their savings. But any such scheme can offer protection only up to a certain threshold as otherwise it would be unaffordable. Wealthier savers are expected to know that their money is not protected above that threshold – it is assumed that better-off customers should be financially literate enough to spread their savings around different institutions. The UK scheme at the time of the Northern Rock collapse ensured that 100 per cent of the first £2,000 of deposits was fully protected, then 90 per cent of the next £33,000. The theory was that many customers would be fully protected and that those with £35,000 would get most of their money back in the event of a failure. The 90 per cent rather than 100 per cent had an element of 'moral hazard' about it – an incentive for customers to do some homework on the banks they were entrusting with their money.

The British deposit protection scheme, as it happened, was one of the least generous of leading economies. Run by the Financial Services Compensation Scheme, an independent body funded by a levy on financial services firms, it covered a relatively low level of savings in the event of a bank default. The US had a higher level of protection following the toppling of the savings and loans institutions in the previous decade. There had been lengthy debates about deposit protection inside the European Union in the 1990s. A baseline safety net was agreed with member states allowed to 'gold-plate' if they wished. The UK chose to remain at the harsher end of the scale with depositors expected to take a small chunk of risk should a bank collapse. The thinking was that it was unhealthy if savers did not care how strong or weak their banks were. But as one senior government source put it subsequently 'in stress conditions it's a dangerous set up and was a mistaken judgement'. It seems to have been a judgement by officials rather than a political one by ministers. But it resulted in a flaw which made Northern Rock's problems a lot worse than they might have been.

The stark reality was that if you had more than £2,000 in an account at Northern Rock, there was every incentive to queue to get the money out. 90 per cent protection above that level might have sounded reasonable before September 2007. But when a bank was unstable enough to need a Bank of England loan and there seemed plenty of alternative homes on the high street, depositors reasoned that instead of potentially losing 10 per cent of some of their savings it was better to withdraw the money and secure the full 100 per cent elsewhere. This explains Mervyn King's comment to Alistair Darling as they watched TV pictures of the Northern Rock queues in the margins of the Portugal meeting: 'They're behaving perfectly rationally, you know.' Darling later reflected ruefully that 'it was helpful advice, which you come to value'. But King was stating the obvious truth given the low level of deposit protection in the UK – there was no compelling reason to leave money in the Rock during the first couple of days of the run.

Deposit protection was improved considerably after the Northern Rock queues had ebbed away. On 1 October it was extended to cover all of the first £35,000 of a customer deposit. A year later, at the height of the banking crisis, it went up to £50,000 and then from early 2011, the threshold rose again to £85,000. That brought protection in line with where the United States had been in 2007 but the American threshold protection has since been raised to $250,000. The Bank of England had examined the question of deposit protection some years before the run on the Rock. Mervyn King had argued during these Bank discussions for more extensive protection after the Asian-owned bank BCCI had collapsed in the early 1990s, also prompting queues outside some of the UK branches. He had made the case for 100 per cent insurance up to a higher level – 90 per cent, he felt, was simply an invitation for depositors to try to get their money out of a stricken bank. The issue was never pursued and the UK was left with what many acknowledged was inadequate protection once the Rock foundered. In September 2007, full coverage up to something closer to £85,000 – and properly publicised – might well have reassured savers and prevented the queues.

Senior policymakers who had to handle the Rock debacle are clear that in another vital area the British regulatory system's readiness for a bank run was woeful. The UK, unlike most other members of the G7 group of leading industrialised economies, did not have a resolution regime – in other words, a toolbox allowing a doomed bank to be wound up rapidly and efficiently. There was no legal framework which would allow regulators to seize control of a bank, and to 'resolve' its future by selling off parts to other institutions and winding down others. Yet the lack of a resolution regime was well known to policymakers before the Rock's collapse – it had been identified in 'war games' carried out by the tripartite authority in 2006.

These preparatory exercises were designed to identify weaknesses in regulation and contingency planning. They were carried out in conjunction with American regulators who wanted to test their own systems with a scenario involving a crisis and banks toppling. The exercises identified what turned out to be a central problem in dealing with Northern Rock – the absence of legal authority to sort out a bank's problems over a weekend, away from the gaze of the markets and not in conflict with rules on disclosure to shareholders. In 2006, a senior regulator at the Financial Services Authority had written to other members of the tripartite authority pointing out the flaws in both the resolution capability and the deposit protection scheme. However, the recommendations after the 'war games' seem to have sat in the Treasury's in-tray and got no further. When Alistair Darling arrived in the Chancellor's office in June 2007, he found no recommendations for action or legislation and the need for a resolution regime was nowhere near the top of the list of priorities presented to him by civil servants. He later reflected that the contingency planning 'might as well not have been done for all the help it was to us', while acknowledging that in the summer of 2007 the prospect of a bank crash seemed remote and not worthy of extensive consideration. Darling, though, recalled a planning exercise on London Underground when he was Secretary of State for Transport which identified a host of problems for emergency services, including oxygen supplies not working. Better equipment was procured and training modified so that by the time of the bombings in July 2005, the response was much more effective than it would otherwise have been.

Ironically, further 'war games' had been planned for October 2007. Ministers and civil servants had been asked to clear diaries for a few days that month. A scenario had been planned with the Americans that involved a bank going under and telephone calls being handled in a mock 'bunker' at the Treasury. It never happened. By October, Whitehall had been confronted with the real thing and been found wanting.

A resolution regime was created in February 2008. Legislation at that time covered the nationalisation of Northern Rock and provided for regulators to take control of fatally wounded banks in similar situations. It was used to good effect on Bradford & Bingley in September 2008. In February 2009, an updated version became law and this was swiftly put into practice with the Dunfermline Building Society in March of that year . There was a simple but effective sequence of events each time. The Financial Services Authority would announce the institutions were no longer fit to take depositors' cash at the beginning of a weekend. By the end of it, regulators had stripped out whatever was impossible to sell and shunted it on to the government's balance sheet. A buyer was found for the marketable part and the transaction was executed swiftly. Repeated messages that depositors' cash was safe were broadcast. Every leading policymaker involved in fighting the fires at Northern Rock in September 2007 agrees that the resolution regime in place after February 2008 would have made a big difference if it had been on the statute book six months earlier. It is conceivable that if those tools had been available to regulators, the bank could have been 'resolved' over the weekend before the fateful events of Thursday 13 September. Lloyds could have taken on the 'good' parts of Northern Rock and the queues would never have happened.

As recriminations reverberated and the blame game began, attention focussed on the Bank of England's handling of the crisis. Much of the criticism was aimed at the Governor. The heat was turned up on Mervyn King by many in the City of London, indignant at what they saw as his failure to support the needs of the financial sector. One prominent commentator, reflecting the views of banking boardrooms, predicted at the height of the row that King would be gone within 24 hours. But the

Governor's reign continued. Battered by the storm of briefings against him, King soldiered on. He was determined not to follow some other central banks and, as he saw it, pander to the needs of reckless investment bankers. The banking industry, in turn, believed that King had failed a fundamental requirement of central bankers – to provide succour to sclerotic financial markets at a time of crisis.

The central criticism of the Bank of England was that it had failed to follow the European Central Bank and the US Federal Reserve in providing funds in exchange for a wide range of collateral once the credit markets had stalled in August. The Frankfurt- and Washington-based central banks had offered loans to banks and taken as collateral mortgages and other loans. The Bank of England stuck to its existing arrangements, offered liquidity in exchange only for high quality collateral, UK government bonds (gilts) and for relatively short periods. King's reasoning was that these facilities would provide any struggling bank with the money it needed without appearing to make life easier for an institution which was the author of its own plight. Senior Bank sources believed that the ECB had over-reacted and created a sense of panic simply by the act of dramatically upping its support for the markets. But bank chiefs could not understand what they saw as King's overly academic stance, seemingly infused with a cogently argued but impractical concept of moral hazard. The Bank's facilities, some argued, were designed with the narrow aim of helping control inflation by ensuring a stable overnight interest rate and had underplayed the need to provide liquidity insurance.

Inside the Bank there was not unanimity behind King's position. Some senior officials believed that a central bank's role, as originally set out by the nineteenth-century constitutional expert Walter Bagehot, was to bail out struggling banks at penalty interest rates but also to provide blanket funding for the market as a whole. A bank on the verge of failure could go to the central bank and be bailed out under cover of an industry wide scheme. In that way there would be no stigma if recipients of Bank of England loans were revealed. Healthy banks could access funds temporarily at rates of interest comparable to others in the market so there would be an incentive for them to do so. The Bank of England could even persuade a range of banks to take funding through this route even though they did not need it – a ruse to give the impression of a market-wide solution. A bank desperate for Bank of England cash to survive, meanwhile, would pay a penalty rate which was kept confidential – that was necessary to underline the point that banks in trouble because of their own recklessness could not expect easy money as a lifeline. The Financial Services Authority pressed hard for the Bank to adopt such measures, arguing it was the central bank's responsibility to oil the wheels when normal market mechanisms were grinding to a halt.

Allies of King maintain that the Bank of England's existing liquidity facilities in August 2007 were adequate. These operations were described in a set of rules codified in a Bank of England 'bible' known as the Red Book. It had been updated by Paul Tucker the previous year and was considered to meet the needs of modern banks. The commercial banks could choose what reserves they held at the Bank of England and could access a 'liquidity window' at regular intervals topping up their reserves in exchange for top-notch collateral. King's reasoning was that there was no point in forcing liquidity on banks which did not ask for it. Commercial bank chiefs did not want to use the window because doing so they feared might suggest they were having problems. But it was suspected in the Bank of England that the bank bosses did not understand how the system worked, leaving such apparently mundane matters as money market dealings with Threadneedle Street to more junior staff.

Those close to King argued that liquidity was provided under the radar even if there was not a high-profile scheme such as that announced by the European Central Bank. The billions lent to Northern Rock flowed out into the wider banking market. By early September the Bank of England had expanded its balance sheet commitments, yet the ECB's net position, after repayments are taken into account, was the same as at the start of the previous month. At senior levels of the Bank there was a suspicion that the banks that had been briefing against the Governor to the press were the very banks struggling to raise funding. HSBC, by contrast, was awash with liquidity as investors sought to deposit their cash in what was seen as safe haven in a crisis. A leading Bank of England official later reflected that coping with hostile briefings in the City and othe sources were 'far and away the hardest part' of tackling the crisis.

Within a few days of the Northern Rock embarrassment, King announced that he was letting the liquidity taps flow more freely. The Bank agreed to supply funds over a three-month time period and accept mortgages as collateral, though at a higher rate of interest than prevailing in the money market. A £10 billion tender would take place at weekly intervals. It looked like a U-turn but King defended it, arguing that circumstances had changed in the markets since the run on the Rock and the liquidity made available to individual banks was not large. But when the banks were invited to tender for the Bank's cash there were no takers. The penal rate of interest was unattractive to those banks which were not struggling to raise funds and those who badly needed the cash were worried about their reputations if the markets knew they had to resort to the Bank's offer.

Some inside the Bank continued to be sceptical about King's position. They recall a very difficult autumn with demands for more action by the Treasury and Financial Services Authority intensifying. There was a feeling that at the highest level of Threadneedle Street there was a failure to absorb how serious the situation had become even with the relative calm after the Northern Rock bailout. But the Bank's thinking did eventually change. By the following spring, it had launched a bigger and more ambitious lending plan, called the Special Liquidity Scheme (SLS). A wider range of collateral, including credit cards loans as well as a range of mortgage debt, would be acceptable at the Bank in exchange for funding in the shape of liquid assets easily tradeable in markets and over a three-year period. Over a period of less than a year, £185 billion was lent to banks. SLS was hailed as a great success and precisely the sort of initiative that a central bank should be pursuing during times of stress in the markets.

Looking back, and accepting the wisdom of hindsight, King's critics are clear that if a bold policy based on the same thinking as SLS had been adopted in late August or early September, Northern Rock could have been saved. The scheme would have dealt with the Rock's immediate funding needs – others would have found it attractive enough to take part too so it would not have looked like a rescue of one troubled institution. Northern Rock would probably not have survived as an independent bank but, with another six months' breathing space, the authorities could have pushed it into a merger or takeover by another player, as was to be the case with Alliance & Leicester. Instead, Northern Rock hit the buffers and UK policymakers had to live with the consequences.

Some see Northern Rock as an important wake-up call for regulators and ministers. The lack of preparedness and weaknesses in the banking system's defences had been painfully exposed. Lessons would be learned, procedures tightened and the financial watchdogs put on high alert for the next crisis. The Northern Rock experience paved the way for the post-Lehman Brothers response in September and October 2008. Kitty Ussher's view is that vital lessons were learned:

> 'Mervyn did not get his head round the responsibilities of a central bank, we at the Treasury did not get our heads round the respon-sibilities of government and in particular the need to act very quickly. However it made us realise the enormity of the situation we were in – our neurological pathways were opened up to act much faster second time round when the order of magnitude was so much greater.'

Ussher believes that if a Bank of England window had been opened in July or even August, offering liquidity to any bank that wanted it, most obviously Northern Rock, the run would have been avoided. And, with hindsight, she concedes the Treasury should have announced that all Northern Rock deposits would be guaranteed as soon as the news broke that Thursday night.

On a mundane level, government staff around the UK were sent on scouting missions to banks and building societies in their local areas. Their mission was to check whether there were attics and cellars which could be used by customers to wait in the event of another panic instead of queuing on the streets. Regulators ordered Northern Rock to change the layout of branches to allow for more customer space. It was evoca-tive of air-raid preparations for the Second World War and little did they know that the financial equivalent of an attack on the UK was only a year away. The Treasury, meanwhile, summoned back any staff who were out on attachment to other departments to bolster the defences for what they saw would be a long period on a war footing.

Other banks, though, seemed too ready to accept that Northern Rock might be a one-off, brought down by its mismanagement. Rock staff reported that Alliance & Leicester employees were seen walking up and down queues during the run trying to entice new customers. HBOS continued expanding its loan book after September 2007. Every pound withdrawn by a Northern Rock customer had to go somewhere and many went to other banks, perhaps giving them a false sense of security. There was no sense that the Northern Rock collapse was the canary in the coal mine.

Northern Rock would seem like a prelude rather than the main drama by the time the crisis erupted in the global markets in September 2008. But it had damaged the UK's reputation. Sir John Gieve's view is that the impact was severe and would have lasting consequences: 'Right at the beginning of the crisis we had the public humbling of the UK authorities and we put a big flag on British banks saying "these look dodgy" which was very unhelpful – it drew attention to the weakness of British banks in a way we need not have done.'

Chapter 3

Banks on the brink

'Dynamic', 'focussed' and a 'breath of fresh air in the stodgy world of Whitehall', or 'rude', 'difficult' and 'not a team player'. It was a tribute to Shriti Vadera's impact on government that there were such strongly held views about her. Critics called her 'Shriti the Shriek', admirers hailed her as the most powerful woman in Whitehall and 'Gordon Brown's representative on earth'. She shunned publicity and never courted the media to build a profile. Indeed, she steered clear of journalists and photo opportunities. What cannot be contested is that Baroness Vadera played a central, and largely unsung, role in the government's response to the financial tornado which swept through the economy in 2008. With colleagues and contacts she strived to ensure that enough work had gone into preparing the defences before the storm hit land.

Vadera was a tough operator who had worked her way up through the macho world of investment banking. Colleagues admired her quick thinking and understanding of corporate finances. One said he thought he was good with balance sheets, spotting a problem after 10 seconds of looking at a page of accounts, but Vadera would always do so in three seconds. Familiar with the sink or swim mentality of investment banking, she did not take easily to the more consensual and deferential world of Whitehall where her impatience was sometimes too obvious.

Shriti Vadera was born in Uganda in a family who were comfortably off and owned a tea plantation. They were expelled by Idi Amin with other Ugandan Asians and after a brief stay in India she arrived as a teenager in the UK. After a spell at a private girls' school in North London, she studied Politics, Philosophy and Economics at Oxford and then began a career in the City. After joining SG Warburg in 1984, which became part of the UBS investment bank, she rose rapidly up the ladder, working on major corporate deals but also advising emerging African economies. Aside from her banking responsibilities she took a close interest in development issues and in her personal time wrote papers with policy recommendations. She was later to become a trustee of Oxfam. Through her interest in development she met Tony Blair, then leader of the opposition. He in turn recommended her to Gordon Brown when he was Shadow Chancellor. Her work on debt relief impressed him and he admired her commitment to social justice and the alleviation of poverty.

In 1999, Vadera was recruited by Brown to be an economic adviser at the Treasury. She specialised in public-private partnerships and dealt with issues like the financing of London Underground, over which she had some bruising battles with management. It was the row over the rail infrastructure operator Railtrack in 2001 which propelled the little-known Vadera into the glare of a media profile. She had been deeply unsympathetic to Railtrack shareholders who were to lose out when the company was pushed into administration by the government. Email correspondence between Vadera and civil servants came to light which included the derogatory description of Railtrack small shareholders as 'grannies' who stood to lose their blouses. In fact, Vadera did not use the phrase but her involvement in the email chain allowed journalists to build up an image of Vadera as a hard-nosed and often confrontational player at the heart of government.

One of Vadera's roles at the Treasury was monitoring public spending across different departments. Treasury people involved in this sort of policing work are never popular across Whitehall and are often regarded as hostile and interfering by civil servants in spending departments. Her encounters with mandarins over budgets made her enemies and encouraged the idea she was difficult to deal with. She also had a brush with Alistair Darling and his senior officials when he was Transport Secretary. There were suspicions, strongly rejected, that Transport had over-spent. In the end the Treasury and Vadera won the argument.

In July 2007, soon after Gordon Brown became Prime Minister, Vadera was appointed to a junior ministerial job at the Department for International Development. To take up the post she joined the House of Lords as a baroness. International Development was an ideal department for her talents, given her specialised knowledge of sub-Saharan economies. But being there meant she missed the immediate response to the biggest crisis to hit the Treasury in decades – Northern Rock. She kept informed as to what was happening in her former department and had some informal chats with Alistair Darling, who expressed to her his frustration about the narrow vision and attitude of some of the civil servants.

In January 2008, Vadera was back in an area of economic policymaking, this time as a minister at the Department for Business. And there she could pursue her natural curiosity about the ominous developments confronting the British banking system.

As banks tightened their purse strings, concerned about their ability to get access to funding for loans, mortgage availability was contracting. Housing market activity was on the slide and ministers were becoming more concerned, mindful of the potential electoral consequences of sliding house prices. Their main worry at this stage was the choking of the supply of credit to the economy. The health of the banks' balance sheets was not seen to be in danger. Alistair Darling commissioned the former HBOS chief Sir James Crosby to carry out a review of the mortgage market.

Vadera and the Treasury civil servant Tom Scholar were asked by Darling to analyse other aspects of the credit crunch and how it might affect the economy. Scholar, after a spell at the Treasury and the IMF, had been chief of staff to Gordon Brown at 10 Downing Street and in 2008 was moved back to the Treasury to head the financial services section.

The close working relationship of Vadera and Scholar was to be central to the eventual official response to the crisis after the Lehman Brothers collapse. Scholar was a sometimes lugubrious figure who in his rare appearances at press conferences never gave much away. Seeing him arrive at work on his bike, clad in yellow cycling jacket and shorts and looking windswept, would not have led to the automatic conclusion that this was one of the highest flying civil servants and ablest administrators in Whitehall. His was a classic fast-track mandarin's career, including serving a long stint as Gordon Brown's principal private secretary at the Treasury when New Labour took office in 1997, at which point Scholar was in his late twenties. That had given him extensive experience of financial services regulation, including the Bank of England independence legislation and the creation of the Financial Services Authority. He knew his way around the highways and byways of economic diplomacy and the International Monetary Fund. His father, Sir Michael Scholar, had been a renowned Whitehall Permanent Secretary. Scholar Junior and Vadera were both trusted aides of Gordon Brown and had served him all through the long march towards Number 10. Crucial to the success of their partnership was that Scholar remained at the Treasury with Darling yet was open to working under the radar with Vadera, now an outsider at another department and who could be portrayed by Treasury old timers as an interfering Brown acolyte.

Vadera and Scholar took on their new roles early in 2008, just as the Northern Rock drama was limping to a conclusion. Months of on and off negotiations with various consortia bidding to buy the Rock had failed to find a solution. The Prime Minister and Chancellor, fearing that a private sector buyer would get Northern Rock on the cheap, decided to bite a bullet they had been reluctant to touch – nationalisation. The very thought of state control of a bank had been anathema after the collapse of Northern Rock. For New Labour, it was a dread concept buried with Clause 4 and the socialist old guard. One Whitehall insider observed later that Brown had been 'really tortured' by the nationalisation taboo and had been 'very scared over being perceived as left wing'. The Railtrack experience, when the privatised operator was taken back into state ownership, was seen to have gone badly wrong and scarred ministers. But once the plans for Northern Rock were announced and there was no collateral damage to the government, a weight was lifted from Brown's shoulders. It helped him make decisions about intervention on a much bigger scale six months later.

In March 2008, chill winds were blowing from Wall Street across the Atlantic. The once-mighty investment bank Bear Stearns had imploded within hours after discovering it was unable to raise cash in the markets. In an ominous foretaste of what was to come later in the year, Bear Stearns had been caught in the vice of a falling share price, plunging values of mortgage investments and other banks refusing to provide short-term funding. It was a reminder that when the market place loses confidence in a financial institution, its time can be up within a matter of hours. In a hastily cobbled together deal, the Federal Reserve agreed an emergency loan to Bear Stearns to be provided through the safer haven of JPMorgan. After a frantic weekend of talks, the bank was bought by JPMorgan for $10 per share, down from $150 at one point the previous year.

The humbling of Bear Stearns ratcheted up nervous tension in all of the world's leading financial markets. If such a big beast could be felled, who might be next on the danger list? In the UK, one name more than any was causing sleepless nights for regulators – Halifax Bank of Scotland (HBOS). Formed from the merger of a leading player in the building society world that then became a bank, and the grandest name in the Scottish banking world, HBOS had ridden the wave of the credit boom. The chairman, Lord Stevenson, was a luminary of the arts world and well connected across Britain's boardrooms. The chief executive was a high-flying former retailer, Andy Hornby. Critics would later bemoan their lack of experience in banking and highlight Hornby's supermarket-style focus on boosting footfall in branches and growing market share. However, few such assertions were being made by analysts or commentators in the spring of 2008. But HBOS had been on a lending spree, spraying money at the sort of areas which were beginning to look decidedly flaky, like industrial estates, retail parks, golf courses and housing developments. Much of it was riskier than Northern Rock's portfolio and HBOS was a much bigger beast than the Rock. In each case the model was straightforward – borrowing cheaply on wholesale money markets and lending at a profit to whoever wanted it.

Since the shameful Northern Rock episode, the tripartite had been determined to up its game. Alistair Darling had made it plain: 'I can't afford another bank failure on my watch.' The Treasury had drafted in new staff and was determined to stay ahead ahead of events rather than being buffetted by them, likewise the FSA. In the email and memo traffic between regulators and civil servants, HBOS was always on the list of areas of concern. The bank was struggling to raise money in the markets and regulators were watching HBOS funding data like hawks. The FSA drew up a paper on how to deal with HBOS if there was a funding crisis, or to use the industry jargon, 'resolve' it. The alarming possibility of the collapse of Britain's biggest lending and deposit-taking institutions was being contemplated. With Bradford & Bingley and Alliance & Leicester also on the watch list, regulators at least knew they had the powers of legislation to wind up banks which were not available for Northern Rock. According to a source present at tripartite meetings: 'We were monitoring everything all of the time – there were hourly updates on the solvency of major institutions.' Such was the concern about a leak, the banks were code-named as planets. There were about a dozen banks and building societies on the list. Crucially, the tripartite system seemed to be working, with all three pillars of the regulatory architecture in harmony.

If regulators were worried about HBOS, it was not surprising that some in the markets were looking a little more closely at the bank's balance sheet. A week after the fall of Bear Stearns, HBOS endured a torrid day on the stock market amidst rumours it was facing a funding crisis. On an extraordinary morning, the shares tumbled 20 per cent and were suspended for a brief period. The Bank of England, usually never willing to comment on vulgar market speculation, felt obliged to deny rumours it had cancelled all staff leave over the impending Easter weekend to tackle a crisis. HBOS vigorously denied what Andy Hornby called 'unfounded and malicious rumours'. The FSA, in similar vein, blamed what it alleged was the spreading of false rumours by market participants who were seeking to profit from them. 'Short-sellers' were made out to be the villains of the piece, using the old practice of agreeing to sell a share at one price in the hopes it would fall again, allowing it to be repurchased at a lower level. The clear impression given to journalists by the FSA was that there was market manipulation based on lies about a sound institution, that of course coming from a regulator which was drawing up secret emergency plans for the event of a possible HBOS crash. A senior player in the tripartite later admitted that there was 'heavy-duty contingency planning' at this stage because of concerns that the bank was facing big problems.

The HBOS share price recovered some of the lost ground by the end of the day, ending down about 7 per cent. Traders, journalists and regulators headed off for their Easter breaks. The FSA got down to an inquiry into the possibility of deliberate attempts to make money from a falling HBOS share price based on spreading false rumours. A senior HBOS executive revealed a few years later that the bank had been saved by the FSA's robust line on the day and that depositors had started to withdraw their cash. Whatever the FSA may have been discussing in private about the true state of HBOS, its argument that the bank was the victim of a market plot to depress the share price restored confidence. The FSA had never intervened in such a way before, having always steered clear of giving a running commentary on the state of individual institutions. The move reflected concern at the highest levels that, given the febrile state of the market confidence, HBOS might have toppled without an official vote of confidence.

By April 2008, the state of the banking market remained high on the list of priorities of Downing Street. But the concerns were framed around the state of the UK economy. On the day Gordon Brown was scheduled to meet bank chiefs for breakfast at Number 10, a survey suggested house prices were falling at their fastest rate for 30 years. For the Prime Minister, the worry was that the mortgage market would start to contract as lenders reined in in response to plunging property values. The bankers, blaming the contraction in wholesale markets where they accessed funding for mortgages, called for further measures to boost liquidity. Seeing Sir Fred Goodwin of RBS and Andy Hornby of HBOS striding confidently up Downing Street gave the impression they were contributing constructively to an important national debate. There was certainly no sense they were sitting on time bombs which were set to explode and would threaten to bring down the entire British banking edifice.

There was one banker at the Downing Street breakfast who was more worried than most. David Soanes of UBS was not the chief of a big high street bank but a smart, well-connected dealmaker who knew the financial markets inside out. He had seen the carnage in the markets after the collapse of the US hedge fund Long-Term Capital Management in 1998 and taken on board how the Federal Reserve had come to the rescue of a banking system which had become over-confident. In February 2007, six months before credit markets began to seize up, Soanes had become concerned about the growing reliance of British mortgage lenders on wholesale financing. He had spotted that much of the funding, something in the order of £500 billion, came from overseas lenders. The UK simply did not have a significant market for buying mortgage securities. British lenders would be highly vulnerable if there was a 'buyers' strike' and foreign investors turned their backs on the UK. Soanes had written to a senior player in government to set out his concerns.

After Northern Rock, Soanes had begun to worry about HBOS, Alliance & Leicester and Bradford & Bingley because of their reliance on the wholesale money markets, and in effect overseas sources of funding. He could see their survival was on the line if these markets pulled down the shutters as they had lent out so much more than their total inflows from depositors. Many foreign investors had packed up and gone home after seeing what had happened to Northern Rock. Soanes had met Alistair Darling in late 2007 and passed on his concerns about the vulnerable institutions. In February 2008 he had been at a meeting at 10 Downing Street and warned again of the dangers to the mortgage market. If wholesale markets stayed in reverse, argued Soanes, the supply of funding for new mortgages would be impaired and the housing market could take a bath. At the April breakfast meeting, he had been surprised how unworried the bank chiefs appeared to be. There seemed to be a lack of awareness, he thought, of how potentially serious the market problems could become. However, he later reflected there was one notable exception, who happened to be the only senior retail banker still in post after the crisis.

However confident they appeared, by early 2008, banks were beginning to realise they were in need of more capital – that is, financial reserves which could be called on to cover future losses. The housing market downturn had raised concerns in bank boardrooms about the possibility of more loans going sour. Managers at Royal Bank of Scotland were already on edge because of the challenge of integrating ABN Amro, aquired with a consortium the previous autumn. RBS decided to go to shareholders to raise £12 billion in April 2008, the largest such fundraising in British corporate history. RBS used what was known as a rights issue, a vehicle allowing companies to raise funds by selling new shares, with existing shareholders being offered the 'right' to buy them first, typically at a discount. At that time, regulators and the Treasury itself did not seem worried about capital levels in the banking sector and were content to let RBS decide what was needed. But Shriti Vadera and Tom Scholar were beginning to question those assumptions.

In late July, as the international climate worsened, Halifax Bank of Scotland announced that its attempt to raise more capital through a £4 billion rights issue had been a flop. Only 8 per cent of the shares on offer had takers, the rest being left with the investment banks who were underwriters to the share issue. Bradford & Bingley, meanwhile, struggled to get its rights issue away in July as conditions deteriorated and had to cut the price at which the shares were on offer. By the deadline in August, just 28 per cent of the new shares were taken up by shareholders. In both cases investors were simply not interested in buying shares in banks perceived to be exposed to the deteriorating housing market.

As banks found it tougher to raise money in the markets, Vadera and Scholar began to wonder where future financing of capital requirements would come from. They had looked at the market in the United States and noted that banks there had been through lots of rounds of fundraising (including rights issues) and when share prices subsequently fell, investors had very obviously lost out. In the US, the appetite for investment in banks had waned. What, Vadera and Scholar reasoned, was to stop the same thing happening in the UK market? Vadera's financial market training told her that there was no good reason to invest in banking shares. Her investor contacts passed on their sceptical views; which coincided with hers. The valuation of banks' assets was becoming increasingly difficult, so doing the usual homework on the health of a bank was proving near impossible.

The fortunes of banks are always closely tied to the fortunes of the wider economy. A deteriorating housing market and falling commercial property prices will infect bank balance sheets as loans turn sour. That will make banks draw back from new lending, which will in turn cause further damage to the economy in what analysts call a 'feedback loop'. Although it was not clear at the time, the UK was already in recession by the middle of 2008. In July Alistair Darling summoned ministers and senior civil servants to a two-day gathering at the Chancellor's official residence, Dorneywood. Their aim was to review the state of the economy and the implications for the public finances. Over dinner they chewed over possible policy options. Kitty Ussher raised the idea of an old-fashioned Keynesian response to a downturn, more government spending or, to use the jargon, 'pulling the fiscal lever'. Senior Treasury mandarins, programmed to veto ministerial demands for higher spending, scoffed at the suggestion. One even laughed, which left Ussher thinking that despite her economics training she was 'put back in a box more appropriate for someone younger and female'. She was later told her intervention had gone down badly at the highest level of the Treasury. Yet just a few months later the government was indeed pulling the lever with a fiscal stimulus.

Whatever resistance there may have been at the Treasury, Darling later revealed that he had become convinced at the time of the Dorneywood summit that economic storm clouds were gathering and that a much sharper than expected downturn was not far off. He gave an interview to *The Guardian* a month later in which he said the outlook for the UK economy was 'arguably the worst in 60 years'. The language he used was not dissimilar to views expressed by the IMF a few weeks earlier when referring to challenges facing the global economy. But Darling's remarks caused a media frenzy and fury at 10 Downing Street. It marked the first signs of a rift between Chancellor and Prime Minister. It was not long before Darling's downbeat assessment was proved correct.

By early August, Vadera had looked more closely at the balance sheets of the major banks. Her private calculations told her that more capital would be needed. But walking through Trafalgar Square to Whitehall with Scholar one day, she had a sudden and scary realisation – there was no obvious source of the new bank capital. She challenged Scholar and they both agreed that much more funding would be needed to shore up the balance sheets, but there was nobody left to supply it. Reaching the Treasury, they both wrote notes on the issue and emailed each other, backwards and forwards with endless refining of the argument. From Vadera's original email headed 'Is it capital?', another 20 emails flowed. From that moment they both focussed intensely on the question of bank capital and the ability of banks to raise enough to cover future losses.

As Vadera and Scholar exchanged emails there was no such sense of urgency elsewhere in government. The Treasury worked on a review of capital in the industry but one observer remembers it was carried out in rather a desultory fashion as befitted the usually dead month of August. The Financial Services Authority had not at this stage showed any renewed interest in the issue following their efforts to get RBS and HBOS to raise money earlier in the year. The Crosby review of mortgage financing had not highlighted the lack of banks' capital as an immediate concern or potential barrier in the supply of home loans. Vadera meanwhile was flagging up her concerns with Number 10 chief of staff Jeremy Heywood and Gordon Brown. The question she was pushing was where capital would come from if not from private sector investors? All roads, in her view, led to the government picking up the tab and investing in the banks. It may have been just a month before Lehman Brothers collapsed and some time after Northern Rock had been nationalised but the idea of state involvement was simply not on most agendas in August 2008.

As Scholar and Vadera experienced their moment of illumination walking through central London on that August day, they had mused: 'What's the betting Gordon will say to us, "Have you tried every source of capital?"' And that proved an accurate prediction. Brown began to take interest in the email traffic between Number 10 and the Treasury. He was curious about where banks might try to raise funds to plug holes in their balance sheets. The idea of the government having to stump up for banks' capital was far from obvious at that stage. It was not what governments did in the twenty-first century global economy. Northern Rock had been bad enough at the time of the nationalisation earlier that year and ministers were keen to write it off as an isolated and exceptional event.

In that torpid late summer, a time of year when political leaders usually take time to recharge their batteries on the beach and the news agenda slows almost to a standstill, Brown was hyperactive. He was beginning to sketch out his thoughts on a big canvas. He feared another 1929-style global collapse and he wanted to work out how governments could stop the rot. Brown realised that state provision of capital had to be part of the answer, ideally adopted by governments for their banking systems in all leading economies. The Vadera/Scholar thinking was materialising at just the right moment for the Prime Minister.

Brown became, according to one observer, 'obsessed' with the Japanese precedent. Japan's so-called 'lost decade' had turned into two lost decades. A colossal market boom had been followed by a stock market and asset market collapse in the early 1990s. Banks were confronted with mounting bad debts but chose to sit on the toxic assets, hoping they would eventually return to full health. Because they were concerned about future losses on these problem loans, they hoarded capital which otherwise would have been used to support new lending. If there had been big enough capital buffers, the banks might have been able to afford to realise losses on the toxic debts, to draw a line and resume lending to growing companies. But because the issue of the 'zombie banks' (as they came to be known) was not tackled by the Japanese government, the economy stayed in the doldrums. Brown feared a repeat performance in the UK if inadequately capitalised banks could only tread water rather than generate momentum for the economy.

The Prime Minister always took a stack of books on his holiday, but never crime thrillers or footballers' memoirs. Books on politics, history and the economy were his reading material of choice. This time he asked for anything available on Japan and the lost decade and also the lessons of the 1930s. He also took with him early writings by the Fed chairman Ben Bernanke on the Great Depression and the US central bank policy known as quantitative easing (QE) – colloquially described as 'printing money'. It was certainly a rich and intellectual diet, especially so for a holiday in the Suffolk seaside town of Southwold. Brown's wife Sarah had insisted on a two-week break with their sons, reportedly at a British retreat to avoid the accusations levelled at Tony Blair for taking exotic foreign holidays.

Local press reports described the Browns enjoying themselves on the beach, going to the cinema in Lowestoft and visiting a pig farm. Whether Brown himself had much time for the family back at their rented house is doubtful. In his book *Beyond the Crash*, Brown admits that 'much to my family's irritation' he had read great tomes during his holiday. And apart from voracious reading on economic history he was in regular contact with his aides over the banking issue. Vadera came up to stay the night to discuss Brown's thoughts on what the next steps might be. Jeremy Heywood also made the journey up from London. For the Prime Minister, a view was forming – something had to be done to thaw banking markets which would allow the flow of credit between financial institutions and out into the economy to return to its normal velocity. He later acknowledged that the thinking behind the bank bail-outs in October had its origins on the Suffolk coast.

The introduction of the radical quantitative easing policy in the UK may also have had its genesis in Brown's Suffolk musings. The creation of new money by a central bank to stimulate an economy was well known from the textbooks and had been used for real by the Japanese central bank as part of the response to the 1990s downturn. The results in Japan had been mixed. At that stage it was not clear whether any

Bank of England official had considered it as appropriate for the UK, but it had certainly not materialised in any public policy debate. This was before the Bank of England began the rapid series of interest rate cuts to cope with the crisis – the official lending rate was 5 per cent. Brown was ahead of most, then, in considering the relevance of quantitative easing for the UK. He even told Vadera to read Bernanke's paper on QE.

Some considered it extraordinary that the Prime Minister had time for these intellectual policy discussions when he was on holiday, when he was also trying to keep tabs on what was happening in the country and working out how to fend off a political challenge to his authority inside the Labour party.

Quantitative easing might be a longer-term policy option for the UK economy. Shorter term, as Brown realised, measures to underpin the banking system were of paramount importance. Back from his holiday, he acted as if there was not a moment to lose. Even with increasing reports that rebellious Labour MPs were demanding a leadership contest, the economy remained his main focus. He demanded that Vadera, Scholar and Heywood come up with a plan. Vadera then asked Scholar if he could calculate a figure for the total potential holes in bank balance sheets that the government might need to fill. Something between £50 billion and £100 billion appeared at that stage to be not unrealistic. They hoped the Treasury might have some analysis on the underlying state of bank finances. Work in that area had started at the Treasury but was not complete – poring over bank balance sheets was a task for specialists and trying to calculate the true value of bank assets was something even directors of those institutions found impossible.

The Treasury may in those weeks of the summer recess have been less than totally focussed on the intricacies of bank capital, the Financial Services Authority likewise. But there were stirrings over at Threadneedle Street. Some policymakers still believed that the problem was liquidity with banks' funding drying up and that this was where any solutions to the crisis should be addressed. But Mervyn King had been arguing since soon after the Northern Rock debacle, both inside the Bank and amongst other policymakers, that the main problem was solvency. In other words, banks might not be able to cover losses on loans as the economy deteriorated. More capital, King believed, should be the priority. One Treasury source acknowledged that whatever the frustrations with the Governor, 'Mervyn King deserves a lot of credit – his conclusion on capital was absolutely right and he hung onto that premise throughout'.

Providing liquidity, i.e. loans to banks in exchange for collateral, had been the major debating point in late 2007, with King accused of dragging his feet. The commercial banks blamed the seizure of the money markets for their problems – once those markets reopened, they argued, all would be well so they only needed temporary credit lines. But in April 2008, the Bank had introduced the Special Liquidity Scheme, which had met the banks' demands. Funding was available in return for a range of collateral, including mortgages and consumer car loans. In the eyes of the Treasury, that had restored King's credibility and he came back to the table with renewed conviction about the capital problem which needed to be resolved.

King's colleagues at the Bank had initially seen solvency and liquidity as two sides of the same problem. Boosting capital was the way for banks, it was argued, to persuade the markets to lend to them. In the summer of 2008, first estimates of economic activity did not suggest a recession. Inflation was high, fuelled by rising global commodity prices, and was seen as among the main concerns for monetary policymakers. The possibility of a serious downturn, which caused major losses on domestic loans and so generated the need for more bank capital, had not been factored in to the Bank's calculations. The threat of a wave of defaults and bad debts had not been considered. But that had changed by August. Papers moved around inside the Bank with leading officials raising questions about the need for more capital in the banking system. Andy Haldane, the young Turk in the financial stability policy area of the Bank, was one of those doing the probing and also some complex arithmetic. These notes were circulated in what one insider said was 'quite an un-Whitehall way of doing things'. This would result in missives being written to which the Treasury had to react.

As the crisis unfolded, Mervyn King himself was pressing for forced recapitalisation – making every major bank in the City raise extra funding, including if necessary from the government. He was 'slightly more on the aggressive side of the agenda' according to one insider. In response to this, the Treasury started looking at the idea but according to the same source 'civil servants weren't very keen'. They acknowledged that capital was a significant challenge but believed that it should be voluntary not mandatory for the banks. So it was King who was pushing hard on the capital front, although Treasury sources don't remember any specific ideas from the Governor on how to achieve the goal. He raised his views on solvency and capital with the Prime Minister more than once that summer, but the Governor had not worked up detailed measures with his Bank subordinates. Some in Whitehall remember King making his intellectual arguments, but do not recall Bank staff coming to tripartite meetings with calls for urgent intervention.

The Financial Services Authority, meanwhile, was not banging the same drum and seemed agnostic about the idea that banks might need to build up their capital buffers. Cynics muttered that to admit there might be a capital problem so late in the day would be embarrassing for the body which was supposed to regulate the industry. Inside the FSA there was a more immediate struggle. The order had come from Downing Street that after Northern Rock there were to be no further bank runs or collapses. So FSA staff had focussed energies on smaller building societies, standing ready to shepherd them towards takeovers by large institutions like Nationwide if there was a hint of trouble. The former mutuals Bradford & Bingley and Alliance & Leicester were also under close watch. Ever since the autumn of 2007, the FSA had been on high alert with fraying nerves as staff feared a much bigger calamity than Northern Rock would descend on them. There had been little time to stand back and think big thoughts about recapitalisation.

Senior players at the FSA later argued that the need for capital *had* been on their agenda. They took credit for pressing RBS, HBOS and Bradford & Bingley to raise money during the summer. Their view was that the Bank of England had to provide more liquidity to the banks and it was odd for a central bank to neglect this side of its responsibilities and bang on solely about capital. Tension between these two members of the tripartite was clear. A Treasury source wearily noted the divergence of opinion: 'The joke was that on any issue the Bank said the problem was capital, the FSA said it was funding – at the Treasury we wished they would all stop arguing and get on with it.'

As August turned into September, the threat of a change in the financial climate on the horizon had materialised as thunderclouds hovering overhead. After months of wrangling, the US government announced on Sunday 7 September that it was taking control of two giant home loan organisations, Freddie Mac and Fannie Mae. They were to be run under 'conservatorship', a form of temporary public ownership. The extraordinary bailout, described by media at the time as the largest in US financial history, was a reaction to continued deterioration in the American housing market. It was believed the two entities had bought or underwritten nearly half the $12 trillion outstanding mortgage debt in the United States. Defaults on home loans and plunging house prices had undermined the value of mortgage securities held by Freddie Mac and Fannie Mae. They had run up a combined $14 billion of losses over the previous year.

15 September 2008 is a day etched in infamy, to coin a phrase from American history. The Japanese attack on Pearl Harbor in the Second World War had pulled the United States into a global conflict. Now, in the early twenty-first century, the world's largest economy was facing its own formidable enemy – the risk of financial meltdown. The investment bank Lehman Brothers had collapsed after a last-minute rescue bid involving other banks had failed. The Bush administration had decided not to intervene to shore up Lehman – with the New York Federal Reserve it believed there were no legislative powers to do so.

Until late the previous day, the US Treasury Secretary Hank Paulson had hoped Barclays would pursue a rescue takeover of Lehman. The British bank wanted the authorities to guarantee Lehman trading liabilities for 30 days or more before a Barclays shareholder vote on the transaction could take place. The US Treasury persuaded Wall Street banks to take on sufficient bad assets from Lehman to give Barclays enough reassurance to press on with a takeover. But neither the US or UK authorities could agreed to underwrite Lehman until a shareholder vote took place. Paulson felt British regulators were needlessly blocking the rescue. Darling made it clear to his American counterpart that he could not countenance a deal which could push a liability onto the

British taxpayer. That spelled the end of a Barclays rescue of the US bank. The bank's bosses maintain that they had lost interest anyway once the chance of a guarantee for 30 days or more had evaporated. A day after insolvency proceedings began at Lehman, Barclays moved swiftly to pick up some of the bank's prize assets in New York.

Markets assumed the authorities would stand back and allow other institutions to fail. After the rescue of Bear Stearns earlier in the year, there had been an assumption the government might stand behind Lehman. There was shock that it had not done so. Panic was spreading across Wall Street. The safety of other banks like Morgan Stanley was being questioned. The giant insurer AIG was on its knees, pleading for a government lifeline. Capitalism was wobbling.

The closure of the Lehman office in Canary Wharf in East London was a dramatic illustration of how this was a global crisis, with no leading economy immune. Images of staff carrying their possessions out in cardboard boxes emphasized the human dimension – 4,500 jobs were on the line (although more than half were later secured when some of the Lehman business was bought by Nomura). Nerves were on edge across the UK's financial centres of Docklands and the City of London. The FTSE 100 index of leading shares plunged by nearly 4 per cent, as Wall Street tumbled that afternoon. And nowhere was confidence more fragile than at the major mortgage lender HBOS.

Regulators had been concerned about HBOS for months. Rapacious short sellers of the shares had been blamed for dramatic drops in the share price on a couple of days earlier in the year. But the banks funding problems were becoming all too obvious to investors – they could see from the bank's accounts how much funding was needed to cover short-term liabilities. The Bank of England and the Financial Services Authority were both keeping a close watch on HBOS throughout the summer. It was on a regulatory critical list along with Bradford & Bingley and Alliance & Leicester. The latter was nudged into the safe haven of ownership by the Spanish bank Santander. The other two were causing bigger headaches, even more so after their cash-raising rights issues misfired. For a time, HBOS pushed hard to be allowed to take over Bradford & Bingley. Depositors' cash in the Yorkshire-based bank looked highly appealing to the HBOS board as it struggled to maintain its own funding. For a while, regulators toyed with the idea. But the possibility of allowing a Bradford & Bingley deal only for HBOS to subsequently founder rang alarm bells loudly enough for the option to be blocked. As one regulator put it: 'We felt you couldn't ladle Bradford & Bingley depositors into a bank which might get into trouble – the first objective had to be to put them somewhere secure.'

As the Lehman fallout widened that Monday, HBOS shares plunged by 18 per cent. The following day a key credit rating of HBOS debt was downgraded, the share price slide continued and the outflow of corporate deposits gathered momentum. At this moment of peril a chance of salvation flickered before the eyes of the beleaguered HBOS board in the shape of a rescue takeover by Lloyds. The two banks had talked on and off about a merger for several years. Letters had been exchanged between the two banks' chief executives recording the mutual interest as long ago as 2000. In 2006, the HBOS chief executive Andy Hornby and Lloyds chairman Sir Victor Blank, who knew each other from their time as directors of another business, had a discussion about some form of deal. For Lloyds, the attraction of linking up with HBOS was that it would propel it from lower in the UK market pecking order to number one or two. After cautious management, high dividend payments and the risk of stagnation under his predecessor, the Lloyds chief executive Eric Daniels was keen to generate some growth. Expanding in the UK mortgage market was a major priority. It would have been a dream deal as far as Lloyds bosses were concerned. But it was thwarted by the sheer scale of the planned merged entity. Lawyers advised that the competition authorities would never allow such a financial giant to be formed and sit astride the high street banking market.

Competition concerns had kicked the idea of a Lloyds/HBOS marriage into touch. But the market upheaval of late 2007 into 2008 allowed the ball to be returned to the field of play. It appealed to Sir Victor Blank, a consummate City deal-maker with a bulging contact book from his years in investment banking. Widely respected for his charity work, Blank was a cricket fan who hosted an annual match at his country home where the worlds of politics, finance and show business rubbed shoulders on and off the pitch. Blank reasoned that the banking world had been turned upside down by the Northern Rock fiasco and nationalisation. In the middle of 2008, HBOS was known to be struggling and the government, he thought, might be amenable to the idea of an agreed rescue takeover by Lloyds. Blank consulted his board, including the chief executive Eric Daniels, and was given the go-ahead to talk informally to the Prime Minister to find out how the idea might be received. Daniels, meanwhile, had tentative conversations with Andy Hornby.

Blank's opportunity came in July on a flight back to London from Israel. He and Gordon Brown had both been at a charity function and were sitting next to each other on the plane for the return journey. Blank raised the subject of a possible Lloyds interest in HBOS and stressed that the only hurdle was the competition rulebook. A deal would resolve the HBOS problem, argued the Lloyds chairman, but it needed a government commitment to waive or suspend the rules. Brown said he would give the matter some consideration. For a few weeks after that, informal contacts were made between the banks but there was no word from Downing Street.

Once Lehman had collapsed and the world's markets took fright, the game changed for Lloyds and HBOS. There was renewed urgency behind attempts to get them up the aisle together. Hornby called Daniels in early September and asked that a deal be put on the table as quickly as possible. The involvement of the government in the eventual marriage of Lloyds and HBOS, shotgun or not, has been intensely debated. It later emerged that Gordon Brown and Sir Victor Blank, accompanied by Daniels, had been seen chatting at a drinks reception hosted by the US bank Citigroup that Monday evening, a few hours after Lehman had imploded. Blank later confirmed that the Prime Minister, following up their previous conversation, had informed him that the normal competition rules would be suspended to allow Lloyds to pursue the deal even though it would become a dominant player in the market, with nearly a third of UK mortgages and current accounts. Critics of the takeover claimed that Brown had encouraged the Lloyds chairman to press on with the deal to avoid the need for a government intervention to save HBOS.

Alistair Darling later reflected that the Lloyds interest in HBOS had indeed been a welcome development. He remembered that a year earlier, major banks had steered clear of Northern Rock and had come up with no alternative to a government-organised rescue: 'Twelve months later I was very alive to the fact we might have to do this on our own but when this Lloyds thing came up and they were willing to do it, that would be fine.' The Chancellor, in fact, had told officials to prepare two statements that week, one covering nationalisation of HBOS, the other a Lloyds takeover. Darling dismisses the idea that Brown might have been pushing Blank towards an offer for HBOS: 'Bollocks! You cannot fix up a takeover of a bank over a glass of warm chardonnay in the full glare of an autumn drinks party.' As far as Darling was concerned, the conversation was simply about how the government might deal with the competition aspects of the takeover.

On Wednesday morning, 17 September, the BBC's Robert Peston broke the story of the impending deal. The revelation came before talks between the two sides had concluded but it had the effect of stopping the freefall of the HBOS share price. The takeover was formally announced 24 hours later. Sir Victor Blank hailed it as a unique opportunity to create the UK's leading financial services group. Eric Daniels, the Lloyds chief executive added: 'There shouldn't be any impression this is a shotgun marriage or a forced marriage, this is something that's been looked at for a good long while.'

In calmer times, what might have seemed a bygone era, Adair Turner, Baron Turner of Ecchinswell had been appointed by Alistair Darling in May 2008 to take over as chairman of the Financial Services Authority. (Sir Callum McCarthy had decided not to seek a second five-year term as FSA chairman and was due to stand down in September 2008.) A seamless transition was envisaged with a minimal handover required as Turner was a seasoned political and financial operator. Tall, amiable, self-confident and with an effortlessly successful career already behind him, Turner can hardly have envisaged the challenges of his new role. Heading the employers' organisation, the CBI, and then a wide-ranging review of pensions provision including some bruising scuffles with Gordon Brown would not have prepared him for the financial devastation a few months ahead, but then nothing would have done.

Turner's contract said he would start at the FSA on Monday 22 September. But on the previous Monday, as Lehman collapsed and markets plummeted, McCarthy called Turner. Entering his final week at the Authority, the chairman suggested Turner might like to start at the weekend, in other words just after midnight on the Friday night. It sounded as if he assumed there would be another bank bailout and that Turner might as well be there to see it through before the Monday morning announcement. Turner's contract was duly amended. There had been nothing in his briefing documents or any advice from the Treasury or FSA before September to suggest he might be walking into a market meltdown. In fact, he had slightly regretted not being in place for Northern Rock and the aftermath of the Bear Stearns rescue in the US.

But in the week after the Lehman collapse, Turner realised the scale of the task ahead. He could see from the markets that much of the banking sector was in deep trouble and that lending between institutions was freezing up. But within minutes of starting the new job for real on the Monday morning at the FSA's headquarters in Canary Wharf, he realised just how severe and unprecedented this banking crisis was. Reports on liquidity coming into the FSA suggested the system was seizing up. Banks which had previously lent to each other for three months were lending only overnight so the next day there was the problem of three-month debt having to be rolled over as well as the one-day money from the night before. He later reflected that what followed was the most extraordinary fortnight of his professional life. He felt that the ceiling of the building he had taken over was falling in.

On Wednesday 24 September, Turner went to the Bank of England for dinner with the Governor. It had been arranged a month before as a welcome for the new chairman. Mervyn King had said a fine bottle of wine would be produced from the Bank's cellar. But there was no time for pleasantries or enjoying the venerable vintage. King spelled out that the UK money markets had not been as badly damaged since the outbreak of the First World War – conditions were worse even than during the Great Depression. The Governor made it plain that radical and bold action was required from the authorities. This, he argued, had to involve a mandatory new capital plan for the banks with the government the source of funding and owner of the share stakes.

The following day, King and Turner met Darling. The leadership of the tripartite authority, Treasury, Bank of England and Financial Services

Authority agreed there had to be a step change from the approach hitherto which had been to fight fires as and when they broke out – one
week Alliance & Leicester, the next Bradford & Bingley. Recapitalisation
and liquidity guarantees were discussed and the three tripartite heads
agreed to get teams of staff working on schemes in these areas. Turner
later described the conversation and the stark reality facing them: 'I
said I wanted to just state my strong support for Mervyn's belief that we
were heading towards a severe crisis and that we would have to do some
sort of banking system-wide rescue, not address the problems bank by
bank.'

Chapter 4

The Financial storm breaks

As the small group from the Treasury and 10 Downing Street, backed by the FSA, continued to try to pull together the threads on recapitalisation that had been developed in Suffolk and Whitehall, they were confronted with a potential problem in the shape of the American response. In the face of a market maelstrom after the collapse of Lehman, the US Treasury Secretary Hank Paulson was battling to come up with a comprehensive plan to restore confidence in American banks. He told his aides it was 'the economic equivalent of war' and the market was ready to collapse.

Paulson's approach was to use hundreds of billions of US government dollars to pump into the banks while sucking out the toxic material which was troubling the markets. The Troubled Asset Relief Program (TARP) was planned as a government-funded vehicle to purchase rancid loans from banks. Removing these stressed assets from the system, it was envisaged, would allow the banks to lend more freely without the fear of future losses from the loans which had soured. But this was not the route the British Prime Minister wished to go down. Contacts between the Treasury and its American counterparts to try to discuss a joint approach had not got far.

Brown believed that a TARP-style approach would not work in the UK. It would be inefficient and probably unaffordable for the Exchequer. But if he embarked on a different plan to support the financial infrastructure, doubts might be raised about the UK's credibility. Why, sceptics might ask, does the British government know better than the titans of Washington, those at the heart of the world's biggest economy? One insider guessed the likely reaction of the markets: 'They would essentially believe we were "Reykjavik-on-Thames" and had a specific UK problem.' Reykjavik-on-Thames was a term coined by former Bank of England policymaker Willem Buiter. He highlighted the risks of economies with large banking sectors which had borrowed in foreign currencies and would struggle to repay them if their own currency tumbled.

Brown and his advisers were convinced that a universal banking solution on both sides of the Atlantic was the best way forward. And the only way to achieve this, he reasoned, was go to the US to make the case.

Brown and a British delegation were due in New York the following week for the start of the annual UN General Assembly. This, he reasoned, offered a chance to pursue the urgent financial agenda both covertly, in the margins of the Assembly, and if necessary overtly at the White House. One immediate dilemma was how to include Shriti Vadera, who at this time was officially a minister at the Department of Business and did not hold a brief with any relevance to the UN agenda. Brown wanted her to undertake a secret mission on Wall Street, testing opinions on Paulson's plan and exploring support for the logic of boosting capital throughout the banking system. It was decided she would travel on the same flight as the Prime Minister and his wife as a friend of Sarah Brown. Vadera even paid for her own airfare. With the media still reacting to Brown's party conference speech in Manchester, framed very much in terms of his response to potential Labour rebels, the Premier and his party took off for New York.

The main talking points at the UN did not get much of the Prime Minister's attention during his time in New York. He embarked on an intensive round of discussions on the financial crisis with different sets of political leaders and economic experts. One such was a meeting with Tim Geithner, then President of the Federal Reserve Bank of New York and a key player in attempts by the US authorities to put out the fires blazing across Wall Street. It took place around the dining table at the apartment of of Sir John Sawers, UK representative at the United Nations. Brown was careful not to give too much away about British intentions but pressed the issue of the US government injecting capital directly into the banks. Geithner made the point that the TARP legislation would allow direct purchases of bank shares if required. The New York Fed chief indicated that he agreed with Brown's analysis on the need for capital but warned that President Bush would not. He suggested Brown might like to raise the issue with the President. There were no clues given on whether it was likely the US administration would back recapitalisation but Brown left the meeting reassured that it remained a possibility.

Vadera meanwhile was pressing the flesh on Wall Street. Her task was to find out whether the major banks backed TARP and whether they thought recapitalisation might be better. At most of the meetings, including a larger gathering with investors attended by Brown, the message was clear. The American institutions confirmed that the banks were under-capitalised and that the TARP approach would not work effectively. Banks that feared an injection of government funding were against the idea of raising capital – most others seemed in favour. For Brown this was heartening and confirmed that he was on the right track with his thinking on a UK plan.

The British Prime Minister managed to convene a meeting of leaders from G20 economies at the UN building in what he described in *Beyond the Crash* as 'one of the dingiest rooms ever to be visited by such a company . . . around a bleak, oversize table'. There they laid the foundations for formal G20 summits – hitherto it had been a forum just for finance ministers. They agreed that the G8, which included the traditional heavyweights plus Russia, was too limited a group for considering joint action in a global economic crisis. In discussions with the then French president Nicolas Sarkozy, Brown had agreed that they should press for an emergency summit of G20 leaders – but they still had to persuade the American President.

The Prime Minister decided he must see George Bush. His foreign affairs aide Tom Fletcher was deputed to pull every White House string to get an appointment with the President. Schedules were rapidly changed and the prime ministerial plane was set on course for Washington from New York on Friday 26 September. The group of journalists at the back of the plane grumbled about the lack of notice and then complained when they were told there would be no time for a press conference in the White House Rose Garden. They had no idea of the Prime Minister's real agenda.

Brown and three advisers took their seats in the Oval Office opposite George Bush and three administration officials. The ice was broken as attention focussed on Shriti Vadera's finger, which had been broken and was in a large cast – an earlier injury which had not healed rapidly. The leaders made small talk and even joked about Vadera's injury. Brown then got straight to the point and said he wanted to talk about capital and the idea of governments recapitalising the banks. Bush looked puzzled: 'What's capital?' He did not appear to have a grasp of one of the building blocks of banking – although he might legitimately have argued that the vast majority of US voters would be in the same boat. Bush seemed taken aback and had clearly not thought about the concept of boosting banks' capital. His response was that Hank (Paulson) did all the technical stuff and that right now the focus was on getting TARP through Congress. Brown tried again to explain the politics of bank rescues as well as the financial arguments, but the most he got from the President was a promise to talk to Hank.

The other key subject that Brown wished to raise at the White House was the urgent need to hold a G20 leaders' summit. The German Chancellor Angela Merkel and French President Nicolas Sarkozy had promised to throw their weight behind the idea when they had audiences with the President. Brown explained to Bush the consensus reached at his hastily-convened gathering in the UN's dingy meeting room the previous day. Bush replied that he could not be seen to leave the United States with an election approaching. Brown, despite knowing that Sarkozy was keen to host the event in Paris, suggested that the summit could take place in Washington. Bush agreed, subject to Brown sorting out the agenda and the outlines of a communiqué. Both leaders knew that an international leaders' summit in the middle of a financial crisis which broke up with a thin or ambiguous set of words would damage rather than sustain market confidence.

Brown pointed out that Bush would have to chair the meeting if it was to be held in Washington and suggested that the President tell Sarkozy that it had to be held on the Western side of the Atlantic. Bush, while voicing scepticism that there would be time to get every leader behind an agreed position, gave his assent. And so, the G20 leaders' summit was born and since the first gathering in Washington in November 2008, then London in April 2009, it has evolved into the primary forum for economic debate amongst world leaders.

Some of the UK governmental team in Washington at that time were later to reflect that the extant American political system was not necessarily well suited to handling a global financial crisis. While Geithner and Paulson might be trying to achieve one thing, Bush might want another. The President had understandably delegated authority to put out the financial firestorm to those he considered experts at the Fed and the Treasury. So there was always going to be a risk of 'salami slicing' rather than one centrally co-ordinated plan. There was no single source of political nous, financial expertise and grasp of the global economic challenge in the leadership of the US. The British political system has been criticised for an excessive centralisation of power. But at a time of financial crisis and with a breakneck pace of developments it had a leader with an understanding of the problem, the beginnings of a plan and a chance of delivering it. Brown's fellow political leaders in Europe at that stage either failed to grasp the severity of the problem and blamed the US anyway, or realised that action was needed but did not know what was required.

Emerging from the Oval Office, the British team was informed there was an urgent transatlantic call. They were ushered into an anteroom in the White House. It was Jeremy Heywood on the line from Downing Street. He told Brown that Bradford & Bingley was being taken into state ownership that weekend with retail branches to be sold to Santander while the deteriorating mortgage book would be held in state ownership. Brown then spoke to Alistair Darling who ran through the terms of the nationalisation and break-up. It did not take them long to agree on it. Those present noted that it must be the first time the affairs of a British building society had been discussed so vigorously in and around the President of the United States' office. It seemed like another weird twist in the astonishing chain of events which was unfolding daily.

Heywood had other urgent business to get through before the Prime Minister and his entourage left the White House. He told them to stay in the Oval Office anteroom and wait by a fax machine because he had documents to send over. They represented the various views of the Treasury, the Financial Services Authority and the Bank of England on bank recapitalisation – the collective wisdom of the tripartite body. There were numbers and estimates which had been crunched and collated by officials. Heywood felt the paperwork was so sensitive that he only wanted to fax over one copy and he made it clear that it was not to be given to White House staff to photocopy. So Brown and his team had to hunch over a single set of documents.

Unexpectedly, there was an extra paper, distinct from the tripartite work, which had been included in the fax-traffic. It was written by Mervyn King, who had requested that it be conveyed direct to the Prime Minister. It contained the Governor's own estimate of the capital requirement for the leading banks – a staggering £100 billion.

The figure was higher than proposed in the main paperwork, which struck the Prime Minister's group as odd because King's colleagues had been working with the Treasury and FSA on the numbers. It was also clear that the Bank of England Governor was on a different planet to the FSA when it came to estimates of what the banks needed to shore up their finances.

Brown and his team climbed back onto their plane ready for the journey home and some time to think and rest. The party of journalists, who had no idea of the agenda being pursued by the Prime Minister, again grumbled about lack of photo opportunities and proper briefings. Brown promised he would brief journalists and turned left to move to his first-class seat. He stayed up throughout the whole flight, mulling over and discussing options with Vadera and Downing Street staff. He resolved to press ahead with the recapitalisation of UK banks, regardless of what the US government did. He describes in his book what decision he reached on that flight: 'We needed a comprehensive plan centred on capital, and, if necessary, Britain would have to go it alone.' And going it alone meant pursuing a very different strategy to the Americans, who were still focussed on making TARP work. The danger, Brown reflected later, was that it might not be enough to gain the confidence of the markets and might put the UK's credit rating at risk. But the risk of doing nothing while the banks wobbled was even greater. Even if Bush and Paulson changed their minds, there would be no immediate change of plan. But Brown left the United States relieved that TARP could be used if necessary to purchase chunks of shares in banks. Seeds had been sown with the US administration.

As the plane cruised high above the Atlantic, there was an opportunity at last for the prime ministerial team to reflect. The talks with the Americans had been constructive and had shed important light on the administration's handling of the crisis. But the reality was that for the

UK's struggling banking sector another week had been lost while Brown had tried to shift US opinion about TARP. One aide remembers feeling nervous that time was running out for Britain's banks and that another depositor run which would dwarf Northern Rock was on the cards: 'It was clear that while we could wait a few days I was completely convinced you couldn't wait much longer – some banks were struggling to fund themselves overnight; the spectre of no cash in the ATMs was becoming extremely real.'

Instead of reclining in their seats and switching off, Brown and his advisers sat with tables down, running through the Treasury's document and Mervyn King's fax. The Governor had pushed for the government to insist on taking share stakes in all the leading banks, including the well funded HSBC and Standard Chartered. His argument was that the banks should not be given any leeway and that market confidence would be best maintained if there were not two classes of bank, those needing state funding and those which could raise money in the markets. The Prime Minister and his aides tossed around this idea. The legal issues seemed paramount. Could the Treasury force the banks to take taxpayer-funded capital? The answer was not clear. And because of that uncertainty it did not appear an attractive option.

As the plane touched down Gordon Brown had made up his mind. He wanted to press ahead with recapitalisation and he was minded to do that the following week. But there was a reshuffle to carry out and he wanted to consult Cabinet colleagues. He wondered if giving the Americans a bit more time might bring them behind capital rather than purchasing troubled assets. And he felt he should talk to European leaders and try to get them on board. One adviser remembers thinking 'Oh my God, don't hold your breath on that one – they are still in an Anglo-Saxon problem-mode, blaming others for the crisis'. But the Prime Minister seemed convinced he could persuade President Sarkozy. The problem for Brown was that time was fast ebbing away.

Back at Heathrow on the Saturday morning there was no let-up for Brown and his team. At the Treasury the rescue of Bradford & Bingley was in full swing. The Prime Minister went straight to Downing Street to be briefed by the Chancellor on the plan. The stricken building society had come out of the summer in terminal condition. Any hope amongst policymakers that it could stagger on unaided had evaporated. The disastrous fundraising exercises of the previous months had tarnished the bank irrevocably. The attempted 'beauty pageant' had left just one contender to pick up the pieces at Bradford & Bingley after HBOS had been dismissed as an unattractive option. The Spanish bank Santander, already owner of Abbey National and Alliance & Leicester, was ready to take on another historic name from the building society world which had transformed itself into a bank and then over-extended itself.

Regulators were able to use the new powers available to them thanks to the Banking Act of earlier that year. Much of the grief over Northern Rock was avoided – there was no leak about the need for a rescue before plans were in place and there was no prevarication because of uncertainty over the legalities. Queues were avoided even though the plight of Bradford & Bingley had become increasingly clear during September. The FSA and Bank of England had told Bradford & Bingley to ensure branches had plenty of space for customers to line up inside. The bank was instructed to have plentiful supplies of cash in the branches. Staff had received extra training in case there was a large build-up of customers at any time. With prompting from regulators, the bank had done what it could to improve IT systems to ensure online services worked smoothly, as one of the contributory factors in the Northern Rock panic was the website crashing. There was a determination to avoid the queues which had provided such damning TV images during the run on Northern Rock. Bradford & Bingley was not the only institution under scrutiny in this regard. Other banks and building societies had been told to draw up contingency plans to ensure extra staff could be brought in if queues at their branches started to build up.

It was the first 'bank resolution' of its kind in the post-Northern Rock era. The FSA simply told Bradford & Bingley that it was no longer licensed to take deposits, in effect ordering the bank to close its doors. The Bank of England's Deputy Governor, Sir John Gieve, later reflected that 'the resolution worked very well – it was the first time we used the powers – it was a very complex exercise which was well handled'. There were complications over the role of the depositor compensation scheme and whether EU state aid rules might come into play. But regulators found Santander easy to do business with. It helped that the Santander chairman was the former Treasury Permanent Secretary Sir Terry Burns. His Whitehall contacts and familiarity with the workings of the government machine were useful in ensuring the deal could be transacted swiftly.

On Saturday 27 September Alistair Darling had made one last effort to find a private sector solution for Bradford & Bingley. He summoned all the leading bank chief executives to the Treasury and urged them to come in through the back door to avoid the being caught on camera. In his book *Back from the Brink*, Darling describes his offer to them to take part in a rescue plan. They did not take long to reject the opportunity. 'They recognised that nationalisation was the only way out, and perhaps it was a sign of the times that they were entirely happy with that.'

On Sunday the structure of the deal was made public. The bank was to be nationalised, wiping out shareholders and Santander would immediately take on the nearly 200 Bradford & Bingley branches with the deposits of 2.7 million customers. Santander was to pay £600 million for the transaction. Around £50 billion of mortgages would be left in the hands of the government and become a liability for the taxpayer. They were to be added to the existing book of former Northern Rock loans. It was a clean solution on paper. But Santander had to make it work. Transferring bank accounts from one institution to another is never easy, and it is even more difficult when confidence amongst depositors is fragile. Santander had to ensure the technology would function, bringing the Bradford & Bingley customers on board and running the new accounts with their own systems. Some regulators feared the possibility of an IT fiasco and even a spate of customer withdrawals. But their concerns proved unfounded and the nightmares of Northern Rock were not repeated.

Five years on, the so-called bad assets from Bradford & Bingley lumped together with Northern Rock's toxic loans did not look so rancid. There is every possibility of government loans being repaid in full, a possibility which would have seemed insanely optimistic in the days after the Bradford & Bingley carve-up.

As Alistair Darling did a round of media interviews on the following Monday morning and later made a statement in the Commons, the banking crisis was lapping around the world's financial centres. Confidence was ebbing by the hour. For the UK, it was Bradford & Bingley; in the US Wachovia was tottering and had to be rescued by the government and Citigroup in a government-brokered deal (though Citigroup subsequently pulled out after Wells Fargo tabled a rival bid). A few days earlier, JP Morgan had taken over the struggling mortgage lender Washington Mutual. The Benelux equivalent was Fortis, which had to be nationalised by three governments. The Belgian bank Dexia was not far behind in requiring a bailout with Belgian, French and Luxembourg taxpayers' money. The whiff of fear in financial markets was becoming more pungent.

Events on that Monday evening (European time) ensured that this was to be a dramatic and desperately challenging week for policymakers in the capital of capitalism. Hank Paulson's TARP legislation was unexpectedly and sensationally rejected by the House of Representatives. This was despite an agreement between congressional leaders to support the $700 billion package. In New York, traders watched the televised events on Capitol Hill in disbelief – Wall Street saw its worst day for leading shares since 1987. Nerves jangled in every other leading financial market. What had been billed as Uncle Sam's Big Bazooka solution to the crisis had been ignominiously spiked. To some it seemed as if the world's largest economy was powerless to stem the tide and that there was nothing left in reserve.

Darling's problems took a turn for the worse on the Tuesday. He woke up to hear news on the radio that the Irish government had unilaterally announced a guarantee of all bank deposits and loans to banks, both by individuals and institutions. Immediately the prospect of a flight of savings from UK banks to government-backed accounts in Ireland was looming. Ulster Bank, part of RBS, looked especially vulnerable to a flow of deposits from the North to South of the border. The Irish move heightened the impression in the markets that governments were not working together and were being dragged along by the rapid pace of events rather than setting the agenda. The President of the European Central Bank, Jean-Claude Trichet, announced he had not been consulted which added to the sense of chaos. Darling took a call from Christine Lagarde, then French minister for finance, in which she voiced her concern about the Irish decision. She wanted to know if the British would follow. Such was the febrile atmosphere at the time that Lagarde reported she had heard a rumour that her own President was planning to introduce a deposit guarantee but she knew nothing about it. She called again later to reassure Darling that the rumour was not true.

Both Brown and Darling spoke to their Irish counterparts. Darling voiced his irritation in a terse conversation with the Irish finance minister Brian Lenihan and received an apology of sorts. He pointed out that the Irish banks' balance sheets, like the UK's, were considerably bigger than the total Irish government spending. Lenihan's tongue-in-cheek response was that he hoped people wouldn't notice. But it wasn't long before international investors did notice the scale of the potential liabilities for the Irish government as a result of their sweeping guarantee. Little more than three years later the Dublin authorities had to negotiate a European and IMF bailout.

October 2008 will remain etched in British economic history as the month when the banking system nearly imploded. And the month dawned with a dramatic, but highly confidential move by the authorities. HBOS had limped along over the previous fortnight with some protection from the perceived safety net provided by Lloyds. Once investors knew that HBOS was set to fall into the arms of Lloyds, the pressure on the share price eased a little, though there was no ink on the deal. But even so the funding pressures were still intense with the bank struggling to borrow money even for a day at a time. So, on Wednesday 1 October, the Bank of England started lending money to HBOS covertly under a programme called Emergency Liquidity Assistance (ELA). Highly liquid Treasury bills, which HBOS could easily sell in the markets, were exchanged for mortgages. The existence of these loans, which were also extended to RBS the following week, was kept quiet for more than a year. Neither Parliament nor the media were informed. In retrospect, it was extraordinary and surprising too that the news never leaked. Bank of England sources later explained that they were in effect on a 'war footing' and the disclosure of such lifelines to banks would have jeopardised the 'war effort'. They feared a leak at some stage that, as one source put it, would have put them 'in a very difficult place'. If news had got out about the emergency loans in late 2008 and the recapitalisations had begun to lose credibility, the entire rescue package could have crumbled. But, to the great surprise of senior Bank officials, their secret was never exposed.

The plight of HBOS was well known to regulators, not least because 50 per cent of total funding requirements came from wholesale markets. And after Northern Rock, any institution with that sort of funding ratio was seen as vulnerable. From April, the FSA and the Bank had begun contingency planning for a rescue of HBOS. This included the likely need for emergency funding. HBOS was closely monitored throughout the summer. But after the collapse of Lehman in mid-September and the consequent freezing of the wholesale markets, it was surprising that HBOS had managed to stagger through until the end of the month. Only on 1 October did it request assistance from the Bank of England, the need for funding by now urgent. Four years later, an independent review of the Bank's handling of the situation suggested it could have intervened sooner and pre-emptively to provide a helping hand to HBOS. The bank continued to draw funding from the Bank of England through until 13 November, with a total debt owing of £25.4 billion. It was repaid in early 2009.

As the Treasury fought fires at Bradford & Bingley and battled to hold the line after the shock of the Irish deposit guarantee, it was hard to focus on the urgent need to prepare the wider action plan for the banking sector. Darling had instructed officials the previous Friday to work with the Bank of England and the FSA on a recapitalisation initiative. This was on the same day the paperwork from the tripartite had been faxed over to Washington along with Mervyn King's big number estimate of the hole which had to be filled. But since then it had been hard for Treasury civil servants, who had more immediate challenges to deal with, to move this agenda forward.

Vadera had arrived back at Heathrow mindful of Brown's demand that work on a rescue plan must begin immediately. If there was one lesson to be learned from the United States, they reasoned, it was to be ready for the financial storm which could make landfall at any moment. Vadera knew that injecting equity capital into the banks – in other words, shareholders' funding – had to be the centrepiece of the plan. And if it couldn't come from shareholders it would have to come from the government. But she thought this would take time to implement because of the legal hurdles to be cleared. She also believed that a device to underpin bank lending was essential. She and Scholar had worked on proposals from Sir James Crosby to stimulate the mortgage market. This would have involved the government providing guarantees for mortgage-backed securities. There had always been doubts surrounding this approach, but Vadera believed it would be feasible to extend the idea to the entire inter-bank lending market. If one of the threats to lending in the wider economy was the banks' reluctance to lend to one another, then any scheme to remove the risk from that market would have wider benefits.

The biggest challenge was to work out how to make the banks raise more capital and if necessary make them take it from the government. But that, so the thinking went, could be easier if the carrot of the funding scheme was dangled in front of them – if you want the funding guarantees, you will have to raise capital first. Then there was the question of how much capital each bank should have to find. What would happen if the FSA came up with estimates and the bank disagreed? Would the FSA have to come up with new regulations? Vadera's view was that you could leave it to the markets to impose the solution. All the regulators had to do was say what they thought was the requisite amount of capital and investors would force the banks to raise it. The final piece of the jigsaw would be provided by the Bank of England extending their special liquidity scheme. Introduced in April, the plan was to allow banks easy access to funding in exchange for mortgages and other loans. It had proved highly successful and King, somewhat reluctantly, had pushed back the closing date from September to January. Now he would be asked to double the funds offered from £100 billion to £200 billion.

Vadera bounced her ideas off Tom Scholar. They tallied with his thinking and some of the work beginning to emerge at the Treasury. But the question was how to move them forward quickly. External expertise was needed but bringing in outside advisers risked a leak. She decided to call on City bankers she knew and could trust. UBS was a good starting point as Vadera had spent much of her career there. Robin Budenberg was the first on her contact list at UBS and she called him on the Wednesday evening. A laid-back character, diplomatic and with a sharp eye for the workings of corporate Britain, Budenberg was described by colleagues as very sane and level-headed. He was used to working with government, having been an adviser on the evolution of Network Rail in 2001 when he crossed paths with Vadera, then at the Treasury. He was also involved in the sale of the government's stake in British Energy, which covered much of the UK's nuclear industry, a few weeks before the collapse of Lehman. Budenberg later went on to head UK Financial Investments, the body which managed the government's share stakes in the banks.

Vadera had to tread carefully. She had to avoid giving too much away. So tense was the atmosphere that any hint of an official government plan in the making would move markets. Talking to bankers in those terms was impossible. She was acting in her capacity as a business department minister, under the radar and quietly 'enquiring' about the state of the bank funding markets. Gordon Brown knew that she was talking to people in the City but she was under no illusion that her involvement had to be deniable. If it leaked, her job would be on the line.

Budenberg, who had had other conversations with Vadera from time to time, sensed there was an urgency about her questioning on this occasion. He had received calls over the previous few weeks from people in government asking what was happening, the usual off-the-record gossip between people in the political and business world. But Budenberg could tell this was different – he was being asked to express a view on something that felt like it could become a project. He said he was ready to talk and would consult his UBS colleague David Soanes, the investment banker who was an expert on banking industry debt markets. Vadera insisted that nobody else be brought into the loop. She also wanted to test opinion on Wall Street and how banks were faring there – so she made a call to Michael Klein, a Wall Street hotshot who had quit Citigroup that summer.

What Vadera really needed to do was speak directly to a major bank to find out more about the funding market. It was much more opaque than other financial markets as there was little quoted data by which to judge fully the severity of the stresses and strains. But she could hardly approach the big UK banks which were caught up in the maelstrom – they would not want to divulge their true positions. HSBC was the obvious choice, but because it was a global bank with ample sources of funding it was one of the few institutions still lending to other banks. Its perceptions might not be typical of the market as a whole. That left Standard Chartered, a British bank but with almost all its activities outside the UK. Vadera reckoned it would at least know what was going on in the market so she contacted the chief executive, Peter Sands.

The call to Sands was wide-ranging, Vadera asking for his opinion on the state of the markets. There was no hint that a plan was being hatched. As a member of the Department for Business ministerial team she had an understandable interest in how banks were funding each other. Sands told her that his finance director, Richard Meddings, would know all about who was doing what in the relevant markets. Meddings, as it happened, was an old friend of Robin Budenberg. Sands suggested that a meeting would be beneficial but Vadera pointed out that it would be impossible for her to host it officially. Sands then agreed to organise it himself at Standard Chartered.

On the afternoon of Thursday 2 October a disparate group of Whitehall people and bankers arrived discreetly at the reception area of Standard Chartered's head office in the City of London, tucked away behind London Wall. There were no press photographers or TV crews present even though in importance it ranked with most other meetings involving policymakers trying to tackle the financial crisis. Shriti Vadera was there and so too was Tom Scholar from the Treasury, also craving anonymity at such a sensitive gathering. Robin Budenberg and David Soanes of UBS slipped into the building. Michael Klein, formerly of Citigroup, also attended. They were whisked up to the boardroom on the top floor of the building. There were plentiful supplies of beer and wine and the atmosphere was rather more relaxed than a normal City business meeting. Soanes recalled that the bottles seemed incongruous: 'I remember thinking that whoever had laid it out was being quite optimistic about what that meeting was for – I was nervous at the speed with which we were having to make decisions.' And as the meeting progressed and the participants grasped the reality of what they were facing, an unsurprisingly sober mood prevailed. There was little appetite for the beer and wine.

Vadera came clean about the severity of the crisis for British banking and the fact that the government was considering a radical response. But she was still careful not to reveal her full hand. She asked the bankers what they would do in the circumstances to try to shore up confidence. Vadera and Scholar were pleasantly surprised that the City representatives came up with areas for intervention which corresponded with what 10 Downing Street and the Treasury were already working on. The business minister was especially interested in the bank funding issue and how to make that work better. One key area of discussion was how the financial markets might react to government underwriting of inter-bank loans and what sort of fees should be levied on the banks. Meddings at one point left the boardroom to consult his group treasurer on issues surrounding bank-to-bank lending. There was not so much debate on recapitalisation, perhaps because Scholar and Vadera did not want to let on too much.

Late into the evening Vadera and Scholar made their excuses and got up to leave. Their final shot was to ask if the bankers would work together on a note summarising the options. As the two returned to Whitehall, those who remained in the Standard Chartered boardroom accepted the challenge and carried on working. When they broke up, Meddings and Budenberg had a quiet word in the corridor. The friends had had many experiences working together in the City over previous decades. But absolutely nothing in their careers to date compared to this. Lehman had gone bust but the idea that RBS might topple seemed quite extraordinary. Until Vadera's bleak assessment at the beginning of that evening's meeting they had not realised the extent of the rescue for the UK's banks which was being proposed. Budenberg remembers the conversation: '[Meddings] said: "Can you believe we talked about what we just talked about?" It seemed unbelievable at that time. I was gobsmacked at that stage.' They chuckled quietly because the very idea that they had just been discussing a plan to save the banking system seemed ridiculous.

The banking team knew the urgency and did not waste any time. Despite a late night on the Thursday they were back at Standard Chartered at 6 a.m. the next day. An intensive six-hour meeting followed. Senior lawyers were consulted and by lunchtime they had finished drafting their document. It contained a three-point action plan:

boosting bank capital, underpinning the bank funding market, and extending the Bank of England's Special Liquidity Scheme. With regard to capital there was an acknowledgement that the government might have to provide it though it was assumed that it would be offered rather than forced on the banks. According to one participant, 'there was still a feeling at that stage this was a liquidity crisis not a capital crisis – that was what evolved the following week and that was why equity (capital) later became more of an issue'. At the time the document was written, there was much more emphasis on those parts of the plan which involved the government and Bank of England tackling funding issues. The full horrors of the banks' balance sheets and the threat to their solvency had not become clear.

The bankers then sent copies to Scholar at the Treasury and Vadera at her office. Both took the document and merged it with other paperwork to be dispatched to ministers. Scholar had to take care with how it was presented in the Treasury to avoid ruffling the feathers of officials who had been deputed to work on this policy area. He had to let Darling know how the thinking and options were developing. Copies were sent over to Gordon Brown and Jeremy Heywood at 10 Downing Street. The Prime Minister noted that the outlines were similar to the thinking developed in Washington and on the flight back. The ad hoc banking team waited for news back from Whitehall. But as the hours ticked by they heard nothing.

There remained one outstanding problem – getting Mervyn King onside. The Governor would have to give his blessing to the proposed big extension of the Bank's Special Liquidity Scheme. Relationships at that time between the Governor and the Chancellor were far from perfect. Some in the Treasury suspected that King had no time for Darling and patronised the Chancellor and his officials during debates on policy options. Wide-ranging discussions on global economic policy were to the liking of both Mervyn King and Gordon Brown, though, and it was felt that the personal relationship between them was good. So the Treasury sent word to 10 Downing Street that Brown needed to work on King to finalise the key elements of the rescue plan. Even during the reshuffle, Brown had meetings with the Governor and they took place almost daily as the crisis rumbled on. Officials would need to check that they remained focussed on the job on hand: 'We would leave them alone for long periods – then we would go in and chivvy them along, and make sure they were getting to the right place.' And the right place involved doubling the Bank of England's liquidity scheme to £200 billion – that is, funding in exchange for old mortgage loans. King was also brought up to date with the government's plans for new bank capital.

Brown's diplomatic skills had been fully stretched in his dealings with the Governor – they were also to be tested in a round of European diplomacy. He had a good bond with the French President. They knew each other well from their time as finance ministers on the sometimes-dreary merry-go-round of European meetings. There was a positive chemistry between them, despite Brown being left of centre and Sarkozy further to the right. Sarkozy was to prove to be an important ally. With France holding the EU Presidency, he had convened an emergency mini-summit for Saturday 4 October in Paris. It was held in the grand surroundings of the Elysée Palace and the aim was to demonstrate that Europe could match the ambition and urgency displayed by Hank Paulson and the TARP legislation, which had passed into law on the previous day. The willingness of EU leaders to attend the hastily-convened summit on a Saturday afternoon demonstrated the heightened state of concern about the financial crisis raging through their banking systems.

British government sources at the Elysée meeting described it later as 'bizarre'. The German Chancellor Angela Merkel made it clear she regarded the banking crisis as an Anglo-Saxon problem, born in the United States and compounded by the UK's failings. Sarkozy chaired the meeting around a large table with Merkel on his right and Brown on his left. Jean-Claude Trichet, president of the European Central Bank sat next to Brown offering support to the British prime minister's call for co-ordinated action. Italy's Silvio Berlusconi and Luxembourg's Jean-Claude Juncker, president of the Euro Group, were the others round the table. Brown explained why he thought the situation, far from being an issue only for the UK and the US, was serious and how it affected every economy across Europe. He pointed out that European banks had borrowed as heavily as others and invested in the same sort of mortgage-backed securities as US institutions caught up in the sub-prime crisis. He urged his counterparts to consider a joint guarantee on bank lending as one part of an agreed Europe-wide action plan. Merkel was especially hostile, arguing it was unaffordable and unnecessary. There was criticism around the table of the unilateral Irish deposit guarantee announced a few days earlier. Sarkozy was more sympathetic – Brown had buttered him up and told him that, with the EU Presidency, France could be seen to be providing leadership in these troubled times.

As well as Sarkozy, Trichet was very supportive of Gordon Brown. Unlike some of the others around the Elysée table, he knew that this was a lot more than an Anglo-Saxon obsession. He understood the potential perils threatening EU economies if banks cut back loans to one another. He pushed the idea of government guarantees on inter-bank lending. Individual economies, he believed, should carry out their own bank recapitalisations. For Trichet, a grand plan implemented pro-actively and ahead of market expectations was the urgent necessity. The summit put its weight behind the idea of a G20 leaders' gathering, the plan pushed by Brown at his White House talks the previous week-end. And the leaders pledged to build a new financial system that would lay to rest the old speculative capitalism. But the summit ended without firm agreements or commitments to co-ordinated plans.

Once back in their respective capitals, the political leaders who had witnessed Merkel's scepticism and occasional hostility at the summit were surprised to see her television appearance on Sunday in Berlin. One of Germany's major banks, the property lender Hypo Real Estate, was foundering that weekend. A rescue package put together by commercial banks had crumbled. The German government was obliged to step in to co-ordinate an alternative bailout deal and underwrite a bigger slice of the liabilities. Merkel, appearing at a media conference in Berlin, was asked whether the government would come to the help of German savers if their money was at risk. She answered: 'We want to tell savers that their deposits are safe.' It was not clear whether the German Chancellor was making a conscious pledge to underwrite all bank deposits, but that was how the media chose to interpret her comments. The unity of the previous day's summit now looked a sham. Germany appeared to be acting unilaterally and in defiance of any co-ordinated European action.

The British Prime Minister and his aides were perplexed. Merkel had made clear the previous day how vehemently opposed she was to open-ended guarantees of bank deposits. Yet here she was doing precisely that and with no warning to her European colleagues. Sarkozy called Brown to assure him that Merkel had been trying to supply a 'political guarantee' to reassure the markets and that there was no new policy for depositors' savings. The German Chancellor later called Downing Street and conceded that the Prime Minister might have been on to something when he had talked of a Europe-wide banking support plan. She seemed, to those officials who were aware of the call, to be more open to guidance and willing to co-operate with any initiatives that might materialise.

Chapter 5

Britain on the brink

Paul Myners was an experienced City hand who knew his way around the financial markets. But he was not a typical public-school-educated financier. Born in Cornwall, his first years were spent in a children's home. He was adopted by a butcher and his wife in Truro and after a scholarship-funded education, he won a place to study at the University of London. A couple of years as a teacher were not to his liking and he found his way into business journalism. From there he moved into investment banking and then to the fund manager Gartmore where he became chairman.

By the time the banking crisis was sweeping around world markets, Myners had become a serial non-executive, with a list of chairmanships as long as his arm. The highest profile was Marks & Spencer where he had helped see off a hostile bid by Sir Philip Green. Guardian Media Group was another. He prided himself on being 'in the City not of the City'. His personal foibles included a chauffeur-driven Rolls-Royce and a large bowl of fresh fruit permanently in his office, the contents of which he would munch through at meetings.

Myners had an abiding suspicion of slick investment bankers. He liked to tell a story of two blue-chip houses which had hurriedly been signed up to represent M&S in the bid battle with Sir Philip Green. Terms of engagement had been drawn up with the fee structure buried in fine print. Myners had read the document and then gone into the board-room to meet the bankers. They looked pleased when he said he agreed to the proposed fees, but less so when he asked for the word 'each' to be deleted. They raised objections. He told them he was off for a coffee and would be back in half an hour by which time he wanted their decision. When he returned, they had agreed to share the one fee between them.

Myners was a Labour supporter and had done advisory work for Gordon Brown and Alistair Darling. He had headed an influential review of the institutional investment industry in 2001 and in the process had got to know Shriti Vadera when she was a Treasury adviser. Even so he was surprised to take call from Number 10 on the afternoon of Sunday 28 September 2008, a fortnight after the collapse of Lehman. Gordon Brown invited him to join the government to work on the response to the banking crisis. It was a short call, the Prime Minister explaining he needed someone to stand 'toe to toe' with the banks.

Myners certainly had his own views on the excesses of the banking world before the crash. He had witnessed at first hand the extraordinarily lax terms required by banks lending to Guardian Media Group for the acquisition of the publisher of *Auto Trader*. He had sat on the governing body of the Bank of England, known as the Court, so he knew all about what the experts called 'mis-pricing of risk' and what others might have simply called a lending frenzy to any borrower, regardless of the credit rating. From the Prime Minister's point of view, Myners was a bruiser who could see through the special pleading of the banking industry. His knowledge and negotiating skills were beyond the experience of any Whitehall civil servants. Those who later worked with him at the Treasury remember him as a 'Marmite minister' – you either loved him or hated him.

Nobody ever accused Myners of lacking drive and energy and, having agreed to help, he was keen to get started immediately even if it was a Sunday afternoon. But he was told to wait a few days. The Prime Minister wanted to announce the appointment along with others the following Friday in a mini reshuffle which would include the return to government of Peter Mandelson. Myners would later reflect that five days were wasted because of the need to choreograph the ministerial changes.

The headlines on Friday 3 October focussed on the recall of Peter Mandelson and the promotion of Ed Miliband from the Cabinet Office to head a newly formed Department for Energy and Climate Change. Questions at the parliamentary lobby briefing for political journalists were directed largely at the politics behind these two appointments. There was little comment on the announcement of Myners' role or a new post for Shriti Vadera who would take an economic portfolio in the Cabinet Office, moving from the Business Department. These two may have seemed insignificant to lobby correspondents at the time, but they were to be at the heart of the response to Britain's biggest peacetime crisis.

Paul, soon to be Lord, Myners arrived at the Treasury late that Friday afternoon. He had dropped all his directorships as required by rules for ministers. This meant giving up a clutch of prestigious posts amongst the corporate elite. Chairmanships of Land Securities and the Tate were among those dropped. He later reflected that he would not have given up the City posts if he had not thought there was a serious job to be done. But the government mission was to consume far more of his waking hours that he could have imagined. He asked for as much information as the Treasury officials could muster on the state of Britain's leading banks. There had been some scratching of heads over what ministerial title Myners would take. He thought 'Financial Secretary' would be appropriate but that post had already been allocated to Stephen Timms. Civil servants had to dream up the title 'Financial Services Secretary' and they had to find at very short notice a staff and an office space for Myners to occupy.

One Treasury civil servant remembers Myners walking in the Treasury courtyard known as 'the Drum' carrying piles of briefing notes and puffing away on a huge, Churchillian cigar. It was not a familiar sight in the conventional no-smoking environment of Whitehall. On one occasion he was ticked off by a security guard for smoking in that area and, according to eyewitnesses, gave a robust and terse response. But it did not take Myners long to read the documents and to come to the conclsion that serious trouble was looming. One observer remembers him looking 'ashen'.

Back in the Treasury the following morning, Myners had his first full set of meetings with ministerial colleagues and officials. He had no idea before joining the government of the extent to which HBOS and RBS were dependent on funding provided by the Bank of England. He could see a 'waterfall' of deposits reaching maturity the following week and needing to be repaid. Usually, large corporate deposits of cash were 'rolled over'; in other words, extended. But the financial climate was unprecedented and lack of trust in banks was reaching epidemic proportions. Clients would rather take their money out and pay a penalty than leave it with a bank that might become vulnerable. RBS was struggling even to attract money overnight for repayment the next day. Myners later said: 'You realised that if more deposits were not replaced over the next week, the banks would become deeply dependent on Bank of England funding lines.'

That same weekend marked the start of the phase of maximum crisis. Banks around Europe were teetering on the brink as big business customers pulled back their cash. Iceland was close to bankruptcy. American and Asian investors had sniffed danger around British banks. The maths told them that RBS and Lloyds/HBOS each had total assets larger than the annual output of the British economy. Some of those assets looked less than wholesome. Corporate treasurers and others with big cash deposits could see no advantage in leaving their money in banks with question marks hanging over them.

This was what Paul Myners, minister charged with dealing with the banking crisis, had walked into. He was only one day in the job. Clichés about 'a steep learning curve' might seem trite: the curve for Myners was almost vertical. RBS was worse even than he had feared. By noon that Saturday he had concluded that there was much less time to come up with a solution than he had hoped. A plan to reassure the markets that RBS had access to capital was needed within days. But he was impressed with the quiet determination and capability of senior Treasury civil servants and the amount of preparation and thinking that had already taken place.

The head of the Treasury, Permanent Secretary Sir Nick Macpherson, and senior mandarins John Kingman and Tom Scholar were clearly on top of the complex and frequently changing brief. Intensive work with the Bank of England and Financial Services Authority had taken place in preceding days. This had focussed on the numbers and how much funding the banks needed. Contingency planning on how a bailout might be executed had been carried out, including the best way for the government to inject capital into the banks. The document initially drafted after the meeting in the Standard Chartered boardroom had been honed by Vadera and Tom Scholar and then fed into the planning process at the Treasury. The legal complexities had been endlessly debated – lawyers advised that ministers were on weak ground if they wished to force banks to take the money.

By Sunday, the Prime Minister and the Chancellor were ready to sign off the outlines of the plan. They met at 10 Downing Street to talk over how it might be taken forward. What they did not know was when they might be ready to enact it. Darling and his officials felt more time was needed for preparation and ensuring the mechanics were robust. Others were convinced it had to be finished and ready to be announced, if necessary, on the coming Tuesday or Wednesday. They feared the banks' defences might hold out for only a few more days. Telling the markets the government was going to intervene would calm the markets and allow the details to be hammered out the following weekend.

While Darling and his officials and Number 10's key players wrestled with the complexities of the proposed bailout package, Brown had to break away to deal with an unexpected problem. He had announced the return of Peter Mandelson to government on the Friday. But by Sunday his new Business Secretary had called saying he was ill. Mandelson felt so poorly that he was convinced he was having a heart attack. He still had private healthcare from his time at the European Commission and wanted to make use of it to get rapid treatment. After the blaze of publicity about his return to the Cabinet, he felt reticent about appearing on a Sunday afternoon at a hospital accident and emergency unit. Brown's response was that would not be a politically sensible move and offered to send round Ara Darzi, the junior health minister. Mandelson, in exasperation as well as pain, replied 'I don't need a politician, I need a doctor!' He had failed to realise that as well as being a minister in the Lords, Darzi was one of the country's most eminent physicians. Darzi was dispatched to attend to Mandelson and confirm that he had not suffered a heart attack. Instead he was diagnosed with a kidney stone, a painful and debilitating condition, and went into hospital the next day to have it removed. Gamely, he was back at his desk that evening.

So far, so confidential. Nothing had leaked. Few business or political journalists had any suspicions about the gravity of the situation. But while Myners, Vadera, Kingman, Scholar and other senior civil servants worked furiously behind the modern facade of the Treasury building overlooking Horse Guards Parade, the Chancellor was being pressed for information. Darling was appearing on the Andrew Marr TV show on the Sunday morning with his main parliamentary opponents also on the programme. Immediately before the Chancellor's appearance, George Osborne, then Shadow Chancellor, and Vince Cable, his Liberal Democrat counterpart, were asked for their views on the banking crisis. Osborne spoke about banking legislation being introduced in the following week and referred to a conversation he had had with Mervyn King. The banks were weak, said Mr Osborne, and the answer was recapitalisation.

To Darling, Osborne's remarks seemed very well informed. Andrew Marr picked up on them as he questioned the Chancellor, pressing him on whether there was a plan to recapitalise banks with Conservative support. Darling had to stall, going no further than saying the government was ready to do whatever it takes and that other measures would be announced when the time was right. He knew he had to give as little away as possible because the plan was not finalised. So he could not answer Marr's questions directly. Likewise, he could not deny outright that there was any such possibility. Thinking on his feet in the BBC studio was no mean feat. He suspected Osborne had used information garnered from the conversation with Mervyn King about the government's intentions. Treasury staff were 'livid' according to a source and had to accelerate and amend work in preparation for a statement by the Chancellor the next day. Conservative aides later strongly denied that the Shadow Chancellor had used privileged information – they pointed out that leading commentators, including Martin Wolf in the *Financial Times,* had already been calling for a recapitalisation of banks.

On Monday 6 October the House of Commons returned after the parliamentary recess. Darling felt obliged to update MPs after the tumultuous events that had taken place in global financial markets since parliamentarians had headed for the beaches. But he had to do so while the group at the Treasury continued their covert planning. He could tell the House nothing of what was really going on. The intention at this stage was for the recapitalisation plan to be worked up for a few more days and probably not unveiled for at least another week. But he had to go further in hinting at what the government was doing as a result of the Marr programme revelations. He later reflected that making that parliamentary statement had not been wise. MPs and the media were left suspecting something was up but without getting any clues as to what the Treasury was planning. The result was that the government's response to the crisis looked inadequate. The Marr programme raised expectations that were not met. And the Conservative opposition was able to push the line that Brown and Darling were dragging their feet, unable to provide firm leadership just when the economy needed it.

Even as Darling was carrying out his holding operation in the Commons, planning was progressing well at the Treasury. Robin Budenberg of UBS had received a phone call the previous evening from Myners and Vadera. Having submitted the paper written with the Standard Chartered bankers on the Friday, he had heard nothing for 48 hours. His political lines of communication had gone quiet. The politicians appeared to be incommunicado. But the call on the Sunday evening left Budenberg in no doubt that the button was being pressed on the rescue plan. He was asked to be at the Treasury with Soanes at 8 a.m. on Monday. Rather than having discussions and writing papers, their expertise was needed to deliver what a few days earlier had seemed like hypothetical concepts.

The process leading to the appointment of the UBS bankers was unusual by Whitehall standards. Tom Scholar had assumed a beauty parade of City institutions would be required the following day, with each making a pitch for the government's mandate. But Vadera and Myners advised that there was no time for that and the nature of the work was so sensitive that it would be too risky to brief a selection of bankers. The UBS pair was the obvious choice. And they had to be contacted that evening – leaving it till the following day was not an option.

Along with Budenberg and Soanes from UBS, others were called in for their City expertise. David Mayhew, veteran stock market dealmaker and chairman of JP Morgan Cazenove was contacted along with his colleague from the investment banking side, Naguib Kheraj. Their presence was required for a second opinion on the work done so far. So too the doyen of City lawyers, Nigel Boardman of Slaughter and May, with his colleague Charles Randall, renowned for their intellect and unrivalled grasp of corporate law. Mayhew and Boardman had been brought on board because they were seen by Myners and Vadera as the best in the business. The ministers knew them well from City corporate skirmishes down the years. They were the bluest of blue-chip advisers. Myners said later of Mayhew: 'If David said something wouldn't fly, it wouldn't fly.' He knew the Treasury needed the best people from outside to help with the unprecedented and daunting task ahead. Giving the banks the message they were obliged to raise more capital was a dramatic step for ministers to take. They needed to ensure the numbers and detailed plans could withstand the inevitable onslaught from outraged bankers.

There was one important obstacle to be negotiated – the City professionals did not have passes allowing free access around the corridors of the Treasury and usually Whitehall security clearances took weeks to arrange. It needed a few barked internal calls from Myners for the passes to be made up that morning. And once inside, the visitors were told there were no fees on offer for the work that was about to get underway – this was for the greater good and the national interest. Not one of them demurred.

Senior officials from the Financial Services Authority arrived along with Sir John Gieve, representing the Bank of England. Other staff from UBS and Cazenove were called in as the day wore on. Those present all knew up to a point what their brief was to be. They knew the banking industry was in poor shape and that the government was planning action. But events had moved rapidly even since the end of the previous week. And it was not until the gathering was addressed by Myners and Vadera that they all became fully aware how grave the situation was. The two ministers made clear to the assembled group that the government wanted to unveil an urgent response to the crisis and that a fully worked-up plan would be needed ready for an announcement the following Monday or Tuesday.

The bankers, lawyers, regulators and civil servants got down to work. The plan which had been drawn up after the Standard Chartered meeting was circulated. Another plan drawn up in the Treasury was also passed around. There were not big differences between the two drafts but it was decided to work on the bankers' version as it had more practical detail. All day they toiled over the finer points and wrestled with the complexities of the financial instruments required for the bailouts. A few members of the UBS and Cazenove teams worked on through the night.

Some of the bankers sat down with experts from the gilts market, the officials at the Debt Management Office who had to raise money for the government on the financial markets. They pondered how to deal with the small issue of finding £40 billion to carry out the bailout operation. Usually officials managing the government's debt and funding requirements plan their cash-raising well in advance. Auctions are held at regular intervals and the major investment houses are invited to bid for government IOUs, known as gilts. A single auction might raise £5 billion. Yet here the debt managers were being asked to come up with eight times that amount. One observer remembers an expletive and a blunt response to the figure – 'that's a lot!' But after the briefest pause for thought, came the reply: 'Give us three weeks.'

On the Monday evening 6 October, the leading bank chief executives came to a meeting at the Treasury. Douglas Flint from HSBC, Peter Sands of Standard Chartered, John Varley from Barclays, Antonio Horta-Osorio of Santander and Graham Beale of Nationwide had no immediate crisis to deal with. Eric Daniels of Lloyds, Sir Fred Goodwin of RBS and Andy Hornby of HBOS each had their own challenges to face. According to one observer, Hornby looked 'gaunt and drawn – he had completely lost it'. Darling felt obliged to update them after the speculation about the government's intentions which had been raging since the Sunday morning. The bankers, in turn, were keen to find out what sort of action the government might be planning to give them a breathing space – at the head of the wish list being the provision of cheap funding to tide them over. They needed short-term liquidity and, with the funding markets frozen, it had to come from the government. One observer noted that 'the banks were being murdered in the markets by uncertainty and government briefings that the situation was unsustainable'. They feared the same sort of intervention as had happened in the US when the administration seized control of Fannie Mae and Freddie Mac.

The banks had become familiar with the routine for visits to the Treasury or Downing Street. A meeting had taken place the previous week and there had been others stretching back to the spring. There had been a regular dialogue between ministers and banking chiefs, with the government interested to know how the industry saw things. Liquidity and how to provide it was a regular talking point. To avoid cameras they drove straight off Whitehall into the large Treasury courtyard, rather than walking through the main entrance on Horse Guards Parade. This followed the experience of one bank chief who had had to run the gauntlet of photographers when walking into the Treasury, an unpleasant experience he was determined not to repeat. Depending on the time of day they were often offered refreshments, for example breakfast. But Treasury insiders noted that they very rarely accepted offers of food, arousing suspicions that they had eaten earlier together to work out their joint agenda.

Top of the list of requests from the bank chiefs was for the Bank of England to extend its Special Liquidity Scheme, which the Governor had insisted was time-limited. They were also keen for a credit guarantee scheme to be put in place as soon as possible. They didn't trust each other so needed the government to act as safety net if any loans to other banks went sour. But they did not ask for capital or suggest in any way that this was a problem area for them. That would have amounted to a damaging admission of fundamental solvency problems. Sir Fred Goodwin was clear – it was a liquidity problem and his bank would get through difficult market conditions without extra capital. The Chancellor listened politely but he had no intention of revealing his full hand. Any suggestion of forcing the banks to raise new capital would have caused consternation at the meeting and would probably have been leaked. Furthermore he did not want to be dragged to the House of Commons to make another statement. Darling indicated there was a plan but he would tell them more later in the week – he warned them not to brief the media as any reports that a meeting had taken place would be damaging. The meeting was said to be amicable and businesslike. After all, they were competitors and would not have wished to betray a hint of anxiety. But a change in the banks' attitude was becoming clear. As one insider at the Treasury that day put it: 'They were beginning to panic – for the first time in their lives they needed HM Government and they didn't know what, if anything, we were going to do.'

Darling's desire to keep the real plan under wraps for a little while longer was dealt a severe blow that night. His press advisers took a call from the *Financial Times* who were asking seemingly well-informed questions about the meeting and what the bank chiefs were calling for. Darling and his aides knew how toxic the story could be in the febrile political and market environment once the *FT* hit the streets the following morning. The Westminster village would see it in the context of the 'dithering and indecision' narrative around the Brown government. But much more importantly, they knew then that further speculation in the finan-cial markets would be fatal so the time for discussion had passed – they had to take decisive action or at least give the impression of doing that.

Some have questioned whether Darling needed to have the meeting at all. As he was not ready to announce the full range of the rescue plan, there was arguably no point in sitting round the table with the bank chiefs. One cynical government source later reflected that 'I didn't feel you could trust them enough to do it that way – it leaked, what a surprise!' And the leak threatened to torpedo the careful series of steps to tackle the crisis which were being taken in great secrecy. There was immense frustration amongst the team that had been planning the government's pre-emptive strike: 'It was like, what the hell? We have this discussion and it's there, on the street – it was horrible.'

The next day at 7 a.m., Robert Peston covered in his blog a version of the meeting between Darling and the bankers, based on accounts of the talks garnered from unnamed sources. Again, these conveyed the impression that the banks had been calling for intervention from the Chancellor. Headlined 'Banks ask Chancellor for more capital', the piece suggested a trio of bankers from RBS, Barclays and Lloyds had signalled that 'they'd like to see the colour of taxpayers' money rather quicker than he (Darling) might have expected'. They, it was said, were concerned by investor perceptions they were short of capital. They had estimated, according to the piece, that they might need an extra £15 billion of new capital, each. This puzzled some of those who had been at the meeting and who had different recollections of what had been said.

The reasons for leaking the details of the meeting are not clear. The intention was probably to put pressure on the government to come up with a funding solution. Some have alleged that one source could have been within the Conservative party, perhaps one of George Osborne's aides trying to turn up the heat on the government. Conservative sources described that suggestion as 'nonsense' as they knew nothing about the meeting. Others have pointed the finger at RBS, alleging it was in the bank's interest, given the severe strains it was feeling, to suggest that the industry as a whole wanted government action. There was no proof one way or the other that RBS was a source of the story. Whitehall aides later reflected on how incompetent the bankers' handling of the press and government relations seemed. The account given to Robert Peston seemed to over-state what was actually discussed, which had the opposite effect to what was intended. 'They were capable of making these sort of misjudgements and capable of blunder in this area,' said one aide. Several weeks later the Treasury Permanent Secretary Sir Nick Macpherson and Sir Gus O'Donnell, the civil service chief at Downing Street, discussed whether to have a leak enquiry with a full trawl of phone records. But it was never pursued.

Whatever the motive for the leaks, the outcome was catastrophic. Denials were swift but couched in such a way that the markets did not take long to work out that the problems were largely with two banks, HBOS, soon to merge with Lloyds and RBS. Barclays angrily denied it needed new capital – John Varley, arriving at a banking investment conference that morning, went out of his way to speak to a TV crew to quash the idea he was seeking new funding. But the embers lit in the wake of the Andrew Marr programme interviews were now fast spreading flames. The spectre of nationalisation for some banks loomed. Any remaining reasons to hold RBS and probably HBOS shares had vanished. Bank chiefs going to Number 10 and asking for assistance, reflected one insider later, was the 'nail in the coffin'. Late the previous evening, many in the Treasury inner circle believed it would take another week at least to activate the plan. By early on Tuesday morning, the truth of the situation was staring at them in their faces – it had to be rolled out immediately. When the market opened, the RBS share price was plunging and its headlong descent continued. Previous runs on bank share prices had usually been followed by a much more damaging run on deposits, and this was to prove no exception.

The core team of Treasury officials and bankers were gathered as usual at 10 o'clock that Tuesday morning. Sir John Gieve, Andrew Bailey and Andy Haldane from the Bank of England were there too. Collectively, they were proceeding on the basis that the plan needed more detailed work, possibly several days. But they were interrupted when, according to one observer, 'someone comes in and says the share prices are collapsing'. Myners and Vadera jumped up and left the room rapidly. They were joined by the UBS bankers in Myners' office. They knew the game was up and the bailout plan had to be activated immediately. Gieve,

Bailey and Haldane made their excuses and departed in a hurry to return to the Bank.

There was only one option for the Chancellor and his team at that point. They had to dust down, shape and unveil a plan for government money to shore up the banking system. With news bulletins reporting plummeting share prices, a run on RBS and HBOS loomed, fuelled by a growing outflow of deposits. Hundreds of millions of pounds were being withdrawn. Confidence was so fragile that there were growing fears at the Treasury of a retail run. A sense of catastrophe was in the air. They knew that an announcement had to be made to the markets at the opening the next morning. Anything less would open the door to a widespread loss of confidence. But all that year's contingency planning had focussed on a possible collapse of HBOS. Nobody had thought through how a crisis at RBS might be handled. As a bank-failure candidate, RBS had crept up on regulators and ministers with terrifying speed.

As the RBS share price plunged by up to 40 per cent, major corporate customers with money left in the bank hit the phones. Some had £5 billion or even £10 billion left on deposit. They wanted it back immediately and, in the words of one expert, 'nobody has that hanging around the sofa'. For Northern Rock, the queues of small savers had pulled the rug from under the bank in a classic retail run. For RBS there were no queues of depositors at this stage, but an even more damaging attack was under way, though unseen on television screens. Retail savers can never pull enough money out fast enough to cause instant damage, but this was a wholesale run, when £100 billion could be withdrawn in a morning. RBS bond prices were tumbling too, another sign of distress. When the bank's share trading was suspended, it was as if the death knell was beginning to toll.

Gieve and Bailey, who had become the Bank's trouble-shooter during the crisis as well as Chief Cashier with his signature on bank notes, knew there was only one thing that would save RBS that day – turning on the Bank of England spigots. They had to convince Mervyn King, in the past so reluctant to staunch the wounds of the banks. They told him what they knew from the series of meetings at the Treasury. But King, fully briefed by the Chancellor and the Prime Minister on the plans to recapitalise the system, readily assented. In an extraordinary meeting at the Bank of England, Andrew Bailey sat across a desk from the RBS Group Treasurer John Cummins who, poker-faced, asked if he could borrow a mere £25 billion there and then. Bailey responded that, yes, it would be no problem. What the RBS executive did not know was that the Bank of England had done the same for HBOS the previous week. Bailey and his colleagues at the Bank had spent the months since Northern Rock trying to work out the best way to carry out covert lending. One of the problems, they had realised, was that money leaves a trail. So the answer was not to actually lend money but instead to swap pieces of paper, in this case highly tradeable government bonds (gilts) from the Bank of England in exchange for mortgages from RBS. The gilts could easily be converted into cash in the marketplace by RBS. A complex arrangement involving setting up a trust was required. Bailey explained nonchalantly how to go about it. If Cummins was surprised that the Bank of England seemed so willing to advance £25 billion and knew precisely how it would be done, he did not show it.

The lifeline was activated. Billions of pounds of assets were flowing from the Bank of England's coffers to RBS to keep the stricken bank afloat. The infusion from the Bank also included dollars. By the end of the week it became clear from the very fine print of a technical Bank statement on its balance sheet to the markets, that £85 billion of new lending had been made over previous days. Future statements did not contain such detailed information. It did not take lengthy deduction to work out that much of it was going to RBS. There were conversations with other banks throughout that day as Treasury, Bank of England and FSA staff monitored liquidity requirements and how each institution was faring.

On the Tuesday evening, another gathering of bankers was set to take place at the Treasury. The tone would be very different from 24 hours earlier. The government was now making the running because there was no alternative – the stability of the whole banking network was at risk. Alistair Darling had realised earlier in the day that time had run out for the banks. At a European finance ministers' meeting in Luxembourg that morning, he had been called out by his special adviser Geoffrey Spence, who had been monitoring the RBS share price on a screen in a side room. Spence told him it was curtains for RBS and that the bank's chairman Sir Tom McKillop wanted to talk urgently. They called McKillop who gave him the chilling message: 'Chancellor, my bank is going to run out of money within a few hours, what are you going to do about it?' Darling and Spence later recalled feeling physically sick. The spectre of an RBS failure and the British financial system seizing up began to loom. 'For the UK, it was the pivotal moment,' said one observer.

Darling's European counterparts, noting his frequent departures from the meeting to take phone calls, had nodded sympathetically. Their own staff had informed them of the havoc being wreaked in the London markets. The Chancellor had wanted to brief his European ministerial colleagues on the British government's plan to avoid them being taken by surprise the next day. Memories of the shock around Europe's capitals after news of the Irish government's deposit guarantee the previous week were still raw. But Darling's rapid movements in and out of the conference room told them most of what they needed to know.

Once back in London the Chancellor went immediately to the Treasury to be updated on developments. Myners and John Kingman were taking a lead as civil servants and banking advisers hustled and bustled up and down the corridors. They gave Darling an exhaustive briefing on all the numbers and costings. Then the Chancellor moved swiftly to 10 Downing Street where he and the Prime Minister reviewed the day's dramatic developments. Mervyn King arrived from the Bank of England, Adair Turner from the Treasury and Myners and Vadera joined the meeting as well. They were soon to make the historic decision to stand ready to pump £50 billion of taxpayers' money into the banks and to underwrite £250 billion of lending between banking institutions. The British government was putting its finances on the line to the tune of hundreds of billions, a move without precedent. As one banking source present put it: 'I think the most impressive thing was that in a parliamentary democracy it was possible, in 48 hours, to put £300 billion of taxpayers money on the table – I think that shows actually it's fit for purpose.' For Gordon Brown, it was an immense step into the unknown. The financial implications were hard enough to grasp but for the Prime Minister the politics were potentially nightmarish. Explaining to the House of Commons that he was putting unimaginable sums of money behind the nation's bankers was a task he would much rather have avoided.

As the nation's political and financial sector leaders were agreeing to activate the plan in principle, the team at the Treasury had proceeded on the basis that it would go into action the following morning. They had worked frenetically around the details of the bullet points outlined the previous week. But one remembers someone saying 'hadn't we better write all this down?' The legal expertise of Nigel Boardman was called into play. He got to work drafting a statement which looked robust and rigorous enough to be acceptable to the markets. As one observer described it, 'it just flowed out of his brain'. There was a delicate balance to be struck. People had to be convinced that the government was putting up enough money, but not feel that the figure was so large that a cataclysm was in the offing.

Bank chiefs had already been told to report to the Treasury that evening. As before, they arrived together and were shown into a large waiting room close to the Chancellor's office. The bankers sat stony-faced on one side of a large table, Darling, Myners and the senior mandarins Macpherson and Scholar with Dan Rosenfield and Geoffrey Spence on the other. On the bankers' side, in the middle of the table, was a chair with arms. One Treasury insider noted that whoever sat there in meetings during that week tended not to last long in their job – to this day he avoids using that chair. The bankers were in front of a large painting by the contemporary Scottish artist John Bettany. The BBC's art history educational pages describes his work thus: 'His most characteristic pictures are large allegorical compositions involving hybrid human and animal forms, painted with explosive brushwork and suggesting some vague menace.'

They were told bluntly that the government was going to require them to raise more capital. If shareholders could not be tapped for more funding, then it would come from the state in exchange for shareholdings. This was the first the bank bosses knew for certain of the Treasury's thinking, whatever their suspicions before that day. For most it was a shock. They let it be known they were not happy with what they were hearing. The idea of the state owning a chunk of their shares appalled them. The pill was sugared, however, with the government's pledge to provide a credit guarantee scheme. This would allow banks to lend to one another with the assurance that the government would stand behind the loan if the borrowing institution defaulted.

The Bank of England's restrictions on the supply of liquidity would be relaxed. The existing special liquidity scheme would be doubled in size.

The bank chiefs' starting point was that they wanted to tough it out, assuring the government that their problems centred on a temporary lack of liquidity rather than a shortage of capital. This indeed was the approach taken by Sir Fred Goodwin, adamant even at this stage that liquidity rather than capital was the problem for his bank. One observer remembers that the early position of most of the banks in response to what they heard from the Chancellor was 'no, no, no'. Bluntly, they were saying, 'This isn't going to work, Mr Darling'. HSBC bosses argued strongly that they should not be expected to be involved as they were fully funded and not in trouble. Barclays asked whether there was any room for discussion over the proposals. Others said as little as possible, each afraid to reveal the true state of their books in front of rivals.

Concerned at the bankers' attitude, Darling called Brown to warn him of the resistance he was encountering. He asked the Prime Minister to speak to Stephen Green, chairman of HSBC. In his book, Gordon Brown says the HSBC boss assured him he would raise a token amount of private capital and would not oppose the plan.

There was a trickier conversation in store for Brown when he was put on the line to Sir Tom McKillop. The RBS chairman was very concerned about what would happen to his bank's funding over the night when American and Asian markets would be open. He urged Brown to unveil the liquidity support plan immediately. Brown reassured the RBS chief that arrangements for emergency funding lines had been made with the US Federal Reserve co-operating with the Bank of England. The Prime Minister was struck by the apparent failure at the highest level of RBS to acknowledge that the crisis went a lot deeper than shortage of overnight finance.

Back at the Treasury, Darling and Myners told the bankers to retire and discuss the government's plan between themselves. They were warned that the bailout announcement would be made the following morning and it was now up to the banks to decide whether they would participate. One banking supremo asked Darling what would happen if they didn't like the plan. He was told he was free to announce his own plan to the markets in the morning but it would be much better if a united front could be taken with the banks swinging behind the government's initiative. For every bank to approach the problem from its own angles would not, argued Darling, result in any solution to the industry's problems. The bankers were ushered to another Treasury meeting room and left to get on with it. Darling, meanwhile, after some persuasion from his staff, agreed reluctantly to record a broadcast clip for the late broadcast news bulletins with a pledge to stand behind the banks in any way required to ensure financial stability.

Sir Fred Goodwin was one of the bank chiefs who argued most forcibly for the government with the Bank of England to boost the supply of funding to the markets. He had clashed with Mervyn King over the issue in the weeks after Northern Rock when Goodwin had accused the Bank Governor of ignoring the needs of the City of London. But Myners and the Treasury team knew how perilous the position of RBS was. As the other banking bosses were getting up to leave, Goodwin was tapped on the shoulder discreetly and asked to stay on with his finance director, Guy Whittaker.

They de-camped to another office, the normal territory of Stephen Timms, a Treasury minister who was not present on that day. Sir Fred was told firmly that the RBS situation was very worrying but the RBS boss responded that it was merely a question of market confidence; he was clear that if the Bank of England offered further temporary liquidity support then confidence could be restored. Myners and his colleagues challenged the RBS chief, stressing again the government's view that the bank's problem was solvency and 'too little capital'. Goodwin's retort was that his bank had enough capital, it was just that it was 'the wrong sort of capital'. One observer present remembers then looking at Whittaker, who had remained silent up to that point: 'His face did not convey agreement on these points.' Whittaker chose to remain silent and did not challenge his boss's analysis of the problems at RBS.

An intriguing sub-plot was played out when Eric Daniels, the boss of Lloyds, sat down with the Treasury representatives. The world had changed since his bank had come up with its plan to take over the stricken HBOS in mid September, a couple of days after the collapse of Lehman Brothers. By early October, HBOS was receiving covert emergency funding from the Bank of England. Daniels could have walked away from the deal. On the Treasury side there was a fear that Lloyds might indeed abandon the marriage with HBOS; indeed, some present had reached a resigned acceptance that this might happen. Daniels may have been thinking that the government would make him drop the merger plan and that HBOS would be nationalised. He may also have assumed that pulling out of the deal would fuel the volatility in the markets, to the detriment of the whole banking sector. Whatever was being privately thought on either side of the table, the meeting ended with the Lloyds/HBOS merger still on course. Daniels had not threatened to abandon the deal. The Treasury insiders were pleasantly surprised and relieved. Having to announce a full-scale government takeover of HBOS would had made a formidable task even tougher. One Whitehall adviser remembers the reaction when Daniels pressed on with the deal: 'It was very odd, we never thought they wanted to do it – they could have pulled out, there was nothing to stop them.'

By the time they took their seats around the table together, some of the bankers were realising the writing was on the wall. Sands and Meddings were there with their Standard Chartered hats on. Initially, they had made the same arguments as HSBC, pointing to the strength of their own balance sheet and the absence of any requirement for new capital either from investors or from the government. But as the meeting with their banking counterparts got underway, and mindful of their secret role in drawing up the rescue package, they appealed to the other banks' sense of perspective to at least give the government a hearing. John Varley of Barclays and Stephen Green and Douglas Flint of HSBC were also arguing that their fellow bankers should see the government's initiative as helpful for the whole sector, in effect doing the industry a favour in its hour of need.

The large room occupied by the bankers was a meeting room normally used by the Permanent Secretary, Sir Nick Macpherson. A portrait of David Lloyd George looked down on a large table in the middle of the room. It had a faintly tatty look with an overflowing bookshelf and a few drab artefacts. A framed picture contained old Treasury Bills, exchangeable at the Bank of England, but for rather less than the value of a twenty-first century bank bailout. The room adjoined the Chancellor's office via an inter-connecting door. At one stage

Darling became agitated in case the bankers could hear everything being discussed with his officials.

As the Chancellor and his colleagues waited for a response from the banks, takeaway curries were ordered. Darling's favourite Indian restaurant, Gandhi's in Kennington, delivered food to the Treasury. Some picked away at the contents of the foil cartons with little appetite, the Chancellor by this time thinking he needed some rest ahead of an early round of media interviews the following morning and a crucial Commons statement later in the day. But others could have done with some sustenance. One of the City advisers later chuckled at the thought that the takeaway offer had not been extended to them. Scholar and Kingman, moving from room to room, focussing relentlessly on the progress of the talks, also missed out on the takeaway. The budget for bank bailouts may have seemed unlimited but the refreshments allowance was clearly strictly controlled. In fact, the bankers in their meeting room were offered some of the takeaway but, true to form with other Treasury offers of food, declined.

While the bankers' meeting continued, there was time for ministers and their advisers to look hard at the options in front of them. Pursuing the three-point plan – recapitalisation, a credit guarantee scheme and more liquidity – seemed perfectly logical. But was there a more radical but perhaps simpler alternative? Might it be best if the troubled RBS was to be nationalised? In the early hours of that extraordinary day, that option was discussed. One official said simply 'we could default the bank'. In other words, regulators could have told RBS it was no longer licensed to take deposits and it would have fallen inevitably under the wing of the government . The scenario was certainly considered. It was on the table, albeit briefly. The fact it was even mentioned reveals the dramatic lengths the government felt it had to go to secure the banking system.

There was still no word from the bankers but Darling, immensely frustrated at what he perceived to be their intransigence and keen for some sleep, decided to turn in. He told aides that the bank chiefs could 'take it or leave it'. If they refused to go along with the plan, they would have to take the consequences, which might mean collapse. Come what may, the plan would be unveiled in the morning. With that, Darling left the Treasury and headed back to his Downing Street flat.

The civil servants and advisers who stayed behind, ground down by lack of sleep, were at this stage depressed and concerned. One remembers ringing his wife, warning of a long night and discussing withdrawing savings from their joint back account the next morning. He felt a heightened sense of fear of the unknown, with a growing worry that bank failures might be imminent. Apprehension was everywhere and colleagues discussed their concerns in corners of offices and corridors. Whatever their private fears about an impending disaster, Treasury press officers had to stick to the agreed line throughout that evening. Press enquiries were met with the stock response that the Chancellor would do whatever it took to secure the banking system. And the phone calls continued to come in relentlessly through the evening, hour after hour.

As the exhausting late-night vigil continued, the banking advisers had another piece of business to attend to. An Australian subsidiary of HBOS, BankWest, was being sold to Commonwealth Bank of Australia. The deal was being rushed through to raise badly needed cash for HBOS. The bankers, based at the Treasury and working flat out on the recapitalisation plan, could not work out why the Australian deal was being pushed ahead so rapidly. The sale price of less than £1 billion was seen as a bargain for Commonwealth Bank even at a time of extreme stress in the markets. They later suspected that Mervyn King had thrown his weight behind the sale and been in contact with his Australian counterpart to ensure the process was as rapid as possible. King was anxious that HBOS raise badly needed capital but Lloyds felt it had no say in the matter even though it was proceeding with the HBOS takeover. Lloyds chiefs later argued that the swift sale had made their life more difficult as BankWest had healthy deposits and that the Bank of England had been wrong to get involved. But BankWest's subsequent admission of major losses suggested it would not have been a trouble-free subsidiary for Lloyds.

Some time later a senior Bank of England official commenting on HBOS and the Australian authorities, said:

> 'There were indeed discussions between the two central banks. They were initiated by the Australians who had to form a judgment about the prospective purchase. The content of those discussions should remain confidential.'

In due course word came back from the bankers that they were ready to talk again. They trooped back into a large meeting room where Myners was waiting for them. John Varley, who appeared to adopt the role of unofficial shop steward, told the minister they had agreed to go along with the government's plan. They would do their best to ensure their organisations complied while acknowledging that each one had its own problems. This agreement included HSBC, which was crucial for the success of the plan. Any suggestion that the UK's biggest and soundest bank was not going to participate would have undermined the credibility of the package.

There had been a debate over the previous week on what to do about HSBC. Mervyn King had taken a hard line and told ministers they should make HSBC along with all the banks take government capital even though they did not need it. But the Treasury and Number 10 had argued forcibly that it was not a good use of the £50 billion of taxpayers' money that had been earmarked for the recapitalisations. Every penny had to be deployed on shoring up the holes in the system. Why would you take a successful global bank, it was argued, and shove government funding into it? Such a move could signal to the rest of the world the UK had even worse problems than had been imagined, not to mention cast a shadow over the bank in the eyes of foreign investors. HSBC was awash with funding as depositors fled other banks and headed for what they perceived was one of the safest financial institutions in the world. But allowing HSBC to opt out of taking government money, King's argument ran, gave Barclays encouragement to resist state funding. This created the potential for the weaker banks to be stigmatised. The issue had been taxing ministers and advisers throughout that Tuesday.

Barclays was in many ways the pivotal bank. Ministers were concerned about some aspects of its loan book and assets but sympathised with its determination to steer clear of any taxpayer funding. Keeping Barclays away from the bank bailout was something the Treasury was happy to go along with. Having three leading banks – HSBC, Standard Chartered and Barclays – 'clean' of any state involvement provided some comfort to the government. Bailing out Barclays along with Lloyds, HBOS and RBS might raise questions in the markets about the whole banking sector having to be nationalised.

One Treasury insider reflected later that it was not clear at this stage what the banks were really thinking – they had given nothing away as they filed out of their meeting room in the Treasury at 1 a.m. Ministers had done as much as they could to drum into them the severity of the impeding crisis. The bankers had heard the terms of the proposed bail-out and indicated their willingness to go along with it but not revealed how they would individually react when markets opened a few hours later. They headed off into the night.

By 4 a.m. on the Wednesday morning, the bankers, lawyers and other sundry advisers had done all they could. The announcement was drafted. It might have been tempting to get out of the Treasury for a couple of hours sleep. But none did. They felt they should stay in case of any last-minute calls. The unspoken fear was that HSBC's bosses might change their minds and tell the markets they were not part of the government's initiative. They would be within their rights to inform investors they were well capitalised and secure even as others were struggling. And if HSBC backed off, Barclays might well follow leaving the plight of RBS and HBOS painfully exposed. HSBC pulling out could torpedo the entire deal. And its chiefs had not signed anything by the time they left the Treasury. The nagging fear was, as one participant remembered: 'If this goes badly wrong it's like Black Monday [the 1987 Stock Market crash] all over again, and this could be equally bad for the government, probably worse.'

More than one of the participants on the government side remembers Wednesday morning as the moment of maximum danger. If the markets reacted badly to details of the package, the defences would crumble. The most chilling thought was that there was no Plan B. This was the only plan and there was no fallback. Alistair Darling knew they were walking a tightrope: 'I was very conscious of the fact that on the Tuesday night this was our one shot – there wasn't anything else – if it hadn't worked what else could we have done?'

The trick had been to come up with a figure for the government credit guarantee which was credible but which was also seen to be affordable for the Treasury. In effect, this was like putting a finger up to test the wind. One participant put it like this: 'We tried to think of a big enough number to make them [the Stock Market] think "Wow, that's a big number!" but not so big the gilt market [source of Government funding] goes "Wow, that's a big number!'" Another reflected uneasily on the fact that nobody outside the group at the Treasury had any idea how bad things were and for people to hear the following morning that such a drastic solution was being proposed might in itself cause a panic. The fear was that 'there could be a really serious impact on gilts and on sterling and we would be isolated and nobody else might come in at that point with us'. Might the markets shift the focus from the banks' crumbling balance sheets to the sustainability of the UK's sovereign finances? In other words, so the fears ran, the UK economy might have to stand alone against the force of a new financial tornado.

Sir Nick Macpherson, the Treasury's chief mandarin, took a rather more pragmatic view of the government's ability to afford a banking bailout on the scale envisaged. He argued that in a crisis there were extraordinary methods which an advanced economy like the UK could use to fix the problems if it wished to do so. Plan A involved the government using its borrowing power to raise the cash to recapitalise the banks. But if the markets started questioning the sums and doubted the UK's ability to handle the debt burden, there could be a run on sterling and the market for gilts (government bonds). In this extreme scenario, printing money was seen as the final tool in the box if all else failed. That responsibility would have to fall to the Bank of England.

Discussions had been held inside the Bank of England about what would happen in the nightmare eventuality of the Treasury being unable to afford to fund the bank rescues. The Bank would stand ready to buy up gilts issued by the government to provide money for the nationalisation of the banks. In these circumstances it would then have to provide emergency lending to the banks as well (on the assumption that in this eventuality the private funding markets would seize up, the Bank of England would be the only source of liquidity). Treasury and Bank sources have since indicated that conversations had taken place and preparatory work had been undertaken for this extreme and barely conceivable turn of events. Such a course of action had been considered. The year since Northern Rock had seen intensive contingency planning by members of the tripartite body. 'It was very clear what the tools of intervention would be in the different scenarios of disaster,' according to one insider. Those tools included the Bank of England in effect printing money to fund state-owned banks, an unprecedented and extraordinary move if it ever happened. It would not be long, however, before the Bank began creating money to support the wider economy.

If they had time to stop and reflect, there were no illusions amongst the bankers and officials who had worked flat out since early on the Monday as to what was at stake. David Soanes, who had extensive experience of the City, had no doubts about how perilous was the threat to the nation's financial system: 'If share prices had carried on falling after the announcement, there could have been a retail run and the confidence-sapping nature of a retail run would have been all pervasive.'

Another banking adviser reflected that nationalisation of most of the banks was the most likely outcome if the markets gave the thumbs down to the rescue package. But he noted that the Treasury had acted professionally in the crisis, while the City of London had manifestly fallen short.

For the Prime Minister, the pressure and anxiety was immense. He privately feared disaster if the plan failed to hold the line and the markets charged through the government's defences. In his memoirs, his press aide Damian McBride described his horror at the apocalyptic language used by Gordon Brown as he sat 'ravaged' on a couch in his office at one stage that evening:

> We've just got to get ourselves ready in case it goes wrong tomor-row. And I mean really wrong . . . if the banks are shutting their doors, and the cashpoints aren't working, and people go to Tesco and their cards aren't being accepted, the whole thing will just explode. If you can't buy food or petrol or medicine for your kids, people will just start breaking the windows and helping them-selves . . . it'll be anarchy. I'm serious . . . we'd have to think: do we have curfews, do we put the Army on the streets, how do we get order back?

As he retired to bed at his Downing Street flat, Gordon Brown made a point of keeping his mobile phone next to him in case any disaster blew up in the early hours. In his book, which understandably for a prime ministerial tome does not convey the same state of high anxiety as McBride's, Brown says he was sure he was doing the right thing in moving to shore up bank finances with government money at this time of maximum risk to the system. But there always was a chance it would fail and if so, he would have to resign as Prime Minister. The next morning he warned his wife Sarah that they might have to move out of Downing Street within hours. At around 6 a.m. he met Darling and Peter Mandelson at 10 Downing Street. They discussed the day's politics, and how the announcement should be made. Mandelson made suggestions on the presentation of what would be a momentous policy departure for the government.

Brown said to one aide 'Do you think I will still be Prime Minister at the end of the day?' The aide's reply was simply: 'I don't know, but you will be going out doing the right thing.'

Chapter 6

Britain stands alone

At the Treasury, the team were watching the minutes ticking away until the announcement to the markets at 7 a.m. They were steeling themselves for the acid test of all the work of the last few days – the market reaction. Brown was less concerned about the reaction at Westminster than how the intervention would be seen internationally, hence his desire to make contact with his counterparts in other leading economies. But the Prime Minister was also worried that people at home would not get what was happening and would have no comprehension why the government was acting in this way. Mervyn King later used language which no voter would have trouble understanding: 'We are not trying to save the banks, we are trying to save the economy.'

On the Wednesday morning, markets opened and the announcement was made through the Stock Exchange's regulated news feed. To the immense relief of all Treasury insiders and their guests camped out there, the reaction was positive. Share prices were up a little at the start before moving slowly lower. Wholesale funding and credit markets were calm. It appeared that the £250 billion credit guarantee scheme had provided the most reassurance. This lifeline gave investors the comfort of knowing that struggling banks would be able to borrow short term and meet their financing needs. City bankers later professed their admiration for the Treasury civil servants who had put the guarantee scheme together in a matter of days.

Alistair Darling, fortified by a few hours' sleep, went on BBC Radio 4's Today programme to set out the terms of the deal. His reassuring style and demeanour gave the feeling of a government in control of events, a contrast to the terrifying market gyrations which had dominated news bulletins the previous day. Shortly afterwards, Darling made his way to Number 10 Downing Street for a joint news conference with Gordon Brown. The Prime Minister had been working the phones for much of the time since the announcement. Worried about the UK going it alone, he wanted to bring other leaders on board. He was anxious to ensure the Europeans took their cue from Britain and followed through with a co-ordinated plan. He went through the details carefully with Sarkozy and Merkel, suggesting how it could be made 'Europe-wide'.

Gordon Brown speaking later to the BBC for "The Love of Money" series (2009) recalled his anxiety at how exposed the UK was that day, having unveiled such a dramatic support programme for the banks:

> 'Nobody had ever done that before, nobody had ever talked in these sort of figures before. It could have been an initiative that went entirely wrong because no other country was prepared to support us and I did not have any assurances from the other countries that they would do so.'

Vadera, meanwhile, returned to her own Whitehall office. She had not been there for days and wanted to check on any work building up in her in-tray. She lay on a sofa exhausted, hoping for a brief snooze. But she was awoken by her mobile phone ringing. It was Sir Fred Goodwin. He reminded her that the previous night he had stated forcefully that RBS did not need capital and that liquidity was his problem. Now, said Goodwin, he had reflected on the matter and decided that he *was* going to ask for capital. The RBS chief told Vadera that he had not discussed the matter at that stage with his board and wanted the conversation to remain confidential. This surprised Vadera, who had been led to believe on good authority that the RBS board had already been pushing for an injection of funding. She asked Goodwin how much he thought he needed. About £5 billion was his answer. Vadera told him that wasn't enough.

A couple of hours after the first announcement, a lower-key press conference was convened. With no sleep between them, Myners, Tom Scholar and John Kingman appeared at a platform in front of media representatives. It was a non-attributable briefing. There was a feeling that whatever his considerable financial expertise, Paul Myners could not be expected to head an 'on the record' press conference with big political questions coming at him. Most journalists present, including the author, were impressed with the level of detail being set out before them. But after the formal question-and-answer session, a huddle gathered around Myners pressing and probing for more information. There was no suspicion, however, that the government plan was incomplete at that stage and that the markets could yet derail the package of measures.

Many of the questions that morning focussed on another major headache for the government. On the Monday evening, the Icelandic Prime Minister Geir Haarde had warned his people that their nation was facing bankruptcy. Iceland's banking industry had grown to several times the size of the economy. With ready access to cheap global funding, the banks had gone on a lending spree that included the UK, where some well-known retail assets were acquired. Iceland's banks, like many others, were caught in the headlights of the credit crunch juggernaut. Their sources of wholesale funding dried up. The Icelandic government decided to nationalise one of the larger banks, Landsbanki, and sought emergency loans from the Russian government.

British savers might have wondered how events in Reykjavik and the plight of an Icelandic bank would affect them. But one well-known player in the online savings market, Icesave, was part of Landsbanki, as was another UK-based bank, Heritable. The Icelandic bank Kaupthing, which had a presence in the UK and an online offshoot, Edge, was also being taken over by the Icelandic government as part of the desperate measures to stem the crisis. Savings in these banks were covered by the Icelandic rather than British compensation scheme. So British depositors would have to apply to Reykjavik rather than the London authorities for any form of redress. And even if the Icelandic government had been able to afford to reimburse savers, its compensation scheme was less generous than the UK's.

Darling decided to intervene immediately. He used special powers on the statute book as anti-terrorism measures to seize Icelandic bank assets in the UK. Heritable and Kaupthing deposits were transferred to the Dutch bank ING. Icesave customers were to be protected by a freeze on Landsbanki's business in the UK. The Dutch government took similar action, leaving the Netherlands and British authorities having to reimburse 400,000 savers a total of £3.5 billion. The Chancellor's actions prevented losses for British depositors but triggered a lengthy and acrimonious international court case as the UK government sought to retrieve the money from Reykjavik. Regulators were confronted with complex legal obligations to ensure a smooth transition for UK savers.

Late in the evening, the Financial Services Authority realised it had to deliver legal papers to Scotland, where Heritable was registered, in time for a court case the following morning. All courier delivery firms had stopped for the night, so an FSA official jumped into his own car with the paperwork and drove through the night to Edinburgh.

The response to the Icelandic debacle formed part of Alistair Darling's statement to the House of Commons that Wednesday afternoon. The brand names Icesave and Kaupthing Edge were well known to most MPs as they regularly featured highly in tables of best savings products. The fate of these banking operations and the implications for UK savers and constituents would have worried many parliamentarians more than the complexities of the banking bailout plan. Those members on both sides of the House who were focussed on the government's response to the wider crisis heard Darling explain that banks had agreed to raise £25 billion in new capital, with access to government investment if they wished. Another £25 billion of state funding would be available if required. This conveniently broke the £50 billion rescue war chest down into two more digestible chunks. In the early hours of the morning it had been decided that announcing a '£50 billion bailout package' would create more fear than reassurance about the stability of the system.

If the markets still needed any convincing that policymakers were serious in the steps they were prepared to take to avoid an economic catastrophe, action by the Bank of England should have done the job. In an unprecedented, co-ordinated move with the European Central Bank, the US Federal Reserve, and the Canadian and Swedish central banks, the Bank cut interest rates by half of one percentage point to 4.5 per cent. The Swiss and Chinese authorities took similar action. It was a huge display of firepower by the global economy's guardians. The US Fed had never before co-ordinated a rate cut with other central banks. 'We are now looking at the first page of the global-depression playbook,' was the verdict of the leading US commentator Carl Weinberg of economics consultancy High Frequency Economics.

By the Wednesday evening it was apparent that the recapitalisation, credit guarantee and liquidity package had steadied nerves in the City and at Westminster. To that extent, the move had worked. But it soon became clear that it had only bought time. The FTSE 100 index fell more than 5 per cent over the day. The colour of the government's money was not visible; at this stage there were more words than action. As one observer put it, 'if we thought we had a week or ten days to give precise shape to proposals, it became clear we didn't'. Well-intentioned announcements by the Prime Minister and Chancellor might have impressed players in British financial markets but much less so internationally. Asian and American fund managers took the hard-headed view that where there was still uncertainty, there was an unattractive place to make large cash deposits. There were plenty of safer havens to leave money. All British banks, including the well-financed Standard Chartered, were lumped together in the eyes of the markets. For Myners, Vadera and the exhausted officials at the Treasury, the sobering reality was that the detailed mechanics of recapitalisation had to be worked up in days.

Reinforcements were needed on the advisory front. UBS could not continue with any role on the Treasury side of the deal as the bank represented Lloyds and RBS. So Soanes and Budenberg, after intense activity over previous days at the Treasury, ended their formal involvement. Both would stay in touch and use their network of City contacts when required. Calls were made to other investment banks late on the Wednesday afternoon with the key demand being that there must not be conflicts of interest because of their client list. Rapidly assembled pitches were made and by 6 p.m., Credit Suisse had been hired to act for HM Treasury on working up the detail of the bailout package. The son of a former Governor of the Bank of England now found himself at the centre of the drama.

James Leigh-Pemberton was a City dealmaker to his bootstraps. His father was Robin Leigh-Pemberton, Baron Kingsdown, who had been Bank of England Governor from 1983 to 1993, and he was official financial adviser to the Duchy of Cornwall based on an historic family connection with the Prince of Wales' estates. But those who observed James Leigh-Pemberton's career said he never traded on his name or connections. He had learned the business at Warburg in the early 1980s before joining Credit Suisse and playing a part in some of the largest corporate transactions of the following decades. He had become chief executive of Credit Suisse's UK businesses in July 2008.

That Wednesday evening, 8 October, Leigh-Pemberton and a team of Credit Suisse colleagues (which would later swell to a total of nearly 60) arrived at the Treasury. In making a pitch for the Treasury mandate they had to come up with an estimate of the size of the capital hole at the banks. They discovered that their initial forecast had not been too wide of the mark. But what struck the Credit Suisse team, who had not been privy to the discussions earlier that week, was the escalating pace of events and the growing assumption that a fully worked-up package would be needed quickly. The need for capital was not a surprise but the deterioration of the liquidity position was unexpected. RBS, for example, was close to running out of assets to put up as collateral in return for financing, hence the need for emergency credit lines from the Bank of England.

The brief for Credit Suisse was to come up with a plan which would secure financial stability but also ensure value for money for the taxpayer. The intervention had to be definitive and be seen as a lasting solution to the banking crisis. Another key question was what form the capital should take, the size of the injections and the price paid by the government. Leigh-Pemberton dispatched members of his team to RBS and Lloyds to start the task of due diligence, working out the requirements of each bank.

He based himself at his bank's office in Pall Mall, a small and discreet building in London's 'clubland', more commonly used to host private client meetings because it was more centrally based than the Canary Wharf headquarters. The West End office was to become the nerve centre for the Credit Suisse work over the ensuing days. Here reports and detailed analysis provided by members of the team at RBS and Lloyds were analysed and collated. Briefing papers for ministers were drawn up and it was but a short walk to the Treasury along the edge of St Jame's Park and Horse Guards Parade to deliver them.

By this time, the banks were being asked to report their funding positions three times a day to the Treasury and the Bank of England. Their bosses had realised that they had to work with the government and there was no point withholding information. The time for reluctance about disclosure had gone: they knew they needed the Whitehall lifeline. On the Thursday the banks' staff were told they were required over the weekend and would have to be in position to call board meetings. The chairmen and chief executives were instructed to be in London that Saturday and Sunday to be in a position to get to the Treasury at very short notice. Ministers did not want to find that key players were in Edinburgh or at their country homes. RBS and HBOS were also asked to ensure that their senior non-executive directors were in London. They would be needed to approve the leadership changes that Myners knew would be required as the price for billions of pounds of government support. They would have to be present to put their hands in the blood.

Ministers and regulators, meanwhile, were working furiously on the sums. With the FSA and the Bank of England, the Treasury had to work out how to divide up the multi-billion pound cheque that would be written out by the taxpayer. HSBC and Nationwide had already signalled their intentions for raising new capital. The main focus would be on Lloyds, HBOS, RBS and Barclays. Myners continued consulting his own informal group advisers – friends and colleagues with shared experience honed over decades of takeover and other corporate activity. David Mayhew of Cazenove and Charles Randall, a colleague of Nigel Boardman of the law firm Slaughter and May, were among them. They were not under contract. Their involvement was private, and deniable.

By Thursday, pressure in the markets was beginning to build again. It had not taken them long to work out that of the £50 billion of total potential capital raising unveiled by the Chancellor the previous day, only a small proportion was accounted for by the healthier banks. Through their own announcements, HSBC, Nationwide and Santander had stated intentions to raise a total of more than £2 billion from their own investors. Even after stripping out assumptions about what Barclays might need, most market players were realising that the vast outstanding amount was due for HBOS and RBS. And in the words of one observer: 'The market didn't like the look of that and RBS started to sink again.' With regard to HBOS, the markets were prepared at this stage to give the benefit of the doubt to the bank, as it was supported by the Lloyds merger deal. But with RBS there was no such charity.

As the financial markets began to grasp the outstanding and unanswered questions still hovering over RBS, there was a change of attitude inside the Financial Services Authority. This was clear not only to insiders but also extremely obvious to those who had been part of the round of meetings taking place since early on the Monday. At the start of the week, the FSA representatives had been arguing that the capital 'hole' was nothing like as big as the number which was central to the Standard-Chartered generated paper. By the end of the week, they were talking much larger figures. The Treasury's view had been that the FSA was too relaxed about the capital inadequacies at the leading banks. One witness to events over those days said later of the FSA: 'During that week they changed their tune pretty fast almost day by day, so by end of that week it was much more significant.' Another believed that the FSA 'went from Monday of that week calling for £20 billion for the leading banks to £20 billion for just RBS by the close of the week'. That conversion mirrored the view inside RBS itself – on the Monday the directors had dismissed the government view that more capital was needed, as opposed to liquidity, as outrageous. But the world as seen from the RBS boardroom had been turned upside down in a matter of days. Sir Fred Goodwin's colleagues had woken up to the idea that an injection of funding to plug gaps in the balance sheet was urgently needed.

On Friday 10 October, markets slumped around the world. From the opening in London, share prices plunged across the board. The falls appeared relentless and irreversible. There was no sign of a rally. Confidence was shattered. The cautious optimism of two days previously in London had vanished. The capacity of governments to staunch the wounds was under question as never before. Finance ministers of leading industrialised nations (G7) were gathering in Washington for the autumn meetings of the IMF and World Bank. Those events seemed almost marginal but global policymakers were at least in the same place at the same time. None had come up with tangible plans to tackle the contagion gripping their banking markets. The Americans had their TARP but it had not so far achieved results. Alistair Darling at least had a plan, unfinished though it may have been.

The Chancellor might have preferred to stay at the helm in the Treasury as work on the recapitalisations continued, but staying away from the Washington meetings would have created a bigger sense of crisis. Darling was able to hold bilateral talks with the key finance ministers in the crisis – American, French, German and Japanese. They agreed on the need for a clear communiqué aimed principally at reassuring markets. US Treasury Secretary Hank Paulson later praised Mervyn King for his contribution in helping focus the minds of the assembled ministers and central bankers. Expectations that their gathering would come up with a 'magic bullet'-style solution had begun to gather momentum. The last thing ministers and their governments wanted was for disappointment to follow unrealistic expectations. They aimed for a one-page solution and settled for one and a half, rather than the usual ten pages or more which traditionally came out of these meetings. An early morning meeting with President Bush at the White House was an unscheduled addition to the programme for G7 ministers and central banks. The President told them 'this problem started in America and we need to fix it'. Darling also remembered the President mangling his words, to the quiet amusement of his audience: '"Hank's got a real handle on this liquidity thing – we're going to make sure it dries up." I said "I hope not!"

For Darling and his officials there was one delegation they did not want to meet. The Icelandic finance minister had asked to speak with the Chancellor and the Dutch finance minister to voice his nation's anger at having assets seized to cover deposits in Landsbanki and Kaupthing. There was a moment in the IMF meeting room when the Icelandic minister approached Darling and officials had to steer the two apart. In Luxembourg, on the Tuesday (October 7th), Darling had received a call from the Icelandic Prime Minister from Reykjavik just as he was trying to deal with the RBS chairman – the call was recorded and a transcript was subsequently produced as part of the Icelandic campaign to gain redress from the UK.

Support for the idea of bank recapitalisations had gained increasing momentum amongst the ministers taking part. Darling sensed a lot of interest in what was happening in the UK. He later recalled his conversation with Hank Paulson: 'He said to me "You guys have done the right thing – we will adapt TARP to do the same thing".' The US administration had enough leeway in the TARP legislation to make capital injections into American banks without going back to Congress. Paulson said subsequently in his book *On the Brink* that he had first asked officials to start looking at the possibility of providing capital for banks the previous weekend. But at the time of the G7 meeting, nothing had been said along those lines in public by the US administration. The UK's template was something for other leading economies to clutch hold of.

While Darling handled the negotiations, there was no shortage of calls from Gordon Brown. The Prime Minister was determined to get the G7 finance ministers to endorse the idea of recapitalisation – he badly needed international cover and blessing for the UK's direction of travel. He was worried about the possibility of the US and UK moving in different directions and he still harboured hopes the President would come round to his way of thinking. Darling, meanwhile, felt he was in control of the talks and, while he would update the Prime Minister as much as possible, the focus of US–UK financial diplomacy should that weekend be through the G7 meeting. Brown, of course, had his own retinue of advisers with strong views, including Heywood and Vadera. One Whitehall source detected signs of tension: 'Alistair and Gordon worked very well together during the economic crisis – that was still a positive and the relationship was working – it was that weekend when you started to see some of the cracks appear.'

The final brief G7 communiqué provided everything the British government wanted. All the words were seen to be useful and fit for the purpose of trying to restore confidence. But, given Brown and Darling's key objective, there was no doubt which were the most important lines on the G7 members' aims: 'Ensure that our banks . . . can raise capital from public and well as private sources, in sufficient amounts to re-establish confidence and permit them to continue lending to households and businesses.'

Gordon Brown, meanwhile, was invited to address a meeting of Eurozone leaders on the Sunday evening, October 12th. Neither Germany nor France had come up with coherent plans to tackle their banking problems. President Sarkozy had asked the British Prime Minister to attend, mindful of the progress the UK authorities had already made on bank bailouts and the fact that Brown of all the leaders appeared to have the best grasp and understanding of the financial kaleidoscope. After a smaller gathering with Sarkozy and Merkel, one source remembers Sarkozy taking Brown by the arm and marching him into the main meeting: 'He was incredibly flattering and said the most amazing things.' Darling later reflected on the significance of the

Eurozone gathering: 'Britain would normally go nowhere near that, nor would they have us for that matter – that weekend was terribly important to have a global response.' Brown gathered that some of the other leaders present 'complained bitterly about my presence'. Undeterred, he told his counterparts that the problem for Europe and the United States alike was lack of capital in leading banks. He warned them not to see this as an Anglo-Saxon crisis simply because it had its origins in the excesses of the US housing market – it was by now just as much a European crisis. In contrast to the previous weekend, Brown could now set out the full thinking behind the British response and how it might now be applied as a pan-European solution.

While Darling and Brown flew the flag at international meetings and impressive sounding statements were drawn up, there was urgent unfinished business back in London. Myners, Vadera and the team at the Treasury had realised that a fully worked-up plan would have to be unveiled to the markets on the following Monday morning. Any further delay could be disastrous. One banking source summed up the mood on that Saturday morning: 'I think the supposition was that if it was not ready by Monday morning, the insolvency crisis will mean one or both banks will become wholly illiquid, which will mean they will have to shut.' A new Bank of England liquidity initiative was in place and the credit guarantee scheme was almost ready. Those were important pillars of the rescue plan, but the crucial one was an agreed recapitalisation of leading banks and that was not in any state of readiness. A weekend of intense activity was in prospect.

The weekend of 11 and 12 October 2008 was the most momentous in the government's response to a banking crisis that was threatening to envelop the nation's financial infrastructure. While Darling did his duty in Washington around a table with fellow finance ministers, the small group back at the Treasury had to take on the banks in a poker game with the highest possible stakes. They had to be told what level of capital was required, whether HM Government was to appear on the shareholder register and which of their chiefs were to be ditched. All the struggling banks' top executives were asked to report to the Treasury on the Saturday morning. They had to be allocated different rooms on different floors. Each had a small Treasury team allocated to them, which presented the official analysis of how much new funding was needed. It was an episode unprecedented in any arm of the British government.

The Credit Suisse initial analysis on what the banks might need was complete. But what still had to happen was full acceptance of the numbers by each bank's directors including authorising the issue of new shares and confirmation of the terms of the share issue. And the directors had to accept that heads would roll. This was to prove especially difficult with some of the bank chiefs, who still felt the government was imposing unnecessary demands. At the start of that weekend they regarded the prospective taxpayer stakes as an inconvenience. Their intention was to hold on to their jobs, keeping the Treasury and ministers at arm's length. But the government's advisers were clear about the standard, if brutal, process which had to be played out. One noted that the terms and conditions for putting new equity into a company were simple: 'If a company has been driven into the ground and needs to be recapitalised, normally you need new management to be the steward of the new capital you have put in – it happens the whole time in the normal commercial world and there is nothing particularly unusual or governmental about it, these are commercial facts of life.'

Brown and Darling knew that bank bailouts on the scale being proposed would be unacceptable to the taxpaying public if there were not sweeping changes in the boardroom. Paul Myners had been instructed to insist that some bank head honchos should head for the exit. That would mean dealing with Sir Fred Goodwin and Sir Tom McKillop at RBS and the top brass at HBOS. Another of the government's conditions was that executive pay should be curbed and that dividend payouts should be scrapped until the share price had recovered.

One bank did not take up the Treasury's invitation, however, bosses from Barclays stayed away. The chief executive John Varley was dead set on raising capital from sources well beyond Whitehall. And he was determined to avoid being seen by photographers walking into the Treasury. Any sniff of government ownership was, in his view, to be avoided at all cost. He agreed to be in contact with the Treasury, but only by teleconferencing. The significance of Varley remaining at his head office in Canary Wharf rather than heading over to Whitehall was more than symbolic. He avoided the risk of a ministerial ambush which could have seen him being pressurised into accepting state influence on his bank. In the end, Barclays concurred with the government's view of how much capital it needed. And it agreed to reach the target figure in part by selling assets outside the UK and not by cutting back lending to British households and businesses.

Whether the decision by Varley and his Barclays board colleagues was a good one for their shareholders is a moot point. Their stakes were heavily diluted because of the terms offered to the new shareholders from Qatar and Abu Dhabi who would acquire a joint holding in Barclays on top of what they already owned, taking the total to almost 32 per cent. There is a view, hotly contested by Barclays, that the deal offered by the government would have been more sensible for the bank's shareholders. Barclays, arguably, paid a very high price for its private sector financial solution which brought in £7.2 billion. Five years later, Barclays were being investigated by City regulators and the Serious Fraud Office over some aspects of the Qatari transactions. But it did escape the stigma of a state bailout.

One of the trickiest issues for the Treasury that weekend was what to do about Lloyds and HBOS. Officials had worked out an estimate for the funding needed by each bank as a separate entity and what they would need as a combined new group. The latter figure was lower because of risk diversification. But ministers and their advisers were privately ready for Lloyds to announce that they were pulling out of the deal, even after the chief executive Eric Daniels had indicated on Tuesday evening that he wished to push on with it. So much had changed in the markets since the takeover was first announced in mid-September. The banking world had been turned upside down in the previous few days. It would be hugely preferable for the taxpayer if the merger were completed, but it would be understandable if the Lloyds board felt that pursuing the deal had become a bad option for shareholders. And Downing Street could not force Lloyds to push on and consummate the marriage.

Lloyds clearly knew the original deal was not binding because Daniels, mindful of the deterioration of market conditions, had renegotiated the terms over that weekend. The proportion of Lloyds shares that was to be used to acquire HBOS was reduced. This was acceptable to ministers, as they had to act in the interests of the taxpayer whose money was being ploughed into Lloyds. But if Daniels had set out to pick apart aspects of the original agreement with HBOS, some have argued that he could have been more aggressive and demanded a better deal for his shareholders. The fact that he pressed on even though he could well have dropped the whole deal seemed puzzling to many observers of the banking crisis.

The dire state of the HBOS loan book was not known at the time and it turned out to be far worse than the market assumed. Daniels insisted that he had done his homework. Speaking in 2013 to the Parliamentary Banking Standards Commission, he said: 'We did a very thorough job in terms of our diligence. We understood what we thought were the strengths and weaknesses of HBOS at the time. We also thought that, despite this being a difficult deal, it would serve the shareholders well over time.' But Daniels also acknowledged that the economy was in worse shape than he and his board colleagues realised at the time. A dramatic set of horror stories on the HBOS balance sheet emerged subsequently. Lloyds shareholders were to suffer grievously in the short term from the consequences of acquiring HBOS and its baggage – the share price plunged in late 2008 and early 2009.

Daniels, it seems, went into the Treasury that weekend assuming that every bank would participate in recapitalisation on the same basis, with the government taking a stake in each. His thinking appears to have been that HSBC, Standard Chartered and Barclays would be on board even if they did not need state funding. In effect it would be 'all for one, one for all' with Lloyds in good company with the taxpayer investing in all the leading banks. The realisation that there were to be two classes of banks – those obliged to take government bailout money and those who were raising money from their own investors – was a bitter pill to swallow. One observer present that weekend remembers Daniels being 'obsessed with Barclays'. For months afterwards he complained that Barclays had been allowed to escape the stigma of state funding that his bank had been subjected to. The Treasury's insistence on Lloyds as well as HBOS taking state funding as well also fuelled Daniels' anger.

Nearly two years later in August 2010, and speaking in measured tones to *The Daily Telegraph*, Daniels said: 'At the time we understood that several banks would be in the government programme. We were given this assurance and given an assurance that the state aid requirements would not be onerous. This had been very clear. But it turned out not to be the case. There weren't several banks and state aid turned out to be more onerous.' Friends of Daniels see the sequence of events that weekend more dramatically, as a betrayal of Lloyds by the government. They claim that he was promised that the EU state aid issue would not be a problem, yet that was far from the case and European regulators later forced the sale of 600 branches. They argue that he could have played hardball and demanded better terms. One summed it up: 'In retrospect the way the government treated him was appalling, given the favour he had done for them over HBOS – and he never forgave them. He could have pulled out of HBOS and also then extracted a deal and he didn't, he trusted them, and they really f*cked him.'

Others in the Lloyds camp dispute the idea that the Treasury was ready for them to pull out. They remember a weekend of pressure on the bank, close to arm-twisting, from ministers and officials, all desperate for the deal to go through. Lloyds directors were angry that having been told by the FSA on the Friday that the bank needed £3 billion of extra capital, the figure was hiked to £7 billion on the Sunday. This, they suspected, was a deliberate ploy to deter Lloyds from trying to go it alone. Raising £3 billion from private investors might have been possible but finding £7 billion would probably have needed government money. Lloyds insiders sensed a mood of fear in Whitehall at the very thought of HBOS having to be nationalised. They believed government advisers had realised that the market reaction to HBOS being moved on to the state's books along with a majority of RBS could have been disastrous. Such a possibility might have left ministers no option but to close down the entire banking system for a couple of days.

Lloyds' directors believed that even after the turmoil of that week they still had a worthwhile deal. They reasoned that they had paid £14 billion to acquire a business with £30 billion of net assets. Pulling out of the HBOS takeover, they reckoned, would create even greater chaos in the markets and that would severely damage a Lloyds bank trying to move forward on its own. They clung to the argument that however much of a caning their shareholders took because of the HBOS acquisition, things would have been even worse without it. Economic recovery, they hoped, would reap attractive profits for the combined group. The problem was that five years would elapse before what looked like a sustainable recovery had gained traction.

It was still possible for regulators to pull the plug on the Lloyds takeover of HBOS, citing concerns the merger of the two banks might have on overall stability. In simple terms, regulators could have intervened to save the former from what would have been depicted as the consequences of its own mistaken judgements. There was an argument for keeping Lloyds 'clean' and leaving HBOS to its fate as a state-owned entity. The Bank of England had signed a waiver document approving the suspension of competition rules which would otherwise have stopped the bid. But subsequently there were discussions inside the Bank about blocking the deal. It was understood that there were reservations too at high levels inside the Financial Services Authority. Senior players in both institutions decided not to intervene to unpick the deal, however, given the fragile state of confidence across financial markets.

Myners met Lord (Dennis) Stevenson, chairman of HBOS on the Saturday. Stevenson told the minister that if the government became a shareholder he would not tolerate any interference in the running of the bank. It had to be broken to him that his departure was a condition of the government investment. It was inconceivable to put taxpayers' money into banks which then continued with the same people in charge. The Parliamentary Commission on Banking Standards later described Lord Stevenson as 'delusional'. One observer felt that the description was apt at that stage of the banking crisis.

The meetings continued in different corners and rooms around the Treasury. Myners, Vadera, Scholar and Kingman shuttled from bank team to bank team. In the absence of Alistair Darling in Washington, the Treasury Chief Secretary Yvette Cooper was the senior minister present. Calls went to and fro across the Atlantic. At one stage a key meeting was held up because of a dispute over whether Vadera, a non-Treasury minister, should be allowed to take part. Darling needed some persuasion but gave his consent. Often the bankers had to be left on their own for an hour or more, staring at the walls and contemplating their future. Elaborate attempts were made to ensure that people did not bump into each other. Myners subsequently reflected that he had been involved in some complex deals and transactions in his career, but never four or five simultaneously. As one observer recalled, it was like Chinese entertainers spinning ever more plates on bamboo sticks and hoping none would topple. However badly the tripartite structure had functioned during Northern Rock, it seemed to those present that this was its finest hour. Bank of England executives Andrew Bailey and Andrew Haldane, together with Deputy Governor Sir John Gieve, worked throughout that weekend alongside the Treasury staff and FSA chief Hector Sants. For 36 hours non-stop they toiled without sleep. The Monday morning deadline concentrated minds.

The question of the future of Sir Fred Goodwin loomed throughout the Saturday. The handling of this issue proved to be one of the most controversial of the whole banking crisis, with heavy political flak later aimed at Myners. Goodwin and his RBS colleagues occupied a room on the third floor of the Treasury, in the southwest corner overlooking Birdcage Walk. Myners arrived and told the chairman Sir Tom McKillop and the senior non-executive director Bob Scott they needed to accompany him to a different room. Myners was in turn accompanied by the lawyer Charles Randall. Myners told the RBS directors that Goodwin had to go. McKillop replied that there was no need to worry, Sir Fred had been told of his fate earlier in the day. Myners said that his requirements were simple – the departure must be swift and clean, there must be no rewards for failure and RBS would not be expected to abrogate any legal agreements. Compensation should be kept to a minimum. Scott and McKillop insisted that all these criteria would be met.

Myners accepted these assurances at face value. He had little time for detailed discussions and was obliged to move on to pressing meetings with other banks and catch up with progress at the Financial Services Authority. But he was later criticised by the Commons Treasury Select Committee for being naïve and placing too much trust in the RBS board.

With hindsight, he acknowledges that he could have asked many more questions. It transpired that McKillop and Scott had exercised the discretion which had become customary at RBS. Executives were traditionally allowed an entitlement to a full pension even if they retired early and in their 50s. McKillop and Scott believed that giving Sir Fred the same treatment was in line with contractual requirements, hence the assurance given to Lord Myners. Crucially, Sir Fred was asked to retire rather than be dismissed so that he would qualify for a full pension. It was a sequence of events which generated a firestorm of criticism when news of his £555,000 pension emerged the following year. Goodwin later agreed to accept a lower pension of £342,000. Myners subsequently admitted he had made a mistake but always maintained that the RBS directors had been less than straightforward. Dealing with McKillop himself was problematic. Eventually a compromise was reached under which he stayed on as chairman until a replacement could be recruited.

All through Sunday, the banking advisers and Treasury officials toiled over the official documentation for the injections of government money into RBS, Lloyds and HBOS. Details on issues such as the dividend access share (a mechanism to block dividend payments to private shareholders by giving the government priority over dividends), B shares and preference shares had to be ground through, checked and then signed off by the lawyers. Only then could they be presented to the bank boards who in turn had to consult advisers before signing off on the content. The tortuous process had to be completed by the Monday morning in time for a 7 a.m. announcement and everything worked backwards from that. Members of the team on the Treasury side of the talks were so immersed in the detail that they had little time to think what was at stake for the banking sector and the economy. As the clock ticked on, the focus was only on completing the task ahead of that early Monday deadline.

Some did reflect at the time on the vast sums of money which were being committed. Usually the Treasury and government departments have time to plan for contingencies and overspending, shuffling a few billion pounds here or there from the reserves. But in this case, according to one of those present that weekend, 'suddenly a set of circumstances come up and you are £45 billion pounds wrong – in terms of the management of the country's finances that is an enormous variation on the originally agreed plan – and that was very apparent as it became clear how much money was needed to solve the problem – that's a lot of hospitals'. There were parallels with the Second World War when government borrowing shot up to cope with a national emergency, but that was over a longer period of time and the American government could be approached for loans.

It was inevitable that despite the pressure of the timetable, and the voluminous amount of paperwork that had to be prepared, ministers would occasionally take a step back and ponder the consequences of what was being planned. At one meeting a minister asked the gathering of officials and advisers whether this was the right thing to be doing and whether a lot of money might be lost. The financial market experts were asked to continually check progress and likely outcomes. The conclusion they passed back to the political leaders at the Treasury was that, unless the estimates for the amount of capital required to stabilise the banks were wrong, the bad assets would at some stage be written off or sold and there would be a recovery in the underlying health of the institutions. Ministers were assured they were investing close to the share price lows. As one adviser reflected later, 'that wasn't right but it wasn't wrong either.'

By late on Sunday night agreements on how much money was required by each bank had been hammered out. Alistair Darling had returned from Washington – one Treasury insider felt relieved to see the Chancellor's reassuring presence after two days away from the home front. RBS and Lloyds had been told they would have £37 billion in total injected by the state in return for controlling stakes in the name of the taxpayer. The banks' bargaining positions had melted away. Sir Fred later likened it to a 'drive-by shooting'. But the final paperwork was not complete as Alistair Darling finally retired to his bed. He knew he would have to make a statement to the House of Commons the next day. He needed as much sleep as he could get. Even a few hours later, some of the key papers were still blank. There were spelling mistakes and gaps in the clauses. Anyone challenging this unprecedented intervention, with tens of billions of pounds of government money on the line, might have been able to put together a legal case. But the documents served their purpose. They established in the eyes of the financial markets that real capital was being injected into the banks, backed by serious amounts of money.

The Treasury team could only wait until the 7 a.m. market opening on Monday and the unveiling of the announcement. They had to hope that it would underpin confidence. A plan to make that Monday a Bank Holiday had been discussed but then dismissed. Whether banks were open or left shut would not have any effect on international confidence

– the outward flow of corporate deposits was likely to continue. On the face of it, the plan looked robust. It was a demonstration of the remarkable powers at the disposal of a government when a crisis erupts. The Treasury had within its mandate the ability to commit billions of pounds of taxpayers' money without specific parliamentary approval. This was in marked contrast to the US Treasury and its battles with Congress over TARP.

But the final hours threw up unexpected obstacles which might have derailed the entire plan. At 4 a.m., Lloyds made a last-minute attempt to change the terms of the deal. The bank wanted to renegotiate the amount of new shares which were being created in a bid to reduce the dilution of the interests of the existing shareholders. Lloyds advisers had contacted Treasury staff demanding a rethink. James Leigh-Pemberton had just got back to his flat close to the Treasury, hoping for a few hours' sleep. His phone rang and it was the Treasury asking him to return immediately to decide on the response to Lloyds. Leigh-Pemberton quickly returned, pacing briskly through the deserted streets around Westminster Abbey as he pondered how to tackle the problem. He advised the Treasury top brass to stick to the plan and he would deal with Lloyds. So as the 7 a.m. deadline approached, an important section of the package was not in place. A series of phone calls followed between Treasury advisers and their opposite numbers at Lloyds. Only robust and carefully constructed arguments managed to persuade the Black Horse bank to shy away from the brink and for the Treasury to press on towards the formal announcement.

It was the task of Paul Myners and Shriti Vadera to tell the Prime Minister and Chancellor what they were signing up for. Brown and Darling were extremely reluctant to nationalise the stricken banks, given all the baggage for the Labour Party associated with state ownership. In the early discussions about how to deal with RBS there had been a desire to cap the state shareholding at less than 50 per cent. All involved agreed that the best outcome would involve a bank which had majority private sector ownership. But as the full horrors of the RBS balance sheet had become apparent and the big numbers on capital needs had been calculated, it had become increasingly clear that the government would end up as the dominant shareholder.

At about 5 a.m. on Monday, the inner circle of Treasury advisers were gathered in the study at 11 Downing Street. They were briefing Darling on the final outlines of the deal and the essential points to make in his Commons speech later that day. The Chancellor spotted from the documents that the government stake in RBS would be above the 50 per cent threshold. He made clear he could not make that decision without consulting the Prime Minister. Officials pointed out that there was no alternative and the arithmetic could not be altered. The Prime Minister, they said, had returned very late from the Euro Group meeting and would not be pleased to be woken so early. Brown, it was suggested, already knew of the planned outcome for RBS. But Darling insisted – he needed to be certain that Brown was in agreement over this aspect of the RBS bailout.

With fewer than two hours to go before the momentous announcement on the bank recapitalisations, a farcical scene played out behind the curtains of 11 Downing Street. The Browns occupied the flat there, just as the Blairs had when Brown was Chancellor – it was larger and better for families with younger children. Vadera was dispatched to get the message to Brown. She spoke to the duty clerk, part of the 24-hour staff cover in Downing Street, and asked her to wake the Prime Minister. The clerk refused, pointing out Brown had been in bed for only three hours. Despite protestations that the Chancellor wished to speak urgently to the Prime Minister, the clerk held her ground. So Vadera found herself creeping up the stairs and letting herself into the flat.

She was on familiar territory on the lower floor as she had been to dinners there. But she realised she had no idea where the family's sleeping quarters were. Fumbling around for light switches, she made her way up to the top floor. Still in darkness she kicked over a tricycle belonging to one of the Browns' sons. She then heard Sarah Brown's voice, 'John, go back to bed'. Sheepishly, Vadera had to ask Sarah to wake her husband. Standing at the doorway of the Brown bedroom Vadera briefly and apologetically explained that the Chancellor needed to talk to him. The Prime Minister was alarmed. Vadera reassured him that there was no disaster and the deal had not collapsed, the issue was over the government stake in RBS. Brown barked back that Vadera should tell Darling that this was fine and he knew the figures already. But Vadera persisted and pleaded with him to come down to talk to the Chancellor.

Grumpily, Brown appeared in the study half an hour later. He dismissed the RBS issue quickly and then continued with a discussion about the rest of the package with Darling and his officials. Not much more than an hour after Vadera's nocturnal wanderings, markets were absorbing the news that all leading British banks would be raising new funding as buffers against future losses. The government had made clear it would stand behind RBS, providing whatever capital was needed to shore up the defences. As one observer put it: 'You need to say that capitalisation is so strong that however bad the weather might become, this ship is not going to sink.' This was above all a capital issue, not a liquidity issue. By reassuring the markets that banks had enough capital to absorb future write-downs, the Treasury ensured that liquidity would start flowing between banks again. In other words, if investors believed that banks had been made secure, they would resume lending to them. And that, for a little while at least, was what happened as bank funding re-established itself.

The details of the plan showed that RBS would receive an investment of £20 billion of taxpayers' money. A further £17 billion was to be put into the combined HBOS and Lloyds. In return, the government would take a 60 per cent stake in RBS and just over 40 per cent of the merged Lloyds and HBOS. Barclays said it intended to raise £6.5 billion from private investors without government help.

The Monday statement was seen as being comprehensive and markets were cautiously impressed. The FTSE 100 index had one of its best ever days, leaping more than 8 per cent by the close. One of the Treasury's advisers was pleasantly surprised by the reaction: 'Brill, great, couldn't have been better.' The fact that Barclays had come up with an alternative solution was a particular source of reassurance as it gave people confidence that parts of the banking market were functioning normally. The markets realised that the government had intervened heavily but had not extracted all the value so shareholders were left with something. It was noted that RBS had not been fully nationalised. If it had been taken under state control, according to one City expert, 'there would have been the mother of all runs against other banks – why keep money in a bank which is not government owned in that environment?' A lot more capital was being raised under the plan by all the banks than the financial markets had expected, another source of comfort.

A source of satisfaction for Brown and Darling was that 24 hours later, the American authorities announced their own bank recapitalisation scheme. Hank Paulson called in executives from the leading US banks and informed them the government would take share stakes in all of them. Germany, France, and Italy meanwhile all unveiled plans to inject capital into their banks and to guarantee inter-bank lending. Brown was pleased that after Britain had stepped alone into the unknown other leading economies had done the same. He had taken a lead on the world stage. As the German news group Spiegel Online commented: 'Before the financial crisis, UK Prime Minister Gordon Brown had been all but written off. Now the whole world is copying his bank bailout plan.'

The British Prime Minister would have been particularly pleased with the words of the recently announced winner of the 2008 Nobel Prize in economics: 'Has Gordon Brown, the British Prime Minister, saved the world financial system?' asked Paul Krugman of Princeton University: 'Mr Brown and Alistair Darling, the Chancellor of the Exchequer . . . have defined the character of the worldwide rescue effort, with other wealthy nations playing catch-up.' Closer to home a Treasury staffer who had witnessed the weeks of frenetic activity and ferocious pressure leading up to the day of the announcement had this judgement on Darling: 'He was so calm throughout and, by and large, he saw things for what they were and didn't react emotionally.'

But Brown could not have delivered on his rhetoric and vision, and Darling could not have announced his rescue plans in time to save the system from collapse, without their junior ministers and the small team of advisers. The preparatory work by Vadera, Scholar and Kingman and their banking advisers, combined with the no-nonsense effort of Myners had paid dividends. In the economy's hours of need, there was a plan. At the height of the storm, there was a chart available for those on the bridge, Brown and Darling, to steer the UK away from the rocks. Reflecting on the events of that week a few years later, Robin Budenberg was clear that a global disaster was averted. He believes that if RBS had collapsed, there would have been serious consequences in other global markets because the government would have been seen as powerless in the face of the crisis – all eyes were on the UK authorities who were seen to be in the first line of defence in an immense assault: 'If we hadn't had a cohesive plan on Tuesday night, things would have been far worse and far worse around the globe – if our system had disintegrated then the plan we put in place would not have worked in other countries.'

Budenberg likened the financial forces facing governments during those weeks to a flood. If a dam is built before the flow gets too strong, it does not need to be too big – lower down the river, the force is greater so a larger dam is required. He believes that the UK action in the week of 5–12 October 2008 was like building a dam near the source of the river and that saved other economies from being overwhelmed by a bigger torrent: 'To my mind if we hadn't blocked our stream, all other streams around the world would have got much more deeper and stronger – and it would have taken a hell of a lot more than it actually did not to have a real global crash.'

Gordon Brown and Alistair Darling had stopped up the British stream early on so that others were able to use the same tools to do the same for their defences. Failure to stem the tide in the UK would have resulted in bigger and uncontrollable disasters both in Britain and other economies. And, says Budenberg, that would have triggered global meltdown. By the evening of Monday 13 October 2008, though they may not have realised it at the time, the UK authorities had successfully saved their financial infrastructure from being submerged. A desperate battle had been won. But the war was not over. And the measures taken had a long-run cost, again not obvious at the time, which would have profound implications for the British economy.

Chapter 7

Battle for banking survival

Britain's biggest peacetime crisis had been tackled. The banking system had been stabilised in the face of a potentially devastating financial tornado. The government had put £300 billion of British taxpayers' money on the line, equivalent to nearly a fifth of annual economic output. But had that money been effectively spent? Had the right strategy been adopted? Were the measures likely to be in the long-term best interest of the UK economy?

All those present, and most commentators at the time, believed that the best course of action had been taken in the circumstances. A nightmare hand had been played as well as it could. Market confidence had been restored. Short-term lending between banks, an essential lubricant of the financial machinery, had been secured. A bold assessment of banks' balance sheets and the likely holes had been made, and plans put in place to ensure there were capital buffers to cover losses. The delicate balance between ambition with the scale of the response and prudence with the UK's public finances had been retained. But in the cold light of day, had the taxpayers' investment been well made?

The Treasury brains trust had made the critical decision not to nationalise RBS and Lloyds/HBOS but to allow the banks to continue as 'stand-alone' commercial entities, albeit with a large government shareholding. There were minority private shareholders with rights which had to be protected. The philosophy was to be that the banks would operate at 'arm's length' from Whitehall. RBS was eventually to have an 82 per cent government stake; Lloyds/HBOS was to be just over 50 per cent state-owned. This thinking had dominated the final weekend's efforts on the details of the individual recapitalisations. Alistair Darling's view was that fully nationalising RBS would inevitably lead to speculation that Lloyds/HBOS would be next and then Barclays. It was argued that because the government had not quite gone to the end of the road with RBS, the line could be drawn at the edge of RBS.

One of the Treasury's key objectives, which was made plain to the banking advisers and civil servants, was that the bailed-out banks should retain their listing on the London Stock Exchange and conduct themselves like other leading banks in the FTSE 100. The Stock Exchange listing requirement is that if any shareholder owns 90 per cent or more of a quoted company, they are obliged to make a bid for the rest of the shares. So the government had to stay below that level, with a bit to spare, to avoid any future confusion over the arithmetic.

At the time, both during the frantic first week in October and the months after that, the focus in government was on stabilising the banks and ensuring they had adequate capital. As one observer put it: 'How do you keep them alive, not how you make them run fast?' Discussions centred on reviving the banks and getting them to a stage where the government could start selling off their shares. The idea that RBS and Lloyds should be vehicles for boosting lending in the real economy was not at the forefront of official thinking. Mervyn King was later to argue that as the banks were, in effect, under state ownership, the Chancellor could order them to lend more to small businesses and consumers. This was an issue which would come back to haunt successive governments presiding over the prolonged saga of the bailed out banks. An increasingly loud constituency would demand that RBS and Lloyds should be used as government lending vehicles as the UK's economic recovery struggled to gain traction. But in the autumn of 2008 this argument was not voiced in or around the Treasury and Downing Street.

Advisers were asked to structure the deals on the basis that minority shareholders were to be retained. In other words, the final package for each bank had to keep a ceiling on the state shareholding. This tied the hands of the advisers when they were calculating what taxpayers would receive in return for the capital they were injecting. RBS needed £20 billion of government money however that was engineered. And the lower the taxpayer stake, the more would have to be paid for each share.

One of the advisory team is clear that the requirement to stop some way short of outright nationalisation resulted in a more expensive bailout as far as taxpayers were concerned: 'The UK government had to pay more for RBS shares than it might have done because of the need to keep the government stake to 82 per cent. The non-voting shares were created to allow that, and to provide requisite value to the taxpayer in return for the subsidy to allow capital to go in.' The same adviser believed that it would have been a lot easier to arrange the deal if the government had insisted on 100 per cent ownership of RBS. But, he believes, managing a bank without subjecting it to the demands of the private sector would be hard to imagine. The existence of minority shareholders was a good check and balance to the state's dominant holding.

The result of the drive to keep a lid on the government's holding at RBS was that a sum equivalent to the 'book value' of RBS shares was paid to acquire them. This meant that the total market capitalisation of the bank, based on the government buy-in price (number of shares in issue multiplied by the price per share), was equivalent to the total net assets of the bank. They were purchased at a discount to the prevailing market price at the time of the bailout, but the price subsequently plunged, leaving the taxpayer nursing a paper loss almost from the outset. The government could have insisted on paying a lower price although this would have upset the arithmetic surrounding the upper limit for the state holding. Ministers could simply have driven a harder bargain, arguing that a state bailout was the only show in town and the taxpayer should not pay more than a token amount for a bank which otherwise would have gone bust. A senior source at RBS later reflected that 'they did overpay, but until you knew how the bad the economy was going to turn out, it was difficult to tell at the time'.

One argument advanced inside Whitehall for the purchase price not being lower is that this would have driven the market price down and undermined what remained of private investor confidence in RBS shares. In other words, if the government was seen to be valuing shares well below the market price, a potentially damaging signal about the official view of prospects for the banking sector would be sent out. But others who advised the government over this period are clear that a smaller amount *could* have been spent on buying the shares and a higher stake obtained. This could still have allowed for a significant minority of private shareholders to continue on the register. One of the banks bailed out by the Irish government, AIB, was 99.8 per cent owned by the state and still quoted on the Dublin Stock Exchange. The outstanding

0.2 per cent of the shares remained in demand amongst market investors. One banker who had been advising the Treasury said: 'We could have gone a lot higher – that's one of the things I don't quite know, how it slipped through.'

Under EU state aid rules, a government purchase of shares at 10 per cent below the prevailing market price is deemed not to be a commercial transaction and so constitutes unfair intervention and remedies are sought. The British government's bailout of RBS was at that 10 per cent discount, so future sanctions were always going to be imposed by Brussels. So, the argument goes, if the RBS rescue was in breach of state aid rules, why not go further and pay a lot less? If you are going to be penalised anyway, why not get a much better deal for the taxpayer, say 20 per cent or even 30 per cent below the market price? Buying at an even bigger discount might even have avoided a clash with state aid rules. If a government can show that the target company is in dire financial straits and thus an extremely low price is being paid, the issue of whether a purchase is 'commercial' or not ceases to apply. But the same banking adviser concedes that going that far would have undermined confidence: 'It would have triggered greater state ownership of banks, greater instability in market price with all the negative consequences for general confidence in banking system.'

The state aid sanctions that were eventually applied would later cause big headaches for the managements of RBS and Lloyds TSB. Both were required by the European Commission to sell off branches. A Lloyds deal with the Co-op involving more than 600 branches foundered, leaving Lloyds having to pursue a different course with a stock market flotation for the branches. Attempts by RBS to sell more than 300 branches to Santander had to be dropped after the prospective buyer pulled out. An auction to an assortment of private investor purchasers then dragged on. In late September 2013, a private equity consortium backed by the Church of England eventually signed a purchase agreement, although the deal was not going to result in formal separation for another two years. In both cases, there was a major distraction for management and unwelcome uncertainty for investors. Staying within the requirements of the EU state aid regime in the first place would have avoided such problems.

The UK's bailout packages were more expensive than they might have been for taxpayers and they still fell foul of EU rules. The US bank recapitalisations were less costly for the American administration because the price paid was equivalent to below the book value of the target banks. The American approach was to tell all the major banks what capital was needed and then to insist that the state would inject that amount and take a share stake in each one. From the healthiest to the weakest, all the Wall Street banking giants agreed to take Uncle Sam's cash. Sir John Gieve later reflected that for all their less agreeable qualities, America's banks had done more to support the national interest than their City counterparts: 'The American system worked better as a club than the UK system – the internationalisation of the City had destroyed that and it was less of a club than Wall Street. The US Treasury Secretary could call in all the senior bankers, who were all Americans and get broad loyalty and agreement – we found it difficult to do that.'

The problem for the UK, however, was that RBS was far bigger in relation to the economy than any of the US banks were to the American system. As a result, the British government had to put considerably more into the stricken Scottish bank than most of the others.

The question that arose in subsequent years was whether the government had erred in paying something around the full book value of RBS, Lloyds and HBOS. Had paying high in 2008 made it harder to sell off the government stakes and demonstrate fair value for the taxpayer? The answer from both City analysts and insiders at RBS is yes. A longer road back to a breakeven price for RBS has delayed the day when the sale of the government holdings can begin. Decisions made for logical reasons in the heat of battle had unexpected and unwelcome consequences which are still playing out several years after the crisis. But for Lloyds/ HBOS, while there may have been a delay, the bank was back in favour by the middle of 2013 and the first 6 per cent of the government's holding was sold in September of that year.

As autumn gave way to winter in late 2008, a bleak mood settled again over those in Downing Street and at the Treasury who were running financial and economic policy. Shoring up RBS, Lloyds and HBOS in October had bought time. But the underlying problems at RBS were, if anything, deteriorating. The banks' assets looked more toxic and depressed by the week. The new boss, Stephen Hester, had been appointed to take over from Sir Fred Goodwin ahead of the chaotic weekend of the recapitalisation talks and the 'drive-by shooting'. Hester had been chief executive of the property investment company British Land, and before that had extensive banking experience at Abbey National and Credit Suisse. He had joined the RBS board as a non-executive director in September 2008, little suspecting the scale of the storm which was about to engulf the bank. A call on the Friday evening 10 October from RBS chairman Sir Tom McKillop had made it clear the bank urgently needed a new chief executive to replace Goodwin. Hester was given half an hour to consider it. He told McKillop he would take the job subject to a government guarantee that RBS would maintain a stock market listing with some private shareholders. Hester arrived at the Treasury on the Sunday to run through the terms of engagement as Myners, Vadera and the Whitehall officials were frantically hammering out details of government investments in RBS, Lloyds and HBOS.

Stephen Hester took over formally the chief executive's seat at RBS in late November. But as he served out his notice with British Land in the weeks before that, he began to take stock of the state of the humbled financial empire he was about to head. Hester believed more capital should have been injected into RBS at the outset and had made that point in his first meetings at the Treasury. Within a few weeks of arriving at the bank's London headquarters in Bishopsgate, he told ministers the bank was in a worse state than he had anticipated. It was becoming clear that the recession was going to be a lot deeper than seemed the case even the previous month. For a bank, the value of assets is closely linked to the state of the real economy – plunging activity and confidence means plunging valuations of loans and investments. For RBS, it was plain that further funding was needed and there was a realisation at the bank and at Westminster that the government would have to intervene again. But this came at a time of immense fatigue amongst Treasury staff. Civil servants and advisers had worked for a lot more hours than was good for them and at weekends for three months. Some recall the situation as 'hellish' with no time to see families, even newly born children. There was a desire to take a breather even in the full knowledge that more had to be done to stabilise the banks.

Whitehall insiders were initially sceptical about Hester's doom-laden warnings at RBS. Was he, they mused, over-egging the bad news, perhaps as a newish chief executive trying the familiar tactic of 'kitchen-sinking' the bank? (In other words, getting all the negatives out into the open quickly so a subsequent turnaround of RBS would look even more impressive.) But as one insider put it, 'the look on his face was one of continued shock and increased anxiety', so it was hard to believe that Hester was really faking it. The heads of the Bank of England and Financial Services Authority, meanwhile, were discussing what to do if things got worse for RBS and HBOS. Mervyn King and Lord Turner debated whether a 'contingent equity' plan should be pursued. Under such a scheme, if the capital ratio fell below 5 per cent the government would automatically inject more capital to bring the ratio back up and in doing so would progressively wipe out existing shareholders. In effect, a creeping state takeover.

The debate had moved on from how to bail out banks to what needed to be done for the UK economy to avoid sliding into a depression. At the initial stage of the crisis, policymakers were reassured that they had got the key decisions right – recapitalisation and the schemes to boost liquidity and bank credit were seen as a success. In contrast in the US, TARP had been a failure at the outset. Credibility was restored for the American administration when government capital was injected into the banks. But as the immediate danger had faded, British government insiders knew that decisions had to be focussed on lending in the wider economy and the general state of consumer and business confidence. HBOS had, in effect, taken itself out of the market and was not originating any significant new lending. Losing a player that size had a significant impact; a big chunk of lending capacity had shut down, leaving many borrowers struggling to renew their loans. So policymakers' attention inevitably turned to how to tackle the burden of bad assets and to better ensure that banks felt free to lend normally without fear of future losses on the wobbly loans.

Doubts were creeping in at the highest levels even a few weeks after the bailouts had been announced. In late October, Adair Turner and his wife were invited to lunch by Alistair Darling at the Chancellor's official residence Dorneywood in Buckinghamshire. The eighteenth-century mansion was made available to the government after the Second World

War for the use of a senior member of the Cabinet, the choice of whom being made by the Prime Minister. Dorneywood is run by a trust and the occupant is billed for its use so there is no taxpayer involvement. Traditionally, it was the residence of the Chancellor of the Exchequer, although for a brief period under Labour the deputy Prime Minister John Prescott was the occupant. Alistair Darling took the keys to the house when he became Chancellor. He did not use it for personal reasons many times, but on this occasion was entertaining friends and acquaintances with his wife Maggie.

Darling and Turner had an opportunity away from the relaxed social chit chat to reflect on the dramatic events on the previous few weeks. They took a stroll around Dorneywood's herbaceous borders, green-houses and lily pond to discuss where they had got to with the bank rescue package. Their attention turned to HBOS and Darling asked the FSA chairman whether it might have been better to have nationalised it. Turner was a little surprised by the question but intimated that perhaps nationalisation would have been the best option, although at that stage they were where they were. Lloyds after all was still keen to push on with the takeover. But a separation of the two banks was still possible – shareholders had not given their blessing in a formal vote at that stage. At Dorneywood that day the question of whether a takeover by Lloyds or a government-owned HBOS was best for the British economy was still lingering in the air.

For Turner, HBOS state ownership would have been a neater solution than the one which subsequently emerged with a Lloyds deal and a complex scheme involving government insurance of bad assets. Punishing the shareholders with nationalisation would send out a message – if you don't stop your company taking unacceptable risks, this is what will happen. In other words, harsh treatment of HBOS shareholders would be '*pour encourager les autres*' (to encourage the others). Turner felt that clarity of understanding would be best served by the nationalisation route. The government would have been in a stronger position to decide precisely what the major banks should be doing in the economy if it had a 100 per cent stake. He thought the same about RBS.

Taking HBOS under the state's wing would, so the same argument runs, have left Lloyds 'clean' and better able to weather the storm and then lend more to businesses in a recovering economy. At a high of level of the Bank of England, there had been concern at the prospect of the Lloyds/HBOS deal continuing. Regulators, it was felt, could intervene to block the merger. But there were no formal high-level discussions between the Bank and the FSA on this issue. The FSA's responsibility was to ensure that documents relating to the deal which were sent to shareholders were clear and accurate. It also had a role in assessing whether the newly merged entity would be stable. But its job was not to look after the interests of Lloyds shareholders – that was for the board and shareholders themselves. So, if it turned out to be a bad deal for Lloyds shareholders, as many of them later argued it was, that was their own collective responsibility. However, there was no denying at the FSA that if in September when the agreed Lloyds takeover was announced they had known how bad the HBOS loan book was, they would have blocked the bid and recommended government ownership of HBOS.

Whatever the reservations amongst policymakers, the Lloyds bid for HBOS stayed on the rails, heading for a destination of a legally agreed merger by early 2009. Ministers and their advisers were increasingly focussed on RBS and what to do about it. Lord Myners said of that time in late 2008: 'Any feeling we had fixed RBS in terms of giving them enough capital began over a period of time to be severely tested by how bad we found the RBS book to be.' It was becoming clear that Sir Fred Goodwin and his boardroom colleagues had been oblivious to what they had on their balance sheet. The need for even more funding to cover future losses was looking more pressing as each week passed. The results for the year 2008 were looking worse than anyone expected. Bigger losses would mean more capital being used to plug the holes – so the likely level of capital in early 2009 when RBS was due to report its full-year results was looking very thin.

The Treasury had by this stage taken full control of the process of handling the state-controlled banks and trying to chart a path for them. Number 10 let the Treasury get on with it and, at first, there were not too many instances of crossed wires or mutterings about interference. Myners later reflected that during those fraught days of early October he had become a minister in a manner akin to jumping onto a charging stagecoach. A couple of months later, however, with the RBS issue to be resolved, he felt as Financial Services Secretary he was more firmly in the driving seat alongside the Chancellor and in control of a significant part of the agenda.

So what were the options for RBS? One was complete nationalisation, for many of the same reasons as could be cited for HBOS. With the government share stake so high, injecting further state capital would make keeping it as a private company unsustainable. So transforming the bank into a wholly owned government corporation would be a logical step. That would involve yet more public money, a difficult step to sell to an electorate becoming ever more outraged about bailed-out banks and their apparently overpaid executives. But such a plan would not involve RBS staying on the country's books for a prolonged period like the coal and shipbuilding industries after the Second World War. It would be a temporary move to allow RBS to be unpicked. The most toxic assets would be separated out from the higher quality loan book and put into a state-owned 'bad bank'. (This would be the same course subsequently taken for the bad assets at Northern Rock and Bradford & Bingley, which were eventually transferred into one government-owned entity called UK Asset Resolution.) At the same time, the 'good bank', with the better quality assets would be groomed for a share flotation. Unencumbered by legacy loan books, the 'good bank', so the theory went, would be liberated and much more willing to lend just when the economy needed support.

The nationalisation idea, followed by 'good bank, bad bank' was strongly favoured by Mervyn King at the Bank of England. He had been pushing for forced state recapitalisation for longer than anyone at the top of the policymaking tree. King was influenced in part by the Swedish bank rescue precedent from the early 1990s. Sweden had experienced a property boom, fuelled by reckless lending, followed by a collapse leaving banks nursing collateral which was worth far less in the market than the value of their loan books. Lax regulation at that time was partly responsible for matters getting out of hand. It was an eerily familiar story and anyone outside the world of finance would have been entitled to ask why the markets failed to learn anything from it in the previous decade.

The Swedish government had taken a very hard line with its floundering banks. They were ordered to come clean about all their losses and then apply for state capital if they needed it. The price of taxpayer funding was a total wipeout of shareholders, with the government taking control of those institutions which could not raise capital from private sources. Bad assets were transferred into a stand-alone vehicle, at arm's length from the government and supported by all the leading political parties. As the economy recovered, banks were reprivatised and the bad assets sold over the ensuing 20 years. In the end, the cost to the Swedish taxpayer was a lot less than initially predicted. One of the architects of the 1990s banking policy was Stefan Ingves who, by the time of the 2008 crisis, was Governor of the Swedish central bank, the Riksbank. He was in regular contact with Mervyn King and the Governor introduced him to ministers on visits to the UK during the autumn of 2008. Ingves, like King, was an academic economist by training so it was not surprising that the Bank of England Governor looked approvingly on him. One of the strengths Ingves was perceived to have brought to the resolution of the Swedish banking crisis was an independent mind, untainted by a lengthy career (at that stage) in financial markets or central banking.

The Treasury mulled over 'good bank, bad bank'. It was firmly on the agenda of policy options which were considered seriously by officials. There was no shortage of investment experts who claimed to have helped devise the Swedish plan and were happy to reincarnate it for the UK. Ingves talked through the politics of going down this route with the need, in his view, to get the opposition on board to avoid it becoming a political football. Finding a culprit (for example greedy bankers) was one of his key observations – do that and a policy involving so much money can be more easily sold to the electorate.

But for ministers, the stumbling block with this course of action was always going to be the cost of nationalisation. Buying out the 15 per cent or so of private shareholders on the RBS register would have a price tag that could be met only by yet more government borrowing. Moving bad assets onto the state's books would involve further cost. The inclusion of a nationalised RBS and its mountainous debt in the public sector accounts sent shivers down Treasury spines. At a time when the government was racking up higher borrowing to fund day-to-day spending, the idea of additional debt to deal with RBS appeared an unattractive option. The underlying priority was to preserve the UK's top-notch credit rating and there were fears that markets might recoil from further lending to the British government. Whereas in the October bailout week, there was agreement that the UK's balance sheet should be used to support the bank rescues, conditions had worsened by the end of the year. There were real concerns that the UK sovereign account could not afford another major financial lifeline for the banks. The fall in the value of sterling, including an all-time low against the Euro in November 2008, demonstrated that foreign investors were sceptical about the UK economy and banking sector.

Ease of execution was another priority for the Treasury. 'Good bank, bad bank' was seen to be a hugely complicated undertaking for an institution the size of RBS. For Northern Rock, splitting up the assets and changing IT systems was operationally challenging but in the end achievable. But at RBS a split could have taken 12 to 18 months to deliver. Valuing the toxic assets was viewed as a near-impossible task because it was so difficult to predict how much worse the economic downturn might become. Ministers feared that a transitional period that long would leave RBS in the doldrums and unable to focus on lending to households and businesses. Senior management in this scenario would be distracted from the task of reviving the bank and bogged down in the detail of dividing up the bank's gargantuan loan book.

As the Treasury carefully weighed up alternatives, Number 10 was getting restless. Brown wanted to see more activity and demanded to know why bank lending was on a downward slide even after the mammoth infusions of public money. He instructed Shriti Vadera to study the issues and explore what new action the government might take. She personally favoured 'good bank, bad bank' but knew that the Treasury was against it. By Christmas the Treasury had not come up with answers and that added to Brown's frustration. He was advised that ministers and officials were struggling to get to grips with precisely what was on the RBS balance sheet. So it was impossible to come up with a policy to tackle a problem, the scale of which had not been fully explored. But nobody across Whitehall was denying that more intervention was needed and that the initial capital infusion was not adequate in itself because the plight of the banks looked worse than it did in October. The banks themselves were on the defensive and highly suspicious of what was going on at ministerial meetings. They were fearful of the heavy hand of the state descending on them. One Whitehall source remembered that 'there was a lot of whingeing from Lloyds'.

By January an outline solution had been reached. The hordes of invest-ment banks allowed in through the door of the Treasury had submitted any number of bright ideas and clever wheezes. The favourite to emerge was a form of insurance scheme, drawing on the principles of the under-writing market. It was to be known as the Asset Protection Scheme (APS). The thinking behind it was that stability had to be achieved quickly if lending was to be kick-started. Bank balance sheets had to be underpinned in a way which was practical and quicker to implement than 'good bank, bad bank'. It was assumed from the outset that APS would be much easier to establish. Some who favoured 'good bank, bad bank' saw the APS as a stepping stone that would, within a couple of years, trigger a full separation and sale of a 'clean bank'. As they were to discover, it did not turn out that way.

The Asset Protection Scheme was later described as the largest private sector transaction ever entered into by a British government, bigger even than Lend-Lease, the loan from the US during the Second World War. The idea was that a bank would insure, for a fee, its dodgy loans so if they fell in value more than expected, the government (in effect the insurance company) would pick up most of the tab. The deal initially reached with RBS involved assets totalling £325 billion. If there were losses on those loans of up to £20 billion, over and above those already factored in, they would be absorbed by RBS. Anything beyond that would see the government covering 90 per cent of the bill. The initial proposal was that the fee, like an insurance premium, would be £6.5 billion. For RBS, the fee was to be paid in shares to the government. The theory was that the bank would pick up the expected losses, given the anticipated state of the economy, and the government insurance would only kick in if there was a bigger downturn. For the Treasury, the chal-lenge was to set that first loss figure (£20 billion): high enough to provide fair value for the taxpayer. But it could not be too high in case market confidence in the banks' ability to handle their liabilities if the climate worsened, what was known in the financial jargon as 'tail risk', was dented.

If anyone needed to be reminded of why RBS required a further safety net, the bank's results announced on the same day (26 February 2009) as the outline APS framework provided it. Billed as the largest ever loss in UK corporate history, the bank revealed that in 2008 it had lost more than £24 billion, largely thanks to a sweeping write-down of the value of assets. Much of the deck-clearing was linked to the acquisition of the Dutch bank ABN Amro in 2007, just before the crisis. The Chancellor, while unveiling the APS details, admitted that the government was having to inject even more capital into the struggling Scottish bank – £13 billion in exchange for non-voting shares. That would take the government's wider economic interest in RBS, if not the voting numbers, from 70 per cent to 84 per cent.

Lloyds was the only other bank at this stage to sign up for the Asset Protection Scheme. The Treasury announced that it was to put £260 billion of assets into the scheme and cover the first £25 billion of losses on that bundle of loans. Everything beyond that, as with RBS, was to be 90 per cent absorbed by the government. There would be a fee of £15.6 billion payable in shares. The government attached an important string to this arrangement – Lloyds was required to boost its loans to house-holds and companies. £3 billion of extra mortgage lending was pledged as well as another £11 billion of loans to businesses. RBS had been told that it had to supply an extra £9 billion of mortgage lending and an extra £16 billion to businesses. These lending agreements were said to be 'legally binding'. The fine print of the paperwork signed with the banks also contained more strictures on executive pay with a demand for what was described as a 'sustainable long-term remuneration policy'.

Paul Myners, who was a key player in devising the plan, described it as a 'neat and elegant sharing of risk'. The Treasury's main banking adviser was Credit Suisse with James Leigh-Pemberton at the helm once again. Citibank was also retained as an adviser on implementing the policy. The beauty of the scheme for the Treasury was that it did not have an immediate impact on government debt, already forced sharply higher because of the October bailouts. Even with the government stake increasing as RBS handed over shares in lieu of 'payment' for the APS insurance, there was no big leap towards nationalisation – a minority stake remained in private sector hands. Markets were reassured that bank capital would not be eroded as unexpected losses would almost all be picked up the government. But it was a colossal potential liability for the taxpayer and, according to a Whitehall insider, it 'could have gone very badly wrong'. Up to £305 billion of RBS losses could, in theory, have found themselves onto the public sector's books.

In practical terms, though, despite not being part of the government's sales pitch when launching the scheme, there was another huge benefit for the banks from APS. If their potential losses were insured above a particular level, the value of their risk-weighted assets could fall. In other words, the risk of the whole loan book had reduced so the banks could lower the assumed value of assets for the purposes of calculating capital required on the balance sheet. It was certainly a neat way of reducing the need for capital – if potential future losses were reduced, then less funding was needed to cover them. Looked at another way, it put a ceiling on the amount of capital that the government would have to inject. And if market conditions took a nasty turn for the worse, spreading a virus further across the RBS and Lloyds loan books, the APS could always be extended to cover more assets. Even in a sharp downturn there would not be a need for more capital – the APS would take the strain. The big fear of ministers was that markets would, in the event of another economic shockwave, judge that RBS did not have enough capital which would in turn provoke another liquidity crisis. APS (in theory) took that risk off the table. For the banks and the government, then, it looked like a win-win outcome on the critical issue of capital. One cynical Whitehall observer described it as 'sleight of hand' that allowed the government to conjure capital out of a hat without any bill attached.

But although the political decision on APS had been announced in January, and the detailed agreements with RBS in February and Lloyds in March, this was only the beginning. The mammoth task of pulling out the assets from each bank, valuing them and then moving them into the APS stretched potentially months into the future. Staff from the banks and the tripartite authority faced the thankless task of combing through the paperwork and agreeing valuations on hundreds of billions of pounds worth of loans. Only then could pen be put to paper by the banks and the Treasury. And this was supposed to be a quicker and more stable solution than 'good bank, bad bank'. One senior investment banker with experience of advising Whitehall was sceptical: 'It was a monsterly complicated thing to do, trawling through the books, asking what was a loss and when it would be recognised.' A senior regulator later expressed astonishment at 'the terrible state of the RBS financial controls – what the due diligence revealed was that it was quite hard to substantiate the backing on the RBS balance sheet'. That view pointed away from the bad bank idea, as it was impossible to say just how bad the assets that might end up on the state books were. The job of extracting these assets from the good bank seemed daunting. The same source reflected that Sir Fred Goodwin's reputation as a great integrator of businesses acquired by RBS was totally misplaced.

It may have been a stratospherically large potential taxpayer liability and the biggest commitment by the state beyond normal public sector activity since the Second World War, but the media and politicians made curiously little noise about the APS. Myners was later frustrated, perhaps unsurprisingly given the ordure which had been heaped on him over Fred Goodwin's £555,000 pension, that an appearance in front of the Treasury Select Committee of MPs was dominated by the Goodwin issue. Three quarters of it was devoted to grilling Myners on why he had not spotted that the RBS chief was heading for the exit with what looked like a very generous package. The APS was barely mentioned. Myners later suspected that the Goodwin payout had been deliberately leaked by 10 Downing Street to deflect attention away from the scheme – the Prime Minister's advisers may have been worried that the huge APS liabilities would get unwelcome media scrutiny.

It was certainly complicated and not easy for the media and politicians to digest. In February 2009, when unveiling the scheme, Alistair Darling told the House of Common: 'Together, these measures will help restructure and rebuild RBS, making one of the UK's biggest banks also a stronger bank, better able to serve the people and businesses of this country.' But for the Liberal Democrats, Vince Cable denounced APS as 'a disgrace and a betrayal of the taxpayer's interests'. Cable argued that the government should purchase more shares in the banks even if that meant nationalisation in all but name. Opposition elsewhere seemed muted.

What was not known at the time was that Mervyn King was deeply opposed to APS. He had been very frustrated that 'good bank, bad bank' was not adopted but would only make that public four years later. King had other things on his mind in the spring of 2009. He and his colleagues at the Bank of England were in the process of launching an unprecedented stimulus for the UK economy. This involved the creation of new money which was then pushed out into the economy in exchange for Government bonds (gilts) held by investors. The idea was that the investors would receive cash for their bonds which they would in turn spend on other riskier assets (such as shares) and in so doing support economic activity. Known officially as 'quantitative easing', as noted earlier, some critics branded it 'printing money' and £375 billion was eventually created.

Like Banquo's ghost, Barclays hung in the air throughout the debate about 'good bank, bad bank' and the APS. It was the one bank that was not physically present but was uppermost in policymakers' minds. Since John Varley had sat in Canary Wharf on the fateful weekend in October that had seen the 'drive-by shooting' at RBS, Barclays had endeavoured to stay well clear of ministers or anyone connected with government. The tall, paternalistic, bespectacled Barclays chief executive had set himself on keeping his bank out of the hands of civil servants and clear of any state shareholding. And as the autumn crisis gave way to winter's nervous chill, Varley had sorted out his capital requirements without a penny of government funding. Qatari and Abu Dhabi investors had been approached and agreed to put up £7 billion, but at a price – Barclays paid hundreds of millions in fees to arrange the financing.

As the Asset Protection Scheme was being launched, there was much speculation in government and amongst financial regulators as to whether Barclays would be obliged to join. The downward adjustment of market expectations on the economy and the impact on banking which had battered the RBS balance sheet was raising questions about Barclays. Exposure to commercial property loans which might turn sour was by no means confined to RBS and HBOS. Ministers were not entirely convinced by the way Barclays marked assets in its accounts. The 'marks', are supposed to be a bank's best up-to-date guess on what loans might be worth relative to their original value. The lower the 'marks' the more realistic a bank's balance sheet is perceived to be. Critics believed they were too optimistic.

The Barclays board predictably said no to the government's offer to join APS, but the bank had to enter into prolonged talks with the Financial Services Authority and submit to a stress test of its balance sheet. Barclays was required, under rules for the industry at that time, to hold core capital of 4 per cent of the 'risk-weighted' assets (the value of all the loans adjusted for varying degrees of risk). That was the benchmark the FSA had to work to as it scoured the Barclays balance sheet to see if there was enough capital. The government, however, had gone a little higher with the state-controlled RBS and Lloyds and demanded a 5 per cent ratio. There was some resentment in the Treasury and Downing Street that Barclays was being tested against the 4 per cent floor.

All this was crucially important for Barclays: fail the 4 per cent stress test and the bank would have to either raise more capital, extremely difficult in the circumstances, or join the APS. Varley and his board-room colleagues were understandably desperate to pass. A war of nerves was being played out with some in government keen to get Barclays into APS and the bank itself determined to stay out. The simmering resentments burst out into the open with a leaking battle in March 2009. The first edition of the *Financial Times* on 26 March ran a story with a headline suggesting Barclays had failed the stress test. Barclays chiefs were furious. They had heard that day, unofficially, from FSA staff that they had passed the stress test although the Agency had pointed out the decision still had to be ratified by the tripartite author-ity. So the *FT* story looked odd at best, malicious at worst. The bank's press team went into overdrive, phoning senior editorial figures at the newspaper. The second edition had a totally different headline, suggest-ing Barclays had passed the test.

The headlines soured the atmosphere even further. Barclays noted that the first edition of the story had been written at Westminster by a politi-cal correspondent. The bank suspected that briefings by 10 Downing Street or others in government had been put out to destabilise Barclays and indirectly put pressure on members of the tripartite who would have the final say on the test. Some government sources were disap-pointed with the second edition headline, believing that Barclays, having only just scraped through the 4 per cent barrier, was trying to pre-empt the tripartite discussion. The bank looked, to some in govern-ment, to be telling journalists that the FSA decision was final and would not be overturned. Whitehall officials considered going on the record to say that Barclays was wrong. But in the end they and the FSA decided it would destabilise Barclays too much if the *FT* story was contradicted.

Barclays, then, stayed out of the Asset Protection Scheme. John Varley and his fellow directors were delighted to steer clear of a structure that had the smell of a government bailout device. It was all in keeping with the bank's strategy since the previous autumn of avoiding what the board saw as the stigma of state intervention. Never mind the fact that some of its major investors included members of the Qatari and Abu Dhabi royal families, the bank had escaped the clutches of the British government. But Barclays had the best of both worlds. It benefitted from the APS without actually being in it because investors regarded the whole UK banking sector as safer after the policy was announced. Once the markets saw there was a government insurance scheme that any bank could join, they judged there was a backstop for the whole sector. On the back of that funding costs for all banks fell, with Barclays like others a beneficiary. And for Barclays, that bonus came without an APS membership card and the subscription to go with it.

In late March there was a reminder, if one were needed, that the banking crisis had not been entirely the fault of high-rolling casino bankers. And not all of the victims were institutions that had gorged themselves on fickle wholesale funding. Sometimes it was plain old-fashioned bad lending which was the problem, and that was the case at the the Dunfermline Building Society. Armed with new resolution powers created in legislation only the previous month, the tripartite swooped on the Dunfermline and forced a sale of much of the society to Nationwide. About £1.5 billion of bad assets were taken under the wing of the Treasury. Regulators argued the Dunfermline was dangerously exposed to commercial lending which was turning sour. The fact that it was Scotland's largest building society, close to the constituencies of both the Prime Minister and the Chancellor, added a political twist to the debate about the intervention of the authorities.

As summer dragged into autumn, progress with APS was slow. Headhunters were hired to recruit staff, interviews took place but for months there were no senior appointments. The Treasury had a

streamlined team of talented and prodigiously hard-working civil servants but it lacked the numbers of people to deal with all the immensely
complex problems that had arisen from the banking crisis. They were
still fatigued, some close to burnout, and now they were faced with the
gargantuan task of dealing with up to £600 billion of questionable
bank assets. They did not, entirely understandably, have the skills or
experience to assess loan books. They had retained banking advisers
from Credit Suisse, Citibank and Blackrock to work on the complicated
task of calculating the value of the assets. But these experts complained
that, despite their best efforts, they could not get proper access to the
loan books at RBS and Lloyds. One source said 'diligence was terrible,
the numbers were all over the place'. The banking advisers told the
Treasury about the problems but officials did not feel able to press the
case.

Another complication lay in pinning down Lloyds. Its membership of
the APS had been announced in March but negotiations had become
tortuous over the summer. The bank's board made it increasingly obvious it wanted nothing to do with the scheme and was set on going it
alone. Spurning the comfort blanket of the APS meant that Lloyds
would need to raise more capital and it was desperate to do just that.
So, in November 2009 it launched the biggest ever cash-raising exercise
(known as a rights issue) seen in the City of London, with the aim of
tapping the markets for £13.5 billion to shore up capital buffers. A
further £9 billion was to be raised from bondholders. Lloyds shareholders backed the deal and took up 95 per cent of the shares on offer. The
board billed it as a vote of confidence by the private sector in the bank,
though the major shareholder, HM Government, had a large part to
play in the success of the share issue by buying all it was entitled to – the
final publicly owned stake was to be 43 per cent. After paying a £2.5
billion fee to the government for the implicit support gained by Lloyds
since the scheme was announced, the bank was allowed to say farewell
to APS.

The Lloyds board's decision to plough its own furrow in the markets
and shun the government's scheme soured its relationships with
Whitehall. Ministers had been keen for it to join the scheme, even if at
a lower level of involvement than had been outlined in February. But
Lloyds was defiant, seemingly hell-bent on avoiding APS at all costs

because of the perceived stigma which went with the scheme. Staying out of the scheme would also help the bank keep the government stake below 50 per cent. On the government side there were suspicions that the Lloyds chief executive Eric Daniels was making derogatory remarks about APS to shareholders, turning them against the scheme. Some commentators have since argued that the rights issue was a less sensible outcome for shareholders as, for those who did not take up their rights to buy, it diluted their interest in the bank. Joining APS, on the other hand, would have helped its capital position without the begging bowl being handed around shareholders. But senior Lloyds sources say they asked the Government not to exercise its right to buy shares. The bank's directors were confident they could raise all the money from private investors and if this had been allowed to happen billions of pounds of tax payers' money would not have been needed. Lloyds' chiefs suspected that, for political reasons, the government did not want its stake to fall.

For RBS, though, there was no escaping the Asset Protection Scheme. The terms were revised by the Treasury to provide better value for the taxpayer. The first loss to be taken by the bank was revised up from £40 billion to £60 billion and the total pool of assets put into the scheme reduced to £282 billion. Yet more government capital was injected into the bank with taxpayers writing out a cheque for £25.5 billion. By this time it was possible to work out the total bill for the bank bailouts. Government investments in the two banks since October 2008 totalled £65.8 billion (£62.7 billion net of fees paid back to the Treasury). In return the state had taken an 84 per cent interest in RBS and 41 per cent of Lloyds. The taxpayer liability of course did not stop there. There were hundreds of billions of pounds worth of lending being underwritten by the credit guarantee scheme and the Bank of England's Special Liquidity Scheme. The die was cast, the taxpayers' billions committed. But the question of whether the extraordinary policy decisions of 2009 would heal the banking system and get credit flowing properly around the economy was far from clear.

Chapter 8

Banks struggle to rebuild

And so the banking system, shaken and stirred, was launched into the new post-crisis era. In the final months of 2009, there were signs that the recession was coming to an end. Any return to growth would provide a boost to banks with the hope that the values of their troubled assets would start to recover. Barclays had pushed on without any direct government assistance while Lloyds, with only a minority government state, was moving ahead without being part of the asset protection scheme. That left just RBS, majority taxpayer-owned, with a large chunk of assets pledged to the APS. The emphasis from Whitehall was very much on turning the banks around and preparing for the day when the government shares would be back in private hands.

As the finishing touches were put to APS, the Labour government's fortunes appeared to be waning. Alistair Darling clashed with Gordon Brown over whether to raise VAT as a means of grappling with government borrowing. Darling's desire to push up VAT in his pre-Budget report in early December was rejected by the Prime Minister. As the Chancellor later admitted, the speech and its measures were not well received and lacked a compelling economic argument. But there was plenty of debate about one of his surprising and headline-grabbing measures. Darling announced he was slapping a tax on bank bonuses, 50 per cent on everything above £25,000. He knew he was tapping into a public mood of revulsion about banks, which had gathered momentum since the bailout. The willingness of bank boards to contemplate bonuses for their already highly paid staff when the taxpayer had been forced to prop up the ailing financial industry was greeted with incredulity by any voters 'vox-popped' on street corners. Yet the City view was that traders and executives needed to be rewarded for helping rebuild profits after the previous year's disasters. HSBC and Barclays could argue that they were not beholden to government because they had not received any direct financial support. Lloyds and RBS resisted what they portrayed as direct government interference in their pay policies. The RBS board even threatened to resign en masse if there was any Whitehall attempt to reduce their planned bonus pool.

Brown and Darling had to endure the wrath of banking chiefs after the bonus tax announcement. There were threats by some to reduce their presence in the UK because of a move they branded as punitive and outrageous. But this public row with bankers did not cause ministers any political damage, far from it. They could count on almost unanimous public support outside a few postcodes in central London. The deep-set problem was how to handle Lloyds and RBS, where the government had the power to call the shots on pay but did not want to be seen to be pulling the strings.

In theory, the government wanted to maintain an 'arm's-length' relationship with the banks, allowing them to focus on rebuilding their finances ahead of a share flotation. Those banks' boards had duties to protect the interests of minority private shareholders so they would not be steamrollered by the dead hand of the state that held the taxpayer-funded share stakes.

A body called UK Financial Investments (UKFI) had been set up to manage the taxpayer stakes in the bailed out banks. At the end of 2009, Robin Budenberg was preparing to leave UBS and take over at the helm of the new entity. He had the job of handling relationships with the bank boards and allowing them to carry out their duties as directors while knowing that no major strategic decision could be made without the approval of the Chancellor. It was a delicate position and critics argued that it could never be made to work. It was argued that either Lloyds and RBS should run their own affairs with no state involvement, or the banks should be run like nationalised industries. The tension went right to the heart of the post-bailout debate. Should the state-controlled banks be agents of government economic policy, expanding lending as a means of stimulating growth? Or should they be quasi-commercial entities focussing on profits and the earliest possible return to normal life on the stock market? The government in late 2009 and early 2010 seemed to favour the latter course.

As the political dogfights were waged in the early months of 2010, Lloyds and RBS continued the arduous reconstruction process and strived to do so away from the spotlight of political scrutiny. One factor moving in their favour was the return of growth and, in the final quarter of 2009, the ending of the deepest recession since the Second World War. Frustratingly for Brown and Darling, the first estimate of the growth in economic output for the fourth quarter of 2009 had showed only a marginal increase. It was hard for them to claim any political brownie points for what looked like an anaemic recovery. But the preliminary estimate is a first draft of economic history and subsequent revisions have taken that quarter's performance up to a more respectable growth rate. The first three months of 2010 also saw a solid continuation of post-recession expansion. For banks, growth is high-octane fuel. A recovering economy makes it easier for banks to sell assets and make profits. For Lloyds and RBS, as well as their competitors, the economy was providing some much needed medicine.

Into this more benign economic environment stepped the new coalition government. The hung parliament delivered by the May 2010 general election in turn produced a Conservative and Liberal Democrat coalition. Setting out plans to reduce government borrowing by more than Alistair Darling intended was a top priority for the new Chancellor, George Osborne. With parts of the Eurozone ablaze amidst fears of possible defaults, the British government felt it had to make plenty of noise about its deficit reduction strategy. But an important set of policy briefings were sitting high in the departmental in-trays of Osborne and the new Secretary of State for Business, the Liberal Democrat Vince Cable. The future of Lloyds and RBS was now open to the new ministers to determine. A new and different path could be chosen if the coalition partners so wished.

George Osborne had made it plain during the election campaign that he favoured a 'people's' privatisation for Lloyds and RBS, with the public being offered shares at a discount to the market price. Lower income groups might be entitled to an even bigger reduction. He called the policy the 'people's bank bonus' and argued that it would be in recognition of the vast amount of financial support which had been provided by taxpayers. Osborne's free market instincts pushed him firmly towards some sort of share sale for each bank. Allowing the banks to seek sustainable profitability in preparation for privatisation seemed the obvious option for the Conservative Chancellor.

Vince Cable had acquired something close to celebrity status thanks to his pronouncements in opposition on the banking crisis. A former economist at Shell, Cable knew his stuff and gained a reputation for incisive analysis about the dangers facing financial markets before Northern Rock crashed. In 2003 he had warned that rising house prices and ballooning borrowing looked unsustainable. Wearing his trademark wide-brimmed hat, long scarf and raincoat he looked rather menacing as he paced the pavements of Westminster answering a steady stream of calls from broadcast news programmes. He seemed pleased to be tagged as a 'Jeremiah' and joked a few years later that readers of the Old Testament would know that Jeremiah was usually proved right. Cable's book, *The Storm*, which looked at the causes of the financial crisis, was well received by a public trying to make sense of the drama. The book's cover tried to reinforce Cable's image as an economic visionary – with dark clouds over his head, Cable looks sternly into the distance. His desire for RBS and Lloyds, made clear during the general election campaign, was that they should stay effectively under public control for a decade. His primary objective for the banks, he said, was promoting lending and supporting the recovery.

The Osborne/Cable axis was never going to be an easy alliance. Their views of what to do with the banks were a reminder that they were poles apart on the political spectrum. The coalition agreement suggested that banking reform was a priority for both parties in government, stating: 'We will reform the banking system to avoid a repeat of the financial crisis, to promote a competitive economy, to sustain the recovery and to protect and sustain jobs.' But the detail of the reforms and how they were to be achieved was the subject of much haggling. The agreement document contained a pledge to set up an independent commission to investigate the separation of retail and investment banking. This was to be the main focus of the coalition's reform programme for the first years of the parliament.

George Osborne was reported to have won an early victory a few days into the life of the new government. The Treasury would take control of the banking reform agenda and the establishment of a banking commission. The Independent Commission on Banking would be chaired by Sir John Vickers, formerly chief economist at the Bank of England, then head of the Office of Fair Trading. The brief was to look at the structure of banking and recommend reform. Vince Cable was keen to break up the major banks, separating what he called 'risky casino banking' from high street retail finance. From an independent perspective, the function of the Commission was to examine how feasible a banking break-up would be. Cable acknowledged that he would not, as hoped, have a formal role in this policy area but he seemed satisfied that the Commission would deliver a genuinely independent verdict on the bank separation question.

There were other pieces of bank legislation in the coalition's armoury, such as a levy on bank balance sheets which ministers hoped would raise £8 billion over four years. The theory was to penalise the riskier end of their operations with the levy applied to wholesale borrowing. It was part of a joint initiative with France and Germany, which made moves to impose similar levies. On top of all that, sweeping changes to banking regulation were planned with the Financial Services Authority having to hand back many of its powers to the Bank of England. Treasury ministers were certainly going to have their hands full in delivering this extensive suite of proposals. It was estimated that the work of the Vickers Commission would take more than a year. With the banking reform agenda likely to be full for some time, little thought was given to how RBS and Lloyds might actually be managed and what their role in the UK economy might be. At that stage, with growth forecasts looking fair there did not seem to be many reasons to challenge the banks' performance or strategies.

But the 'good bank, bad bank' idea had not gone away. Work under the bonnet of the RBS balance sheet had continued, with managers painstakingly working out which lower-quality loans would move into the insured APS. A body to manage the process, known as the Asset Protection Agency, oversaw this process and monitored the management of the assets with the objective of protecting the taxpayer's interest. The agency was managed by Stephan Wilcke, recruited by the Treasury in September 2009 with extensive experience of European financial services. The agency also advised government of the projected scale of the losses and whether they were likely to go beyond the £60 billion 'excess' which was being covered by RBS. In effect, a 'bad bank' was being created inside RBS with the assets that had been put into the APS. To all intents and purposes, everything else was a 'good bank'.

Neither the organisation nor the structure of RBS had been split. But it was clear which parts of the RBS loan book were on which side of the divide.

Soon after the election the question of whether 'good bank, bad bank' should be pursued with a formal division of RBS was raised in government. Those in favour of the idea thought the new government had a promising window. Politically, the coalition could afford to take RBS in a new direction with a radical policy. The honeymoon period, such as it was, had not ended. Economic growth in the UK was looking positive and from June 2010, once the Eurozone crisis had seemed to subside the stock market was climbing steadily. The opportunity to nationalise and then split RBS was, in the view of some advisers, there and worth seizing. On the downside, it would be complicated and would involve unpicking the UKFI structure. The process might also take more than a year but it should be complete by the end of 2011, allowing a flotation in 2012. Failure to press the button in that summer of 2010, the supporters of such a move argued, could close the door for good. Stalling on the policy, they said, could mean the government and the bank being overtaken by events.

The Bank of England favoured activation of 'good bank, bad bank' and there was support too at the Asset Protection Agency which by then had got to grips with what was on the RBS books. But the FSA was against the idea as was UKFI, which feared that any such strategy would alienate the RBS management, some of whom might quit. The Treasury seemed divided and unable to come down either way – whatever private discussions took place, it did not pick up the ball and run with it. One senior source, who backed going ahead with nationalisation and then dividing up RBS, said 'the new government bungled it – they were afraid of taking political responsibility for RBS'. It was easier for the Treasury to let the bank's management keep plugging away without any strong political direction. Ministers probably felt there was enough to worry about with the Vickers Commission at work and the reform of financial services regulation. But the 'good bank, bad bank' proponents were frustrated that an opportunity had been missed.

Relations between Bank of England and Treasury staff had become frayed over this issue. The Bank was driven by a strong belief that running RBS at one remove from government with UKFI as the buffer had been a mistake. At senior levels of the Bank there had been scepticism since the beginning of APS. The idea of RBS operating like a private sector bank with the government standing back despite holding the dominant shareholding seemed wrong-headed to policymakers in Threadneedle Street. Mervyn King's enthusiasm for 'good bank, bad bank' in the final months of 2008 had not ebbed. The Labour government had not heeded his advice – now he was pushing the new Chancellor to pursue the policy.

The RBS senior management had no desire to have 'good bank, bad bank' imposed. Stephen Hester and his team were committed to turn the bank around as it was. Yes, they might have to shed some businesses through asset sales but they wanted to see the task through to flotation. Key to their plan was holding onto the investment bank, which may have been unpopular with politicians but was seen by Hester as a cash generator for the rest of the group. He was later to fall out with Osborne. But at this stage, in 2010, neither Osborne nor Vince Cable had the inclination to square up to him and force a major shake-up at the bank. Hester later insisted that keeping the RBS bad assets together with the good side of the bank had not inhibited its ability to make loans. He argued that 'we created our own bad bank inside RBS and there was no effect on the rest of the bank's lending'. An external bad bank, he believed, would not have been a better answer either for RBS or the government. Hester's view was that much of the economy did not want to borrow and RBS would not have lent more if the bank had been split.

The opportunity came and went. From 2011, the Eurozone crisis dominated market thinking and triggered a highly volatile ride for shares. UK growth had seemed particularly buoyant in 2010, generating hopes of a rapid recovery. But by the following year growth was patchy, with a slide backwards in the final three months of the year. The banks themselves encountered more challenging conditions. Predictions that the Euro would break up sent tremors around European markets. Speculation about a Greek default reached fever pitch. The fear of cracks appearing in the much larger Spanish and Italian economies was seeping around financial markets. Banks across Europe found that their funding costs were higher and, in a repeat of some of the worst weeks of the summer of 2008, inter-bank lending almost dried up.

Senior government sources have since made clear that 'good bank, bad bank' was a serious runner in May 2010 and a case was made for it inside Whitehall. But while the benign conditions immediately after the election led the government to believe that a split of RBS was not an urgent priority, the sharp fall in markets the following year ruled it out at that time. Market volatility and a worsening investment climate made valuing assets near impossible. George Osborne has since acknowledged that he could have acted more decisively on RBS soon after taking office. He said, when asked in September 2013, that not tackling the RBS issue was one of his major regrets.

RBS found the going much tougher in 2011 than it had the previous year. Losses nearly doubled to just under £2 billion partly thanks to write-offs on loans to the Greek government. The Ulster Bank subsidiary was still deeply in the red with exposures to the woeful Irish property market. The process of deleveraging, i.e. reducing the colossal RBS balance sheet, was proving prolonged and painful. More than £700 billion had been removed from the RBS books thanks to sales of assets or loans reaching maturity and not being renewed. When the results were announced in February 2012, Stephen Hester told BBC News that the clean-up process would take a total of five years so there were two more years of pain ahead.

If the RBS board and financial regulators had expected a better 2012 their hopes were soon dashed. The Eurozone crisis raged on with a bail-out for Spain's banks and the European Central Bank President Mario Draghi making a dramatic pledge to do whatever it would take to save the Euro. Economic growth in the UK faltered, apart from a brief spurt around the time of the London Olympics. With a sizeable chunk of British exports of goods and services sold to Eurozone countries, any fragility in that region was sure to undermine confidence in the UK. Against this dreary backdrop, RBS limped along. Losses were racked up for the fifth year in succession. Yet more write-offs had to be taken on loans judged unlikely to be repaid in full – Ulster Bank was again a source of losses on disastrous Irish lending. Fines for previous scandals, including allegations of rigging the benchmark interest rate LIBOR, had to be accounted for. RBS described it as a 'chastening year' during which it had tried to 'put right past mistakes'.

There was one piece of good news for RBS towards the end of 2012. It was able to announce that it had quit the Asset Protection Scheme. The departure from APS came at the earliest possible time allowed under the scheme. The bank had parted with £2.5 billion in fees to the Government by then, but had not made a single claim on the scheme. That did not mean the scheme had not been worthwhile. Its very existence, acknowledged by RBS, had restored market confidence in the bank at a critical moment and then provided a breathing space for implementing a recovery plan. At the start of APS, a vast array of dodgy assets nominally worth £282 billion had been insured. But Hester and his team had successfully chopped out more than half to leave a total of £105 billion. The insurance was no longer needed and there was agreement on that with the Treasury and the Financial Services Authority. Hester described it as 'a significant milestone in RBS's recovery'.

When the 2012 results were published in February the following year, Hester endeavoured to put on a brave face on the result and described them as the light at the end of the tunnel. He predicted that the bank would be ready for some sort of share flotation before the general election due in 2015. Later, briefings by RBS management mentioned the end of 2014 as a time when the bank might be ready for the beginning of a sale process, if the government wished to see that happen. A new script was being written by RBS bosses, aware perhaps of frustration in the Treasury about the slow pace the bank was taking in the long march back to profitability and a future free of the state. The message emanating from the City offices of RBS was that ministers would not have to wait too much longer until there was an opportunity at least to fire a starting gun on privatisation.

By May 2013, RBS chiefs were more openly bullish. They were able to report a profit for the first three months of the year, the first such outcome since before the banking crisis. The chairman, Sir Philip Hampton, said that the bank would be ready for the start of a share flotation by the middle of 2014, possibly even sooner. Stephen Hester said in interviews that the long clean-up of the RBS books would be substantially complete by then. There was a clear and uncoded message to the Chancellor – please give the green light to a share sale and allow us to start preparations for that. There was one obvious problem for Hampton and Hester – getting the share price back within 12 months to

a level that would at least allow taxpayers to break even on their investments. On the day of Hampton's plea to the Treasury, the RBS price
hovered around 290p per share. But, depending on how the government's intervention price was calculated, it would need to get back to at
least 440p, probably 500p, to allow ministers to say a fair value had been
achieved. The silence from the Treasury was noteworthy – there was no
nod to even the possibility of a share sale in 2014.

Little more than a month later, RBS was in turmoil again and the reason
for the Treasury's muted attitude on the day of the results became obvious. In a shock to the City and media alike, it was announced on 12
June that Stephen Hester was to quit as RBS chief executive later in the
year. A rather convoluted explanation was given by the bank. It was said
that UKFI had told the RBS board that the Treasury wanted the bank
to have cleared the decks in readiness for a share flotation by the end of
2014. Given that Hester would have been there for six years by then it
would be likely, the bank argued, that he would not want to stay much
longer. Selling shares in RBS might, it was said, be easier if there was no
doubt about the career plans of the chief executive. Better, so this thread
went, to have a new chief executive in place well before the end of 2014.
That was the official version of events. Another view was that George
Osborne and Stephen Hester simply did not get on. The Treasury
strongly denied that it had blood on its hands. It was the decision of the
RBS board and Mr Hester, officials briefed. Sir Philip Hampton and his
colleagues may have decided that having a chief executive who was
clearly not singing from the same hymn sheet as the majority shareholder was a less than sustainable position.

The City seemed to believe the less charitable interpretation of Hester's
departure. The RBS share price plunged more than 7 per cent the next
morning, although it recovered some losses later in the day, as analysts
publicly blamed the Treasury for interfering with RBS and pushing out
a highly respected chief executive. Lord Myners, still wearing his Labour
hat, suggested that the RBS board was 'doing the bidding' of George
Osborne. It looked like a mess and a reminder of the realities of the
governance of a company with more than 80 per cent of the shares held
by HM Government. Having the RBS board, UKFI and the Treasury all
with fingers in the pie was arguably a recipe for trouble.

In interviews after the announcement of his departure, Hester never pointed the finger directly at Osborne. He remained diplomatic about the circumstances leading up to the decision by the board to find a new chief executive. 'George and I never had a discussion,' said Hester after leaving the bank, 'there were a few things he wanted which I couldn't make a shareholder case for'. Those things included the disposal of the RBS American subsidiary Citizens Financial Group. Valued potentially at £10 billion, Citizens looked to the Chancellor like a pot of gold which could be easily cashed in as RBS focussed on building up UK banking operations. Hester's view was that Citizens should be sold only when the price was right and at a profit.

Hester departed wearily, reflecting on how RBS had become a political football: 'It was frustrating on a human level. Politics and business don't make good bedfellows – everyone had views on RBS, from the Archbishop of Canterbury to the former Chancellor, Lord Lawson. If nobody can agree on what the problem is, then it is hard to find a solution.' There was no easy answer or magic bullet, Hester believed, and if they had existed then the management would have found them. The political uncertainty had in his view slowed down the recovery of the bank and made it harder for bank executives to concentrate on the job.

To compound the frustrations for the RBS board and senior management, a wide-ranging report on the future of banking came up with some thought-provoking ideas and harsh conclusions. The Parliamentary Commission on Banking Standards had been set up by George Osborne in mid-2012 in response to the scandal over rigging of LIBOR, the key market interest rate which influenced many mortgages and business loans. The intention had been for the Commission to focus on the ethics and culture of banking, but under the determined and forensic leadership of the Conservative MP Andrew Tyrie it lifted up many stones across the banking terrain. Having Bishop Justin Welby, later to be Archbishop of Canterbury, on board added to the gravity and stature of the body.

The Commission highlighted the important role of RBS in the wider economy, both because of its scale and history of lending to small businesses. Given that, it argued, 'the current state of RBS and its continued ownership by the government create serious problems for the UK economy'. There was praise for Stephen Hester and his team for their efforts to sort out the bank's balance sheet. But the Commission concluded that after five years, the strategy for returning RBS to the private sector had to be reappraised – the bank was not in a position to provide the lending or competition required to help bring about the UK's full recovery. UKFI, the Commission continued, was not fit for purpose as it had not stopped the Treasury interfering – the body should be wound up.

For RBS, the most significant conclusion of the Banking Standards Commission report was a call for the 'good bank, bad bank' issue to be reopened. Evidence had been heard from supporters of the idea – one leading proponent, Lord Lawson, was actually a member of the Commission. One of the arguments aired in favour had been that the 'good bank' could concentrate on UK retail and commercial lending, freed from the toxic legacy assets which had held back the expansion of new loans. But it was noted that it was not clear whether a split would result in the 'good bank' getting back on the stock market more rapidly than an undivided RBS would. The Commission called for the Treasury to carry out an analysis of the policy and publish it within three months. George Osborne accepted the challenge and set up a Treasury review of the 'bad bank' option. But he rejected the idea of abolishing UKFI, noting that it had valuable banking expertise and was doing a good job of managing government stakes in the banks. He made it clear no more taxpayer money was to be put up in pursuit of any new goals set for RBS.

Lloyds, meanwhile, had steered a course free of political controversy. Sir Victor Blank and Eric Daniels had both moved on by early 2011. Antonio Horta-Osorio, a Portuguese banker who had previously run Santander UK, took over as chief executive in March 2011. After an uncertain start and health problems caused by overwork, which forced Horta-Osorio to take extended leave, the share price had been rising fairly steadily since late 2011. Markets perceived that Lloyds was a better candidate than RBS for recovery and a share sale. When the board announced results for 2012 they showed an increasing underlying profit, stripping out factors like fines for misdemeanours such as mis-selling of Payment Protection Insurance (PPI). Taking everything into account, a pre-tax loss of £3.5 billion the previous year had been cut to

£570 million. Speculation about an impending sale of the government's stake was fuelled by the revelation that the Horta-Osorio's bonus was linked to the share price reaching a level above what the taxpayer had shelled out and staying there for a sustained period.

The Parliamentary Banking Commission had little to say about Lloyds other than that it had 'suffered far less from the effect of public owner-ship and the perception of political interference than RBS'. It was hard to argue for government intervention at Lloyds, said the Commission, and it was better placed to return to the private sector without addi-tional restructuring. In early August, when Lloyds announced a sharp rise in profits for the first half of the year, the Treasury let it be known that a start of the sale of the government's shares was imminent. Although not quite as imminent as some expected, the starting gun was formally fired in mid-September. A 6 per cent stake in Lloyds was put up for the sale by the Treasury and in a late-evening process, banking advisers lined up institutions such as pension funds to bid for the shares. The following morning it was announced that £3.2 billion was to be raised with buyers paying 75p per share – this was a fraction above the average 74p price paid by the government to recapitalise Lloyds back in 2008. The publicly owned stake in Lloyds had been reduced to just under 33 per cent.

No wonder George Osborne was making the most of the developments at Lloyds. He said the news was positive for the taxpayer and an impor-tant step in plans to repair the economy. He kept his cards close to his chest when asked when a second chunk of Lloyds shares might go on sale. He was keen to stress, however, that he would think carefully about an offer of shares to the general public – an enticing prospect for him in the year before the general election. The Lloyds story fitted perfectly his narrative – a bank on the road to recovery, ready to help the economy with more lending, and with the government retrieving money for the taxpayer through a successful share sale. But with RBS he was no closer to getting back any of the state's investment. The RBS saga was drag-ging on and the Chancellor was bitterly regretting not grasping the nettle after the 2010 election.

The fifth anniversary of the dark days of October 2008 was approach-ing. RBS remained a mammoth in the room both for the Treasury and the economy. It was still deleveraging, reducing the burden of historic bad assets. Lending to businesses and consumers was still falling according to data from the Bank of England. Taking into account new loans and debt being repaid, net lending by RBS to households and corporate borrowers was down by £6.7 billion over the year to the second quarter of 2013, leaving the total loan stock at £208 billion. A share flotation seemed as far away as it had done at any time in the previous few years. The possibility of a root-and-branch review hovered over the bank. The brutal truth was that successive Chancellors had not worked out a viable path for an institution that was an important pillar of the whole economy. To put it another way, RBS was still in the mire five years on from the rescue. The question being asked more forcibly was whether a 'good' RBS separated from the toxic loans would generate more lending for the economy and also provide a quicker return for the taxpayer through a stock market flotation.

The coalition government's handling of RBS had taken a hammering a few months earlier. Sir Mervyn King had come out into the open with his hostility to the governance of RBS. Giving evidence at the Banking Standards Commission, the Governor said:

> The whole idea of a bank being 82 per cent owned by the taxpayer, run at arm's length from the government, is a nonsense. It cannot make any sense. I think it would be much better to accept that it should have been a temporary period of ownership only, to restructure the bank and put it back. The longer this has gone on, the more difficult that's become.

King argued that it should still be possible to split RBS into a 'good' and a 'bad' bank, the aim being to create a new, clean 'good' bank which could be a major lender to the economy. And, with a swipe at both Alistair Darling and George Osborne, the Governor said policymakers had not been sufficiently decisive in recapitalising and restructuring the banks. He concluded: 'This has dragged on unnecessarily long. I don't want to blame anyone for this but I think the lesson of history is we should face up to it.'

King's salvo had initially been dismissed by Treasury sources as a frustrated Governor wanting to get something off his chest during his final weeks in office. They made clear that the Chancellor wanted RBS to press on as it was and aim for a flotation at some stage in the next couple of years. Giving evidence at the Commission a couple of weeks earlier, the Chancellor had rejected the idea of splitting RBS as it would require nationalisation of the whole bank and he would not support the use of public money for that purpose. That was in March. But little more than three months later, George Osborne was agreeing to a review of the 'good bank, bad bank' policy. Such was the state of flux around RBS. In November 2013, the review complete, Osborne decided not to split RBS. Instead he demanded a complete ring-fencing of £38 billion of bad assets and a faster process for selling them off as well as a quicker timetable for the disposal of Citizens. Hester's achievement had been to reduce the £258 billion mountain of toxic debt to that £38 billion figure.

At the same time as the decision not to go ahead with an RBS carve-up, an independent report commissioned by the bank said it had performed poorly on small business lending. There was an acknowledgment from Hester's replacement as chief executive Ross McEwan that the bad assets had held back the bank: 'Five years ago we were broke – and when you get broke because you've lent money to the wrong people and can't get it back, you tighten up – we probably tightened up too much and we need to get the bank now back to being more normal with how it works with customers.'

Sir Mervyn King (knighted in 2011 and then awarded a peerage two years later) was not alone questioning the policy adopted for RBS. Five years on from the rescue and bailout of the bank, there has been wider scrutiny of the use of the Asset Protection Scheme and the government taking only a back seat in the management of the bank. Talking to some of the architects of RBS post-crisis and the APS gives the strong impression that they wished they had done things differently. Lord Myners, who played a central part in decision-making regarding RBS in late 2008 and early 2009, conceded that a different course might have been taken. He said: 'The case for nationalisation followed by a "good bank, bad bank" policy looks with hindsight to have been a stronger option than we probably considered it to be.' If any economic forecasters had predicted that it would be several more years before UK economic output got back to its pre-recession peak, Myners argued, then the case for a radical policy in 2008 would have been a lot clearer.

Given what we know now, he suggested, nationalisation of RBS would have been the best option back in 2008.

Lord Turner, who was chairman of the Financial Services Authority until mid-2013, is clear that HBOS should have been nationalised and he thinks that RBS should probably have been taken into full state ownership as well. Having an external minority stake in RBS in his view did not help the clarity of purpose which both government and management needed from the start of the reconstruction process. There was a lack of public understanding about what RBS was trying to do and whether it really was attempting to run itself like a private sector bank on behalf of its minority shareholders. Nationalisation of RBS would, with hindsight, have been the best outcome according to Turner, though he is doubtful about whether a 'good bank, bad bank' split would necessarily have had to flow from that. The most important thing under public ownership, he thinks, would have been to make sure the bad assets were moved into their own workout area.

Alistair Darling, as Chancellor, presided over the creation of the Asset Protection Scheme and took the decision to press on with RBS operating as a commercial bank which just happened to have a large government shareholding. Darling's main concern at the time was to keep RBS in a state that made an early sale back to the private sector as straightforward as possible. There was a widespread assumption that after a deep recession, there would be a sharp rebound for the economy which would allow a disposal of RBS shares within a year or so. Doing that with a stock market listing, he felt, would be much easier than launching a privatisation of a wholly government-owned business.

He rejected nationalisation during the early October crisis because he wanted to create a complete package which involved Barclays and HSBC as well as those who were obviously struggling. As he saw it, they were simply offered a straight choice of raising capital from private investors or the government if there was no other source.

Darling said he wanted a package which had 'the buy-in of all the big British banks – if you had said, by the way, this included nationalising anybody who's a bit slow off the mark, they would have been off'. One of his fears at the time was that nationalisation of either RBS or HBOS, let alone both, would generate unwarranted fears about the health of the whole banking system both at the other healthier banks and in the financial markets: 'At that time, it didn't take much to scare them. We wanted them to see the British government was playing a major role but not saying the entire banking system was bust.'

The Chancellor's anxiety at the time went beyond the well-being of individual banks. He had half an eye on what investors might conclude about the state of the British government's balance sheet. Given that RBS was bigger than the UK's annual economic output, taking it into full state ownership might raise concerns about what was affordable. Darling argues that the cost of any nationalisation would have been a major stumbling block and he was reluctant to run the gauntlet of an adverse reaction in the markets:

> I do wonder, looking back when the world was so febrile, if it looked like the UK government was busy nationalising banks, the market might have said how many banks can you nationalise? I wouldn't have said it at the time because people would have immediately said you are dead right – but five years on I can say you do need to have regard to how much money you are spending, any Chancellor does, but at that time you don't want people to doubt your sovereign creditworthiness.

Darling remains convinced he made the right decisions in late 2008 and early 2009. He does not recall hearing strong arguments at the time in favour of 'good bank, bad bank' and nationalisation. Even if the case was being made inside the tripartite authorities, there were few, if any, independent commentators calling for full state ownership. There does not seem to have been any evidence of dissenting views inside the Treasury. Investment bankers working on APS were clear that it was the most efficient way of boosting the capital ratios at RBS. Taxpayers' money would be needed to nationalise the bank if that route was chosen and more state funding might be required as a buffer against losses in a bad bank. As one senior adviser put it: 'You would need more public money for a bad bank and getting it capitalised – that seemed less efficient if you could achieve the same positive capitalisation at RBS without a huge funding requirement – why would you not do that instead?'

But the premise to the case for the Asset Protection Scheme was that it provided a safety net for RBS with the aim of stabilising it and preparing for the long-term goal of re-privatisation. According to one senior banking source, the focus was on 'how do you keep it alive – not how you make it run fast'. There was no talk in early 2009 of the Treasury using RBS and Lloyds as vehicles for boosting lending in a recovering economy, and no focus on using the state-controlled banks as agents for credit supply. Decisions were made only with a view to preparing the banks for life at some stage in the future without a lifeline from Whitehall. This was the brief to the banking advisers who were hired to devise plans to deal with capital shortfalls at the main banks after October 2008. The question put to them, according to a senior banking executive was: 'What's the most efficient way of effectively creating more capital in RBS? The question of lending more to the UK economy was never an agenda item'.

Beyond Downing Street and the Treasury, critics of the Asset Protection Scheme claimed it was too complicated and that the process of trying to separate the bad assets from the good was enormously difficult and time-consuming. APS, they argued, did not provide bank managements with any incentives to lend – it was simply a clever ploy to reduce the capital needed on the balance sheet. Loans to small businesses under banking industry rules needed more capital allocated to them as they were deemed to be riskier. There was thus a greater incentive for RBS management to put loans in this category into the APS and so reduce the capital required for them. There could arise a bizarre situation where one part of the bank was trying to increase lending to small firms while another was taking exactly the same sort of loans, labelling them 'bad assets' and shunting them into the insurance scheme. One senior banker who had advised the government, though not on this scheme, summed it up: 'You wouldn't do APS if you wanted RBS to play a part in lending and helping revive the economy.' The same source argued that if the government had said the priority was to lend, then advisers would have kept small business loans away from the Asset Protection Scheme.

Proponents of 'good bank, bad bank' like Sir Mervyn King were convinced that once so much public money had been pledged to RBS and Lloyds, there was no point pretending they were stand-alone, quasi-commercial entities. They pointed to the dangers of a Japanese-style slowdown, where banks remained haunted by historic toxic loans, unable to value them with any confidence. As long as this overhang of bad assets stayed there, so the argument ran, banks would be unwilling to take risks with lending on new projects and to vibrant start-up businesses. Better by far to withdraw the poison totally from the more promising areas of RBS and Lloyds and allow them to flourish back in the private sector, lending normally. The toxic waste, meanwhile, would sit out of harm's way on the state balance sheet. Continuing as a single entity, so this line of argument went, RBS was doing the economy no favours.

The Bank of England opposed APS and said it was too complex. 'Treasury civil servants,' according to one well-placed source, 'got themselves completely bogged down by having a massively complicated scheme and it has probably cost them a lot of public money by not going down the right route.' From this viewpoint, the government failed to provide enough capital both in late 2008 and in early 2009 after market conditions had deteriorated and ducked the radical restructuring required. The government, according to the same source, was too hung up on trying to steer clear of any further state support for the banks when the state of their balance sheets required just such an intervention: 'Someone's got to get a grip on them in order to get them back in the private sector as quickly as possible – otherwise they just linger in the public sector or as crippled banks where we have to support them the whole time.' In other words, radical and expensive surgery early in the reconstruction process would have prepared the way for a new, clean RBS to grow and thrive (perhaps using the NatWest brand and dropping RBS altogether).

The arguments about what should or should not have been done with RBS, Lloyds and HBOS and when will run and run. It is always easy with the benefit of hindsight to look back at decisions made in the heat of a crisis and suggest that different choices should have been made. At the Treasury, and amongst advisers who devised APS, there is a view that the best decision from a range of difficult options was made at the time. As far as Lloyds is concerned, those who defend the policies adopted by successive governments point to the eventual sale of some of the taxpayers' shareholding in September 2013. Not nationalising HBOS and allowing it to continue with the Lloyds marriage and then permitting the combined group to steer clear of APS in late 2009 were the key political decisions. But it took more than four years to get Lloyds to the stock market starting gate. Net lending by the group to households and businesses was down by £5.3 billion over the 12 months to mid 2013, although there was an uptick in the final three months of that period. What will never be known is what a 'clean' Lloyds might have done for the economy, while HBOS and its 'dirty' assets were sorted out under the umbrella of state ownership.

The surprising success of those banks that were nationalised and split up is evidence of how 'good bank, bad bank' can operate. Northern Rock was nationalised and then divided, with the government taking on a large chunk of the mortgage book. The rest of the bank, which had come to symbolise the credit crunch with the images of queues at branches repeated in every TV news piece on the financial crisis, finally found a home in the private sector. The retail side of Northern Rock was sold to Virgin Money for just under £750 million in November 2011. The Treasury could receive up to £280 million more, depending on whether the business is floated on the Stock Exchange. The Northern Rock name is no more, with the branches rebranded as Virgin Money, but there were reported to be cheers at the Newcastle headquarters when the deal was announced to staff.

The government resolution of Bradford & Bingley had passed the branches and customer accounts smoothly over to Santander. Most of the mortgage book, including some of the extravagant loans of the boom era, stayed on the government's books. It was combined with Northern Rock's to form a new quango called the UK Asset Resolution Agency. These loans were due to sit like nuclear waste for decades till they were all paid off or as much money as possible recovered from the borrowers. There were indications by late 2013 that a profit might even be made once the process had ended.

What might have been is a familiar debate in many walks of life, partic-ularly sport and politics. What if Brighton's Gordon Smith had scored in the final minutes of the 1983 FA Cup Final against Manchester United? What if Jim Callaghan had called a general election in late 1978 rather than waiting and enduring the 'Winter of Discontent'? The 'what ifs' over RBS and Lloyds in one sense are more important. They are central to the direction of the whole UK economy – jobs and livelihoods. The big banks' presence in the economy and ability to lend to families and businesses was secured by the Labour government's intervention in October 2008. But Alistair Darling and then George Osborne made decisions about the how the banks were structured and organised that could be seen to have impaired the flow of credit from two dominant players in the banking market. What if there had been a free-standing Lloyds, shorn of HBOS and lending freely to households and businesses? What if there had been a 'good' RBS back on the stock market with no government stake and pumping out loans? The problem with 'what ifs?' is only being able to guess at the answers.

Timeline

2 April 2007 New Century Financial, one of the largest sub-prime lenders in the US, filed for Chapter 11 bankruptcy protection. New Century sought protection from creditors after it was forced by its backers to repurchase billions of dollars worth of bad loans.

17 May 2007 Federal Reserve Chairman Ben Bernanke said in a speech on the sub-prime mortgage market: 'We believe the effect of the troubles in the sub-prime sector on the broader housing market will likely be limited, and we do not expect significant spillover from the sub-prime market to the rest of the economy or to the financial system.'

10 July 2007 The *Financial Times* reported that the chief executive of Citigroup, Chuck Prince, had 'dismissed fears that the music was about to stop for the cheap credit-fuelled buy-out boom, declaring that Citigroup was "still dancing"', adding he said that 'the party would end at some point but there was so much liquidity at the moment it would not be disrupted by the turmoil in the US sub-prime mortgage market'. Prince said: 'When the music stops, in terms of liquidity, things will be complicated. But as long as the music is playing, you've got to get up and dance. We're still dancing.'

17 July 2007 Wall Street investment house, Bear Stearns, said that its two troubled hedge funds were virtually worthless following the bursting of the real estate bubble.

19 July 2007 Ben Bernanke warned that the crisis in the US sub-prime lending market could cost up to $100bn. Giving evidence to the Senate, Bernanke said that credit losses associated with sub-prime mortgage failures were 'fairly significant'.

9 August 2007 As the financial markets fell back, international investors feared that the credit problems that began with the US sub-prime mortgage market were accelerating. French investment bank BNP Paribas froze three funds because of the knock-on effects of the sub-prime troubles. Germany's IKB said that it was affected and there were also rumours of serious problems at WestLB, another German bank.

In response to the turmoil, the European Central Bank (ECB) pumped €95 billion into the credit markets to improve liquidity.

The US Federal Reserve said it was also injecting $12 billion of temporary reserves into the US banking system.

14 August 2007 It subsequently emerges that on this date, the Financial Services Authority (FSA) disclosed concerns about Northern Rock to the Treasury and Bank of England.

17 August 2007 The US Federal Reserve cut its primary discount rate (the rate at which it lends money to banks) from 6.25 per cent to 5.75 per cent.

26 August 2007 In Germany, Sachsen, a Saxony-based bank with assets of €68 billion (€46 billion) owned partly by the regional government, announced that it was being taken over by Landesbank Baden-Württemberg (LBBW) after a previously attempted €17.3 billion bail-out failed.

3 September 2007 The German lender IKB Industriebank, already bailed out by other German banks, said it expected to lose around €473 million as a result of its exposure to sub-prime mortgages in the US.

4 September 2007 The London Interbank Offered Rate (LIBOR) reached 6.7975 per cent for a loan over a three-month period, suggesting that banks were reluctant to lend money to each other. It also meant LIBOR was above the Bank of England's emergency lending rate to banks, which is 6.75 per cent.

13 September 2007 The BBC revealed that Northern Rock had asked for, and had been granted, emergency financial support from the Bank of England (in its role as lender of last resort).

14 September 2007 Northern Rock issued a statement on market conditions and trading update. Depositors queued to withdraw their savings from branches around the country.

17 September 2007 The Chancellor, Alistair Darling, made a statement on the situation in the financial markets and announced that the government would guarantee all the existing deposits in Northern Rock.

18 September 2007 The Federal Reserve cut interest rates to 4.75 per cent from 5.25 per cent.

19 September 2007 The Bank of England announced an injection of £10 billion into the money markets in an attempt to bring three-month inter-bank interest rates down.

20 September 2007 The Treasury announced extended protections for Northern Rock customers.

23 September 2007 The press reported that Northern Rock had borrowed 'about £3 billion' from the Bank of England facility.

25 September 2007 Northern Rock announced that they would not be paying the interim dividend due the following month – this retained £59 million within the bank.

1 October 2007 Swiss bank UBS announced losses of $3.4 billion from sub-prime related investments. Citigroup later announced a sub-prime related loss of $3.1 billion.

The FSA increased the limit of Financial Service Compensation Scheme (FSCS) cover for deposits to 100 per cent of the first £35,000 of each depositor's claim. The previous compensation limit was a maximum of £31,700 (100 per cent of the first £2,000 and 90 per cent of the next £33,000 of depositors' eligible claims).

9 October 2007 The Treasury confirmed that the guarantee arrangements previously announced to protect existing depositors of Northern Rock would be extended to all new retail deposits made after 19 September.

11 October 2007 The Chancellor announced that the FSA would be setting out proposals for a review of the UK liquidity regime.

19 October 2007 Northern Rock Chairman, Dr Matt Ridley, resigned from the bank's board and was replaced by Brian Sanderson.

30 October 2007 Merrill Lynch's chief executive, Stanley O'Neal, resigned after the bank unveiled a $7.9 billion exposure to bad debt.

31 October 2007 US Federal Reserve lowers key Fed Funds interest rate to 4.5 per cent from 4.75 per cent.

4 November 2007 Chuck Prince resigned as chief executive of Citigroup, as the bank revealed it was facing an additional $8 billion to $11 billion of losses on mortgage related securities.

16 November 2007 Adam Applegarth, CEO of Northern Rock, resigned.

The deadline for offers to acquire Northern Rock expired.

19 November 2007 The Chancellor made a statement on the future of Northern Rock following the bids received for the company.

29 November 2007 The Bank of England revealed that the number of mortgage approvals had fallen to its lowest level for nearly three years.

30 November 2007 The Council of Mortgage Lenders warned that without more funding available on financial markets mortgage lenders would not be able to offer as many mortgages.

6 December 2007 President Bush outlined plans to freeze rates on subprime mortgages for five years to help people hit by the US housing market crisis.

The Bank of England cut interest rates by a quarter of a percentage point to 5.5 per cent.

11 December 2007 Federal Reserve lowered the Fed Funds rate to 4.25 per cent from 4.5 per cent.

12 December 2007 The US Federal Reserve announces two policy measures: (1) Term Auction Facility (TAF), 'allowing the Federal Reserve to inject term funds through a broader range of counterparties and against a broader range of collateral than open market operations'; and (2) the establishment of foreign exchange swap lines with the European Central Bank (ECB) and the Swiss National Bank (SNB), providing dollars in amounts of up to $20 billion with the ECB and $4 billion with the SNB.

A Liberal Democrat-sponsored debate in the House of Commons called for nationalisation of Northern Rock.

13 December 2007 The Federal Reserve, European Central Bank and central banks from the UK, Canada and Switzerland announced that they would provide billions in loans to banks in order to lower interest rates and ease the availability of credit. The move was co-ordinated by the US Federal Reserve.

14 December 2007 Northern Rock CEO Adam Applegarth replaced by Andy Kuipers.

19 December 2007 The FSA published the consultation document 'Review of the liquidity requirements for banks and building societies'.

Ratings agency Standard & Poor's (S&P) downgraded its investment rating of a number of 'monoline' insurers (which specialise in insuring bonds, guaranteeing to repay the loans if the issuer goes bust). There was concern that insurers would not be able to pay out, forcing banks to announce another big round of losses.

18 January 2008 A rush to withdraw money from its commercial property funds forced Scottish Equitable to introduce withdrawal delays of up to 12 months for its customers. It affected investors in the Scottish Equitable Property fund, Select Reserve fund and Select Distribution fund.

21 January 2008 Global stock indexes, including the UK FTSE 100, had their most precipitous fall since the terrorist attacks of 11 September 2001. The FTSE 100 index tumbled 5.5 per cent to 5,578.2 per cent, wiping £77 billion ($149 billion) off the value of its listed shares. Indexes in Paris and Frankfurt slumped by about 7 per cent, while markets in Asia, India and South America also dropped. The Chancellor made a statement outlining how the private sector rescue of Northern Rock would proceed and how the competing bids would be assessed.

22 January 2008 The US Federal Reserve slashed interest rates to 3.5 per cent from 4.25 per cent, its biggest cut in 25 years, and noted that 'appreciable downside risks to growth remain'.

26 January 2008 The Treasury Select Committee published its report on Northern Rock, 'The Run on the Rock'.

29 January 2008 The government published its regulatory reform proposals, 'Financial stability and depositor protection: strengthening the framework'.

31 January 2008 Major monoline bond insurer, MBIA, posted its biggest ever loss for a three-month period, hit by its exposure to the US.

sub-prime mortgage crisis. MBIA made a net loss of $2.3 billion (£1.15 billion) in the quarter ending 31 December.

7 February 2008 Ben Bernanke expressed his concern about monoline insurers, saying he was closely monitoring developments 'given the adverse effects that problems of financial guarantors can have on financial markets and the economy'.

The Bank of England cut interest rates to 5.25 per cent from 5.5 per cent.

8 February 2008 Figures from the Council of Mortgage Lenders revealed that the number of homes repossessed in the UK in 2007 was 27,100, its highest level since 1999.

17 February 2008 The Chancellor announced that Northern Rock would be taken into a period of temporary public ownership. In so doing, the government rejected the two private sector offers that had been put forward. The draft Banking (Special Provisions) Bill was published.

18 February 2008 Northern Rock shares were suspended. The Banking (Special Provisions) Bill had its first reading in the Commons and, in a statement to the House, the Chancellor stated that 'the government have no intention at present to use the Bill to bring any institution other than Northern Rock into temporary public ownership'.

19 February 2008 The Banking (Special Provisions) Bill had its second reading in the Commons.

21 February 2008 The Banking (Special Provisions) Bill received Royal Assent. The Act defined the circumstances in which the Treasury can take a financial institution into public ownership. This can only occur if either of the following two conditions is met: (1) maintaining the stability of the UK financial system in circumstances where the Treasury consider that there would be a serious threat to its stability if the order were not made; (2) protecting the public interest in circumstances where financial assistance has been provided by the Treasury to the deposit-taker for the purpose of maintaining the stability of the UK financial system.

22 February 2008 Northern Rock moved into a period of 'temporary public ownership'.

7 March 2008 The US Federal Reserve made $200 billion (£99 billion) available to major banks, saying it had taken action 'to address heightened liquidity pressures' in funding markets.

11 March 2008 The Federal Reserve announces Term Securities Lending Facility (TSLF) to lend up to $200 billion of Treasury securities to primary dealers secured for a term of 28 days against a range of collateral. Swap lines with the ECB and SNB (previously announced on 12 December 2007) increased by $10 billion and $2 billion respectively.

12 March In the UK, the Northern Rock plc Compensation Order 2008 was debated in the Third Delegated Legislation Committee. The order determined the framework for compensation levels for existing shareholders.

14 March 2008 Bear Sterns investment bank receives emergency lending from the Federal Reserve (via JP Morgan).

17 March 2008 Wall Street's fifth-largest bank, Bear Stearns, was acquired by larger rival JP Morgan Chase for $240 million (or $2 per share) in a deal backed by $30 billion of central bank loans (the offer was subsequently increased to $10 per share a week later).

18 March 2008 Federal Reserve lowers Fed Funds rate to 2.25 per cent from 3 per cent.

26 March 2008 The FSA published the summary of a review conducted by their internal audit division into the supervision of Northern Rock.

28 March 2008 The Nationwide Building Society predicted that UK house prices would fall by the end of the year.

2 April 2008 Moneyfacts reported that 20 per cent of mortgage products had been withdrawn from the UK market in the previous seven days.

7 April 2008 The Abbey bank announced it was withdrawing the last 100 per cent mortgage deals available to UK borrowers. The offers ended on Wednesday 9 April.

8 April 2008 The International Monetary Fund warned that potential losses from the credit crunch could reach at least $1 trillion and said that the effects were spreading from sub-prime mortgage assets to other sectors, such as commercial property, consumer credit and company debt.

10 April 2008 The Bank of England cut interest rates by a quarter of 1 per cent to 5 per cent.

11 April 2008 The Council of Mortgage Lenders warned that mortgage funding could be cut by half in 2008.

15 April 2008 The Royal Institution of Chartered Surveyors (RICS) said that 78.5 per cent more surveyors reported a fall rather than rise in house prices in March. This was the gloomiest reading since the RICS survey began in 1978. The government's house price figures confirmed a fall in prices in February by 1.6 per cent.

21 April 2008 The Bank of England launched the Special Liquidity Scheme (SLS) allowing banks to temporarily swap their high-quality mortgage-backed and other securities for UK Treasury Bills. Under the scheme, banks could swap illiquid assets for Treasury Bills. However, responsibility for losses on their loans would remain with the banks.

22 April 2008 The Royal Bank of Scotland announced a plan to raise money from its shareholders with a £12 billion rights issue – the biggest in UK corporate history.

25 April 2008 Persimmon became the first UK house builder to announce major cutbacks, citing the lack of affordable mortgages and a fall in consumer confidence.

29 April 2008 Figures from the Bank of England showed that new mortgages approved for house purchases in March slumped to 64,000, down from 72,000 the previous month. This was the lowest level since current records began in April 1993, and was down 44 per cent on the figure for the same month in 2007.

30 April 2008 The first annual fall in house prices for 12 years was recorded by Nationwide. Prices were 1 per cent lower in April compared to a year earlier.

The Federal Reserve lowered the Fed Funds rate to 2 per cent from 2.25 per cent.

2 May 2008 Insolvency Service figures revealed an increase in UK company insolvencies.

The Federal Reserve's Term Auction Facility (TAF) increased to $75 billion from $50 billion; increases its swap lines with the ECB and SNB by $20 billion and $6 billion respectively and broadens the range of collateral that can be used in the Term Securities Lending Facility (TSLF).

22 May 2008 Swiss bank UBS, one of the worst affected by the credit crunch, launched a $16 billion rights issue to cover some of the $37 billion it lost on assets linked to US mortgage debt.

5 June 2008 Moodys and S&P rating agencies downgrade the two largest monoline insurers from AAA to AA, although market reaction was observed as 'calm'.

19 June 2008 The FBI arrested 406 people, including brokers and housing developers, as part of a crackdown on alleged mortgage frauds worth $1 billion.

Separately, two former Bear Stearns employees faced criminal charges related to the collapse of two hedge funds linked to sub-prime mortgages. It is alleged they knew of the funds' problems but did not disclose them to investors. They were later acquitted of the charges.

25 June 2008 Barclays said it was planning to raise £4.5 billion ($8.8 billion) in a share issue to bolster its balance sheet: shares would be sold to new investors, such as the Qatar Investment Authority, and existing shareholders including China Development Bank.

8 July 2008 The British Chambers of Commerce's quarterly report found the credit crunch and rising costs had dented the most important sectors of the economy and that there were serious risks of recession in the UK.

The FTSE 100 stock index briefly dipped into a 'bear market', in which the market suffers a 20 per cent fall from its recent highs.

13 July 2008 US mortgage lender IndyMac collapsed.

14 July 2008 The US government announced measures to shore up the nation's two largest mortgage finance companies, Freddie Mac (Federal Home Loan Mortgage Corporation) and Fannie Mae (Federal National

Mortgage Association). The plan called on Congress to expand the companies' access to credit and allow the Treasury to buy shares in the companies if needed. The two firms own or guarantee almost half of all US home loans – more than $5 trillion (£2.5 trillion) of debt.

21 July 2008 Just 8 per cent of HBOS investors agreed to take up the new shares offered in its £4 billion rights issue, because they are priced higher than existing shares are trading on the stock market.

31 July 2008 UK house prices showed their biggest annual fall since the Nationwide began its housing survey in 1991, a decline of 8.1 per cent.

HBOS revealed that profits for the first half of the year sank 72 per cent to £848 million, while bad debts rose 36 per cent to £1.31billion as customers failed to repay loans.

4 August 2008 HSBC warned that conditions in financial markets were at their toughest 'for several decades' after suffering a 28 per cent fall in half-year profits.

22 August 2008 Revised figures from the ONS revealed that the UK economy was at a standstill in the second quarter of the year.

28 August 2008 Nationwide revealed that UK house prices had fallen by 10.5 per cent in a year.

29 August 2008 One day later Bradford & Bingley posted losses of £26.7 million for the first half of 2008, blaming surging mortgage arrears for a rise in impairment. It warned that it expected arrears to remain at high levels for the rest of the year.

Alistair Darling warned that the economy was facing its worst crisis for 60 years in an interview with *The Guardian* newspaper, saying that the downturn would be more 'profound and long-lasting' than most had feared.

1 September 2008 Official figures from the Bank of England showed a slump in approved mortgages for July.

The pound fell to record lows of 81.21 pence against the Euro and two-year lows of $1.80.

2 September 2008 In an effort to kick-start the UK housing market, the Treasury announced a one year rise in stamp duty exemption, from £125,000 to £175,000.

The OECD, the international forecasting group, forecast that the UK would be in recession by the end of the next two quarters. A day later the ECB cut the Eurozone growth forecast 2009 to 1.2 per cent from 1.5 per cent.

4 September 2008 The Bank of England left rates on hold at 5 per cent while figures from the Halifax showed that house prices in England and Wales were continuing to fall.

5 September 2008 A raft of negative news from around the world saw the FTSE notch up its steepest weekly decline since July 2002.

US labour market figures showed the unemployment rate rising to 6.1 per cent.

6 September 2008 The Halifax warned that the impact of the credit crunch would be felt well into 2010. Chief executive Andy Hornby explained that British banks would continue to suffer major problems in offering loans until they could raise significant sums on wholesale markets, something that would not be possible until US house prices recovered.

7 September 2008 Mortgage lenders Fannie Mae and Freddie Mac were rescued by the US government in one of the largest bailouts in US history. Treasury Secretary Henry (Hank) Paulson said the two firms' debt levels posed a 'systemic risk' to financial stability and that, without action, the situation would get worse.

In the UK, the Nationwide announced that it would merge with two smaller rivals, the Derbyshire and Cheshire Building Societies.

9 September 2008 The Office for National Statistics (ONS) revealed UK manufacturing output fell by 0.2 per cent between June and July, raising a real fear of recession.

The British Retail Consortium reported that retail sales values fell by 1 per cent on a like-for- like basis from August 2007.

The Royal Institute of Chartered Surveyors published figures showing house sales were at their lowest level for 30 years while the CML reported that the number of first-time buyers had hit its lowest level since its survey began in January 2002.

10 September 2008 Wall Street bank, Lehman Brothers, posted a loss of $3.9 billion (£2.2 billion) for the three months to August. The announcement came against a background of further dire economic warnings from the European Commission, which warned that the UK, Germany and Spain would go into recession by the end of the year.

15 September 2008 Lehman Brothers filed for Chapter 11 bankruptcy protection, becoming the first major bank to collapse since the start of the credit crisis.

Former Federal Reserve chief Alan Greenspan dubbed the failure as 'probably a once-in-a-century type of event' and warned that other major firms will also go bust.

US bank Merrill Lynch agreed to be taken over by Bank of America (BoA) for $50 billion.

Eleven of the world's biggest banks have agreed to pool $70 billion in a liquidity fund to help counter disruption in short-term funding markets. The *Financial Times* said the fund was 'intended to act as a kind of self-insurance scheme'.

16 September 2008 The Federal Reserve leaves Fed Funds rate unchanged at 2 per cent.

17 September 2008 The Bank of England announced the extension of the final date of the drawdown period for its Special Liquidity Scheme from 21 October 2008 to 30 January 2009.

Lloyds TSB bank agrees to buy HBOS.

American International Group (AIG), one of the world's biggest insurers, was saved from the brink of collapse after the US Federal Reserve, agreed an $85 billion (£47 billion) bailout of the company. The deal gave the US government a 79.9 per cent stake in the insurer.

18 September 2008 Rumours circulated of a Federal Reserve plan to buy out banks' toxic assets.

The Federal Reserve doubles the size of its swap line to ECB, increasing it to $110 billion, and raising the swap line with the SNB to $27 billion from $15 billion. In addition, new swap lines are created with the Bank of Japan ($60 billion), the Bank of England ($40 billion) and the Bank of Canada ($10 billion).

The FSA announced a ban on short selling of financial stocks and an obligation to disclose significant 'short' positions, a move also adopted by the Irish Central Bank, the financial regulator.

19 September 2008 US Treasury Department announced the establishment of a temporary guaranty programme for the US money market mutual fund industry. The programme will mean that the US Treasury will insure the holdings of any publicly offered eligible money market mutual fund – both retail and institutional – that pays a fee to participate in the program.

The FTSE 100 recorded its largest ever one-day rise after US government plans for a banking sector bailout and new restrictions on short-selling sparked a rally that pushed the benchmark index up by 9 per cent.

Financial regulators in the US, France and Canada ban short selling of financial stocks. In the US, the Securities and Exchange Commission (SEC) said that its action was in concert with the FSA's.

24 September 2008 Warren Buffett's investment company, Berkshire Hathaway, reported taking a $5 billion stake in Goldman Sachs through a private placement in preferred stock.

26 September 2008 JP Morgan bought American mortgage lending institution Washington Mutual.

29 September 2008 US Congress rejected a plan involving $700 billion of government purchases of 'toxic debt'. The US stock market registered its steepest ever fall.

The Federal Reserve adds a further $330 billion to its swap lines with overseas central banks, bringing the total to $620 billion.

Citigroup bought parts of Wachovia, the Federal Deposit Insurance Corporation, and agreed to take responsibility for losses over a set level.

In the UK, Bradford & Bingley was broken up. Its retail side was taken over by Santander and the mortgage and loan books were nationalised.

In Iceland, the government took a 75 per cent share in Glitnir Bank.

The Fortis Group was nationalised by a coalition of the Belgian, Luxembourg and Dutch governments.

30 September 2008 The Irish government guaranteed all deposits (as well as certain bonds and debts) in six Irish banks for two years.

Belgian bank Dexia was rescued by Belgian, French and Luxembourg government money.

1 October 2008 The Bank of England began providing covert liquidity to Halifax/Bank of Scotland; this support peaked at £25.4 billion on 13 November. Information about this covert help was disclosed to the House by the Chancellor over a year later (25 November 2009).

Italy bans short selling of financial stocks.

3 October 2008 The Bush administration's $700 billion emergency bailout for the US banking industry became law. The House of Representatives backed the rescue plan by a margin of 263 to 171, over-turning the vote of 29 September when it was opposed by 228 to 205.

The bill, which allowed the US treasury to clean up banks' balance sheets by purchasing distressed mortgage-backed securities, was signed by President Bush within hours of congressional approval.

Wells Fargo announced plans to merge with Wachovia. Citigroup later withdrew its Wachovia bid.

In the UK, the FSA increased the compensation limit for bank deposits from £35,000 up to a total of £50,000 for each customer's claim.

5 October 2008 In Germany, a €50 billion (£39 billion) package to rescue Germany's second-biggest property lender, Hypo Real Estate (HRE) was agreed. In addition, the German government guarantees all private bank accounts.

In Belgium, an agreement was reached to secure the future of Fortis, the country's second-biggest bank, by selling 75 per cent of its Belgian operations to BNP Paribas. France's biggest bank would also take over two-thirds of Fortis's Luxembourg business.

In Iceland, the government continued talks with Nordic central bankers on a €10 billion capital injection into the island's commercial banks, including its leading player, Kaupthing.

In Italy Unicredit, the country's second-biggest bank, negotiated a fresh capital injection of up to a reported €6 billion.

6 October 2008 The Chancellor made a statement to the Commons on developments in the financial markets.

The Federal Reserve increases the size of the Term Auction Facility (liquidity support for banks) programme to $600 billion.

Sweden increases its deposit guarantee to SEK 500,000 from SEK 250,000.

7 October 2008 The Bank of England began providing covert liquidity to Royal Bank of Scotland; this support peaked at £36.6 billion on 17 October. Information about this concealed help was disclosed to the House by the Chancellor only over a year later (25 November 2009).

The Icelandic government took control of Landsbanki, the second-largest bank in the country, and sought to secure a €4 billion loan from Russia as it worked to avert a financial meltdown.

8 October 2008 The Treasury announced a number of measures including the Credit Guarantee Scheme and Bank Recapitalisation Fund that were intended to: (1) provide sufficient liquidity in the short term; (2) make available new capital to UK banks and building societies to strengthen their resources permitting them to restructure their finances, while maintaining their support for the real economy; and (3) ensure that the banking system had the funds necessary to maintain lending in the medium term.

HM Treasury also reported that eight major banks and building societies had committed to the government that they would increase their capital by £25 billion.

The Bank of England reduced interest rates by half a percentage point to 4.5 per cent, as part of a co-ordinated move with the Bank of Canada, ECB, Federal Reserve, Swedish Riksbank and the Swiss National Bank.

The Federal Reserve cut its Fed Funds rate to 1.5 per cent from 2 per cent .

The Treasury issued press releases on Landsbanki, Icesave and Heritable and on Kaupthing.

9 October 2008 Italian government pledged to provide funds to any of the country's banks if needed.

11 October 2008 The G7 presented a five-point 'Plan of Action' to deal with increasing financial turmoil. This included a promise to: 'ensure that our banks . . . can raise capital from public and well as private sources, in sufficient amounts to re-establish confidence and permit them to continue lending to households and businesses.'

13 October 2008 The Chancellor made a statement to the Commons on the recapitalisation of HBOS, Lloyds TSB and RBS, with the government taking significant shareholdings in the three banks and its capital investment totalling £37 billion. The Chancellor also issued a written statement on the Contingencies Fund and the action taken on the Icelandic banks, Kaupthing and Landsbanki.

France announces a €320 billion fund to provide loan guarantees to banks and other financial institutions, plus €40 billion to buy stakes in French banks in need of capital.

The German government pledged €400 billion in loan guarantees and €80 billion to recapitalise banks in distress.

The Federal Reserve removes limits on the size of its swap lines with the ECB, SNB announcing and Bank of England, 'Counterparties in these operations will be able to borrow any amount they wish against the appropriate collateral in each jurisdiction'.

The Bank of Japan introduced a similar measure the following day.

14 October 2008 The US government unveiled a $250 billion plan to take stakes in nine leading banks. Of the $250 billion (which came from the $700 billion bailout approved by Congress), half was to be injected into nine big banks, including Citigroup, Bank of America, Wells Fargo, Goldman Sachs and JP Morgan Chase, officials told the New York Times. The other half would go to smaller banks and thrifts.

The UK Treasury issued a written statement on the Debt Management Office's 2008–09 financing remit to raise £37 billion to facilitate bank recapitalisation.

15 October 2008 The Dow Jones fell 733 points, or 7.9 per cent, to 8,578, and the wider S&P500 fell 9 per cent. Both performances were the worst since the 1987 stock market crash.

16 October 2008 Swiss government invests CHF6 billion into UBS, and relieves UBS of problematic assets of up to US$60 billion which are sold to the Swiss National Bank (central bank of Switzerland).

17 October 2008 The Bank of England's covert liquidity support to Halifax/Bank of Scotland and Royal Bank of Scotland peaked at £61.6 billion jointly, at which point the two banks were providing collateral in excess of £100 billion.

French savings bank Caisse d'Epargne announced a loss of €600 million in a 'trading incident'.

19 October 2008 South Korea announced a $130 billion financial rescue package to stabilise its markets by offering a state guarantee on banks' foreign debts and promising to inject capital into struggling financial firms if necessary.

The Dutch savings bank ING received a €10 billion capital injection from the Dutch government.

20 October 2008 The Swedish government pledged more than SEK 1.5 trillion (£117 billion) to support its financial firms.

The French government announced it would invest €10.5 billion in the country's six biggest banks by year-end, on the condition that they increase lending to companies and households.

The Reserve Bank of India reduced its overnight lending rate from 9 per cent to 8 per cent with immediate effect.

21 October 2008 In the UK, the Department for Business, Innovation and Skills issued details of further measures to help small and medium sized businesses. These focused on cash flow, access to finance and training for staff.

22 October 2008 The UK government announced new rules to help protect homeowners facing the threat of repossession. New court protocols would help to make repossessions a last resort, and the government proposed that companies engaged in sale and rent back schemes should be brought under FSA regulation.

The Economic Secretary to the Treasury made a statement to the Commons on the latest government measures to help small businesses.

23 October 2008 The Canadian government announced the creation of the 'Canadian Lenders Assurance Facility' to provide insurance on the wholesale term borrowing of federally regulated deposit-taking institutions. It explained that it would 'help to secure access to longer-term funds so that Canadian financial institutions can continue lending to consumers, homebuyers and businesses in Canada'.

24 October 2008 UK gross domestic product in the third quarter of 2008 fell by 0.5 per cent, the first contraction since the second quarter of 1992 when the British economy was at the end of its last recession, and the biggest drop since the fourth quarter of 1990.

27 October 2008 Japanese FSA bans naked short selling until 31 March 2009.

29 October 2008 The Federal Reserve cuts the Fed Funds rate to 1 per cent from 1.5 per cent and new swap lines are established with Brazil, Mexico, Singapore and Korea, each of $30 billion.

30 October 2008 The US economy shrank at an annual rate of 0.3 per cent in the three months to September.

31 October 2008 The UK Secretary of State for Business, Peter Mandelson, gives Lloyds TSB plc's acquisition of HBOS plc regulatory clearance, saying that 'on balance', ensuring the stability of the UK financial system justified the anti-competitive outcome that the Office of Fair Trading identified and that 'the public interest is best served by clearing the merger'.

6 November 2008 The Bank of England reduced interest rates by 1.5 percentage points to 3 per cent.
The ECB cut interest rates from 3.7 per cent to 3.25 per cent

9 November 2008 China announced a £373 billion economic stimulus package to boost its economy.

11 November 2008 Peter Mandelson announced the creation of a new panel to monitor how banks were lending to small businesses.

12 November 2008 The US Treasury abandoned its plan to spend billions of dollars buying up illiquid mortgage assets, and instead concentrated on improving the flow of credit for the US consumer. The plan to help US banks by taking toxic mortgage assets off their hands had been a cornerstone of the $700 billion troubled assets relief programme.

14 November 2008 Gross domestic product in the Eurozone fell by 0.2 per cent for a second consecutive quarter in the third quarter, satisfying the technical definition for a recession.

19 November 2008 The International Monetary Fund approved a $2.1 billion loan for Iceland. The British, Dutch and German governments later confirmed that they would give Iceland a combined $6.3 billion in loans to cover the cost of compensating Icesave account holders.

24 November 2008 In his pre-Budget report, the Chancellor announced a £20 billion fiscal stimulus, including a reduction of VAT from 17.5 per cent to 15 per cent and the bringing forward of £3 billion of capital spending to support the economy, increasing capital budgets for 2008-09 and 2009-10.

The US government announced a rescue plan for Citigroup.

25 November 2008 The International Monetary Fund approved a $7.6 billion standby loan for Pakistan to help the country avoid defaulting on its debt. The US government injected a further $800 billion (£528 billion) into the financial system in another attempt to kick-start the mortgage and consumer lending markets.

26 November 2008 The European Commission announced plans for a £160 billion economic recovery package.

1 December 2008 The US recession was officially confirmed by the National Bureau of Economic Research.

3 December 2008 The UK government announced details of a new Homeowner Mortgage Support Scheme.

4 December 2008 The Bank of England reduced interest rates by one percentage point to 2 per cent.

The ECB reduced interest rates to 2.5 per cent from 3.25 per cent.

The French government announced a €26 billion plan to help the national economy, including a €1 billion loan for carmakers and €5 billion of new public sector investments.

10 December 2008 The UK Treasury announced further details of the Homeowner Mortgage Support Scheme.

11 December 2008 The Bank of America announced that it was cutting up to 35,000 jobs following its merger with Merrill Lynch.

14 December 2008 The Irish government announced a recapitalisation programme for its national credit institutions of up to €10 billion.

15 December 2008 HM Treasury extended Credit Guarantee Scheme (first announced on 8 October 2008) from three years to five years.

16 December 2008 The US Federal Reserve cut interest rates to a range of zero to 0.25 per cent from 1 per cent.

19 December 2008 Japan cut it main discount rate to 0.1 per cent. President Bush announced $17.4 billion (£11.6 billion) in short-term loans to General Motors and Chrysler, with the money coming from the Troubled Asset Relief Programme.

21 December 2008 The Irish government announced €2 billion recapitalisation investment each in Allied Irish Bank and Bank of Ireland and €1.5 billion in Anglo Irish Bank.

31 December 2008 The FTSE closed down 31.3 per cent since the beginning of the year, the biggest annual fall since the index began.

8 January 2009 The Bank of England reduced interest rates by half a percentage point to 1.5 per cent.

12 January 2009 The UK government announced extra help for people unemployed for over six months. This included: employers' golden hellos; new training places; work-focused volunteering options; and help to set up a business.

14 January 2009 Peter Mandelson announced new measures designed to address the cash flow, credit and investment needs of small and medium businesses.

15 January 2009 The European Central Bank cut interest rates to 2 per cent from 2.5 per cent, bringing Eurozone borrowing costs to a three-year low after four cuts in a row totalling 225 basis points (2.25 percentage points).

The Irish government nationalised Anglo Irish Bank, stating that 'the funding position of the bank has weakened and unacceptable practices that took place within it have caused serious reputational damage to the bank'.

16 January 2009 Bank of America was given a new injection of $20 billion (£13.5 billion) by the US government and a guarantee of $118 billion on potential losses on toxic assets. The move came as Merrill Lynch, which had been taken over by BoA, reported a $15.3 billion loss for the fourth quarter. BoA lost $1.79 billion in the quarter. Citigroup posted a loss of $8.29 billion and said it would split in two.

The UK ban on short selling expires but the disclosure requirements regarding short positions continues till 30 June 2009.

19 January 2009 The UK government announced new measures 'to reinforce the stability of the financial system, to increase confidence and capacity to lend, and in turn to support the recovery of the economy'. These included: (1) extending the drawdown window for new debt under the government's Credit Guarantee Scheme (CGS) which was designed to reduce the risks on lending between banks; (2) establishing a new facility for asset backed securities; (3) extending the maturity date for the Bank of England's Discount Window Facility which provided liquidity to the banking sector by allowing them to swap less liquid assets; (3) establishing a new Bank of England facility for purchasing high-quality assets; (4) offering capital and an Asset Protection Scheme for banks, with proposals for this to be co-ordinated internationally; and (5) clarifying the regulatory approach to capital requirements, through an announcement by the Financial Services Authority.

The Treasury issued a statement on the Asset Protection Scheme as well as on the government's decision to convert the Treasury's preference share investment in RBS Group plc to ordinary shares in order to: (1) make available additional core capital to the bank to strengthen its resources, enable it to absorb expected losses and permit it to restructure its finances; and (2) give the bank the opportunity to build its capital further so that it is able to maintain and increase its support for the real economy by facilitating £6 billion more lending to industry and homeowners, over and above existing commitments.

The FSA made a statement on the development of the bank capital regulatory framework.

21 January 2009 The French government announced further €10.5 billion to recapitalise French banks.

28 January 2009 The Federal Reserve kept its target range for the Fed Funds rate at 0 per cent to 0.25 per cent, but added that it was 'prepared to purchase longer-term Treasury securities if evolving circumstances indicate that such transactions would be particularly effective in improving conditions in private credit markets'.

3 February 2009 The Swedish government announced recapitalisation scheme of up to SEK50 billion for solvent banks and certain other credit institutions incorporated in Sweden.

The Federal Reserve extended the expiry of existing liquidity programmes from 30 April to 30 October 2009.

5 February 2009 The Bank of England reduced the Bank rate from 1.5 per cent to 1.0 per cent.

9 February 2009 Barclays Bank reported profits before tax of £6.1 billion for the full year of 2008, down 14 per cent on its profits taken in 2007.

11 February 2009 The Irish government agreed to invest €3.5 billion each in Allied Irish Bank and Bank of Ireland.

23 February 2009 The UK government announced a renegotiated business plan for the state-owned Northern Rock bank. The main elements of the new agreement were an increase in the government's contribution to the bank's capital base of £3 billion and an end to the policy under which the bank would not seek to wind down its mortgage lending as existing mortgages came up for renewal.

25 February 2009 Italy's Finance Ministry approved a €12 billion recapitalization plan for Italian banks.

26 February 2009 Details were announced of the terms of the government's Asset Protection Scheme. Under the scheme eligible institutions were able to insure 90 per cent of losses on existing loans subject to an excess or 'first loss'. The terms of the fee and the extent of the 'first loss' would be decided on a case-by-case basis. The scheme would run for at least five years. Participation in the scheme would also include guarantees of sustained lending to individuals and businesses and the adoption of approved remuneration policies.

The first participant under the scheme was announced as Royal Bank of Scotland (RBS). RBS intended to insure £325 billion of loans for a fee of 2 per cent of the value of the assets insured (£6.5 billion). The first loss in this case was £19.5 billion and the 2009 lending commitments are £9 billion of additional mortgage lending and £16 billion of additional business lending.

The government also announced a further capital injection of £13 billion into RBS and committed to subscribe for an additional £6 billion at RBS's option.

RBS revealed annual losses of £24 billion.

27 February 2009 Lloyds TSB announced profits before tax for 2008 of £807 million.

These profits *excluded* losses by the HBOS group of £10.8 billion.

2 March 2009 HSBC announced pre-tax profits of £6.5 billion and a rights issue of £12.5 billion. American Insurance Group (AIG) announced a $61.7 billion loss in the fourth quarter of 2008, the largest in US corporate history.

The US Treasury Department and the Federal Reserve announced a restructuring of the government's assistance to AIG in order to stabilize the company and enhance its capital and liquidity.

5 March 2009 The Bank of England announced that it would undertake a policy of creating new money, known as 'quantitative easing'. The Bank would purchase £75 billion of assets using the new money. The aim was to boost the economy and prevent inflation undershooting its 2 per cent target. This was accompanied by a further interest rate cut to 0.5 per cent (from 1 per cent). Although the 0.5 per cent rate was the floor for UK interest rates in the crisis, the level of quantitative easing was increased during the subsequent months.

The ECB cut interest rates to 1.5 per cent from 2 per cent.

7 March 2009 The Lloyds Banking Group announced participation in the Asset Protection Scheme and that it would swap £4 billion preference shares held by government for new ordinary equity shares. Lloyds intended to insure £260 billion of loans for a fee of £15.6 billion to be paid for in the issuance of further 'B' shares. Under the agreement the government would not take up voting shares such that its holding exceeds 75 per cent. The first loss in this case was £25 billion, and the lending commitments were £3 billion of additional mortgage lending and £11 billion of additional business lending over the next 12 months.

9 March 2009 The FTSE 100 hit a six year low of 3,460.

12 March 2009 FSA chief executive Hector Sants delivered his 'People should be very frightened of the FSA' speech.

18 March 2009 The Fed steps up its policy of 'credit easing' similar to the quantitative easing employed by the Bank of England: 'to help improve conditions in private credit markets, the Committee decided to purchase up to $300 billion of longer-term Treasury securities over the next six months.' This is in addition to the $1.25 billion of mortgage-backed securities and $200 billion of agency debt that would be purchased in 2009.

23 March 2009 The US Treasury announced details of the public-private investment fund purchase of toxic loans and securities. Using $75–100 billion of TARP funds, the Treasury would invest in the purchase of toxic assets that remain difficult to sell on the market. Reducing risk to encourage private investment, the Fed made available low-interest loans for purchasing securities while the FDIC offered guarantees against losses on loans. The Treasury hoped the investment fund would initially make $500 billion of purchases, potentially rising to $1 trillion; profits would be shared equally by the Treasury and private sector.

26 March 2009 The US Treasury unveiled plans for a new regulatory framework. The framework detailed four components of regulatory reform: addressing systemic risk, protecting consumers and investors, eliminating gaps in the regulatory system and fostering international co-ordination.

30 March 2009 The Dunfermline Building Society – which announced £26 million in losses, principally arising from its residential and commercial mortgage assets – was taken over by the Nationwide Building Society. The Treasury took on approximately £1.5 billion in residual bad assets.

2 April 2009 G20 world leaders' summit held in London's Docklands. They jointly pledged to repair the financial system, restore lending and rebuild trust. There was a commitment to a $1 trillion plan to stimulate the global economy, most channelled through the IMF.

The ECB cuts its main refinancing rate to 1.25 per cent from 1.5 per cent.

1 May 2009 The Treasury Select Committee released the report 'Banking Crisis: dealing with the failure of the UK banks'.

7 May 2009 Barclays announced a pre-tax profit of £1.372 million for the first quarter of 2009 – 15 per cent higher than the first quarter of 2008.

The Lloyds Banking Group announced a £826 million profit for the first quarter of 2009. However, it also issued a profit warning suggesting that it was expecting to make a loss for 2009.

The Bank of England voted to continue its policy of quantitative easing, and increases the size of its asset purchase fund by £50 billion to £125 billion.

The European Central Bank announced that it would lower its main refinancing rate to 1 per cent and continue to provide unlimited short-term and longer-term liquidity to the market for at least a further 12 months.

The ECB also announced its intention to purchase €60 billion of Euro-denominated covered bonds (a particularly safe form of asset-backed security) from primary and secondary markets.

The US Treasury and Federal Reserve release the results of their 'stress tests' under the Supervisory Capital Assessment Program. The Treasury stated that: 'The assessment announced today will help strengthen the lending capacity of banks, with greater transparency and actions to reinforce the amount of capital banks hold against the risk of future losses.' Of the 19 financial institutions facing the test, the Treasury concluded that 10 would require further capital: Bank of America, $33.9 billion; Citigroup, $5.5 billion; Fifth Third Bancorp, $1.1 billion; GMAC, $11.5 billion; KeyCorp, $1.6 billion; Morgan Stanley, $1.8 billion; PNC Financial Services Group, $0.6 billion; Regions Financial Corporation, $2.5 billion; Sun Trust Banks, $2.2 billion; Wells Fargo, $13.7 billion.

8 May 2009 RBS announced a pre-tax loss of £44 million for the first quarter of 2009. Losses rose to £857 million after tax and shareholder payouts.

11 May 2009 HSBC announced that it had made a 'resilient' start to 2009 with profits exceeding those made in the first quarter of 2008.

4 June 2009 The Bank of England maintained its headline interest rate at 0.5 per cent, and voted to continue with its asset purchase facility.

The Federal Reserve Bank of New York President, William Dudley, warned that the revival of the Commercial Mortgage-Backed Security (CMBS) market was 'essential to stabilising the commercial real estate market' adding if it did not revive, a 'vicious circle' would be created that would 'likely further constrain credit availability'.

9 June 2009 Ten US banks in receipt of government support were set to repay the US Treasury a total of $68 billion. The banks include American Express, Goldman Sachs, JP Morgan Chase and Morgan Stanley.

12 June 2009 Barclays agreed to the sale of its Global Investors fund management firm to money market firm Blackrock for £8.2 billion.

25 June 2009 The Bank of England's six monthly 'Financial Stability Report' noted that 'market sentiment has improved in recent months . . . Perceptions of banks' resilience have improved . . . Market contacts report somewhat better conditions in funding markets, with signs that creditors are willing to provide finance without government guarantees, though term funding in unsecured money markets remains constrained. Notwithstanding these positive developments, balance sheets of banks internationally remain weak . . . As long as these balance sheet vulnerabilities persist, there is a risk to the banking system from further adverse economic or financial sector developments, which could in turn affect lending and economic recovery'.

2 July 2009 The Swedish central bank, Riksbank, announces that it will cut its deposit rate to 0.25 per cent, described by the *Financial Times* as 'uncharted territory'.

6 August 2009 The Bank of England increases its quantitative easing by a further £50 billion to £175 billion, while maintaining interest rates at 0.5 per cent.

3 November 2009 The Treasury announced that Lloyds would not after all join the Asset Protection Scheme and would instead raise £21 billion through a shareholder rights issue. RBS reduced the assets insured under APS to £282 billion.

5 November 2009 The Bank of England increases its quantitative easing by a further £25 billion to £200 billion, while maintaining interest rates at 0.5 per cent.

25 November 2009 The Chancellor told the Commons that the Bank of England provided liquidity to Halifax Bank of Scotland and Royal Bank of Scotland from October 2008. The support provided peaked at £36.6 billion for RBS (17 October 2008) and £25.4 billion for HBOS (13 November 2008), and in return the banks deposited collateral at the Bank of England and were charged fees. The *Financial Times* reported that 'although Lloyds shareholders were told [during the acquisition process] HBOS would have to "substantially rely for the foreseeable future" on Bank of England liquidity support, they found out the extent of the stricken bank's problems' only when the Chancellor made his statement to the House. The Chancellor said 'there has been no cost to the taxpayer', and added that the Treasury had provided an indemnity to the Bank in respect of its liquidity operations.

Dubai's Department of Finance asked for a standstill (until May 30) on all financing to the heavily indebted Dubai World and its troubled property unit Nakheel. As a result, the next day the FTSE 100 fell by 3.2 per cent with financial shares badly hit (Barclays shares were down 8 per cent).

9 December 2009 In the pre-Budget report, the UK government announced a temporary bank payroll tax of 50 per cent would apply to discretionary bonuses above £25,000 awarded in the period from the pre-Budget report to 5 April 2010 for each individual employee.

18 December 2009 In its six-monthly 'Financial Stability Report', the Bank of England reported that 'The financial system has been significantly more stable over the past six months, underpinned by the authorities' sustained support for the banking system and monetary policy measures'. It went on to say that 'Activity in many capital markets has resumed, reducing financing risks for some borrowers. The market rally has boosted bank profits and lowered concerns about potential future losses, and banks have raised further external capital'. It added that 'overstretched balance sheets will take time to adjust fully. Around the world, a number of borrowers, including in the commercial property sector, have large refinancing needs in the coming years . . . Banks need to reduce leverage further, extend the maturity of their funding and refinance substantial sums as official sector support is withdrawn'.

1 January 2010 Northern Rock is restructured by the government into two parts: (1) 'Northern Rock plc', described as the 'good bank', which would hold all savings accounts (currently amounting to £19 billion), carry out new lending and hold £10 billion of existing mortgages. It would also hold certain wholesale deposits, and; (2) Northern Rock (Asset Management) plc, the 'bad bank', which would hold the majority of the mortgage book – about £50 billion – and repay outstanding government loans.

24 February 2010 The UK government announced that it would withdraw the 100 per cent guarantee to all savers with Northern Rock bank on 24 May 2010, meaning they would revert to the £50,000 limit applying to all other savers with FSA registered savings institutions. The limit was increased to £85,000 later in the year.

25 February 2010 The Royal Bank of Scotland announced a loss of £3.6 billion for 2009, but said it would pay £1.3 billion in bonuses to staff.

9 March 2010 The FTSE 100 was at 57 per cent above the low point reached a year earlier.

24 March 2010 In his Budget Statement, the Chancellor sounded a note of caution, saying: 'There are still uncertainties. Financial markets are febrile. Oil prices have increased by over 50 per cent. Bank credit, while improved, still remains weak in many parts of the world. Confidence has not fully returned to either businesses or consumers.'

The government also announced its intention to integrate its holdings in Northern Rock Asset Management and Bradford & Bingley, which was viewed as a step towards their sale.

8 April 2010 The difference (or 'spread') between yields of Greek government bonds over their German equivalent (Bunds) hit its highest point since Greece joined the European single currency. The spread was 456 basis points, indicating that investors were demanding a premium of 4.56 per cent to hold Greek government bonds compared to Bunds, even though both were denominated in Euro.

12 April 2010 Euro area member states announced that they had agreed upon the terms of the financial support that would be given to Greece, if requested, including up to €30 billion for financing needs.

Reuters reported that 'together with at least €10 billion expected from the International Monetary Fund in the first year, it could add up to the biggest multilateral financial rescue ever attempted'.

2 May 2010 Greece receives a €110 billion bailout by Eurozone and IMF.

11 May 2010 Conservatives and Liberal Democrats agreed to form the UK's first coalition government since World War Two.

17 May 2010 Government sets up Banking Commission under Sir John Vickers.

28 Nov 2010 Ireland bails out by UK and other European economies.

5 May 2011 Portugal receives international bailout package.

21 July 2011 Greece provided with second bailout package.

9 August 2011 Rating agency S&P downgrades United States.

12 September 2011 Vickers Commission publishes final report recommending ring fence between retail and investment banking activities.

6 October 2011 Bank of England restarts money creation programme (quantitative easing).

27 June 2012 Barclays fined £290 million over attempts to rig industry interest rate LIBOR.

26 July 2012 European Central Bank President Mario Draghi promises to "do what it takes" to save the Euro.

6 February 2013 RBS fined £390 million over LIBOR-rigging allegations.

22 February 2013 Rating agency Moody's downgrades UK.

12 June 2013 Stephen Hester quits as chief executive of Royal Bank of Scotland.

19 June 2013 Parliamentary Banking Commission publishes final report.

1 July 2013 Mark Carney succeeds Sir Mervyn King as Bank of England Governor.

17 September 2013 Chancellor announces sale of 6% stake in Lloyd's worth £3.2 billion.

Source: Woodhouse, John, Jarrett, Tim, and Edmonds, Tim. *The credit crisis: a timeline*. House of Commons Library: April 2010.

Postscript –
Inside the Banking Crisis

It is late February 2014 and on a chilly but bright morning in an unassuming corner of East London, the head of one of Britain's leading banks is visiting a small business. The Trampery offers space to start-up enterprises. It is a customer of Royal Bank of Scotland and an example of the sort of small firm with growth potential which might have once struggled to find credit. No wonder Ross McEwan, CEO of RBS, is hailing the success of the venture as he chats to tenants including fashion and jewellery designers.

But this is no ordinary visit to a client. Cameras follow his every move. TV satellite trucks mount the pavements and obstruct traffic in an area not known for high profile news. Journalists, grumpy at having to make the journey from better known City haunts, mill around. McEwan has chosen The Trampery as the venue for the announcement of the bank's results and the latest developments on its restructuring. The easy-going New Zealander, who started in the job the previous October, is trying to make a point – that RBS is returning to traditional banking roots serving British businesses and consumers.

In a sparsely furnished white-walled meeting room, McEwan makes a speech to business customers and other invited guests. Behind him the screen is blank apart from the words "A bank that earns your trust". He tells his audience that RBS exists to help customers but this is not possible if customers do not trust the bank. "We are the least trusted company", he says "in the least trusted sector of the economy." Shortly afterwards the financial press is herded into the room and a relentless stream of questions on lending, bonuses and bank losses are thrown at the RBS chief.

Later he embarks on a series of TV interviews with the cameras and lights perched uneasily amidst the desks of the young entrepeneurs and designers. McEwan's calm demeanour remains intact despite the often hostile probing about the bank's future strategy and policies on bonuses for investment bankers. There is a steely glint in his eye. This chief executive is letting it be known that he has a mammoth task on his hands, that the bank is not fixed and that a continued period of painful rebuilding is required.

That morning, more than five years on from its near collapse and bail-out, yet more bad news is emanating from RBS. A loss of more than £8 billion for 2013, the biggest since the crisis, has been unveiled. Further restructuring costs and fines for previous misdemeanours such as mis-selling are cited as reasons for the continued plunge into the red. McEwan admits that the bank has lost a cumulative total of £46 billion since the rescue in 2008, equivalent to a little over the sum injected by taxpayers. He talks of slimming down RBS and shedding branches where necessary. He is clear that a full recovery for the bank and a sale of the Government stake might not be possible for another five years.

The hopes of a share flotation and realisation of the taxpayers' invest-ment in RBS seemed at that point as slim as at any point since the dark days of 2008. The strategy of preparing the bank for a sale of the Government's shares, pursued since early 2009 had not borne fruit. The state controlled behemoth had not delivered any economic divi-dend in the shape of higher net lending to businesses. And, while Ross McEwan and his senior executive colleagues had turned down bonuses, the familiar annual row over bonus payments to other RBS bankers was raging again. The saga had become like a broken record.

Whatever signs of life there may have been amongst the private sector banks, including the newer players, Royal Bank of Scotland remained unfixed. The legacy of the near collapse and rescue of the bank hung heavily over the economy. Speculation over whether RBS should have been split would not go away. One senior policymaker familiar with the Royal Bank's balance sheet believes that the "good bank, bad bank" solution might in the end have saved taxpayers up to £10 billion. Assets in a "bad bank" would have been left to recover over the long term rather than being flogged off cheaply as they were between 2009 and 2013. A "good bank", perhaps branded Nat West, would be in the same shape as Lloyds and ripe for a Stock Market flotation. The same policymaker argues that RBS in early 2014 was still "massively stricken" and that the strategy of not doing radical surgery simply had not worked.

George Osborne barely spoke of RBS any more. There was no chance of significant improvement at the bank before the general election, let alone any form of share sale, so there was no political dividend to be gained. Vince Cable would articulate his frustration about RBS bonuses from time to time but with declining levels of conviction. RBS had become like an embarrassing relative who nobody wanted to be reminded about. The bank was in effect a ball and chain hitched to Whitehall, seen but not spoken of.

The fact that banks like RBS had nearly failed and caused chaos on the streets amounted to one of the biggest crises of modern times. The unresolved state of the bank half a decade later added up to a public policy dilemma unprecedented in the late 20th and early 21st centuries. The finest minds in Whitehall and the City had failed to come up with lasting solutions. Whether anyone will any time soon is a matter of conjecture.

The untold story of the banking crisis has no ending. It is a story which matters to borrowers, savers and taxpayers. Future generations should be grateful to the politicians, regulators and advisers of 2008 for preventing a cataclysm which could have crippled the UK economy for years. But they will not thank them for leaving debts and liabilities which could take decades to settle.

Bibliography

Brown, Gordon. *Beyond the Crash: Overcoming the First Crisis of Globalization*. London: Simon & Schuster, 2010.

Brummer, Alex. *The Crunch: How Greed and Incompetence Sparked the Credit Crisis*. London: Random House Business Books, 2008.

Cable, Vince. *The Storm: The World Economic Crisis and What it Means*. London: Atlantic Books, 2009.

Darling, Alistair. *Back From the Brink: 1000 Days at Number 11*. London: Atlantic Books, 2011.

Farag, Marc, Damian Harland and Dan Nixon. *Bank Capital and Liquidity*. Bank of England Quarterly Bulletin, September 2013.

House of Commons Treasury Select Committee. *The Run on the Rock: Fifth Report of Sessions 2007–08*. London: The Stationery Office Limited, 2008.

Martin, Iain. *Making it Happen: Fred Goodwin, RBS and the Men Who Blew Up the British Economy*. London: Simon & Schuster, 2013.

McBride, Damian. *Power Trip: A Decade of Policy, Plots and Spin*. London: Biteback Publishing, 2013.

Parliamentary Commission on Banking Standards. *'An Accident Waiting to Happen': The Failure of HBOS: Fourth Report of Sessions 2012–13*. London: The Stationery Office Limited, 2013.

Parliamentary Commission on Banking Standards. *Changing Banking for Good: First Report of Sessions 2013-14*. London: The Stationery Office Limited, 2013.

Paulson, Hank. *On the Brink: Inside the Race to Stop the Collapse of the Global Financial System*. London: Headline Publishing Group, 2010.

Perman, Ray. *Hubris: How HBOS Wrecked the Best Bank in Britain*. Edinburgh: Birlinn Limited, 2012.

Index